TIME TO CARE

TIME TO CARE

REDESIGNING CHILD CARE

TO PROMOTE EDUCATION,

SUPPORT FAMILIES, AND

BUILD COMMUNITIES

Joan Lombardi

A CENTURY FOUNDATION BOOK

 Temple University Press
PHILADELPHIA

Temple University Press, Philadelphia 19122
Copyright © 2003 by The Century Foundation
All rights reserved
Published 2003
Printed in the United States of America

⊗ The paper used in this publication meets the requirements of the American National Standard for Information Sciences—Permanence of Paper for Printed Library Materials, ANSI Z39.48-1984.

Library of Congress Cataloging-in-Publication Data

Lombardi, Joan.
    Time to care : redesigning child care to promote education, support families, and build communities / Joan Lombardi.
        p.   cm.
    Includes bibliographical references and index.
    ISBN 1-59213-008-9 (cloth : alk. paper) — ISBN 1-59213-009-7 (pbk. : alk. paper)
    1. Child care—United States.   2. Child care services—United States.   3. Early childhood education—United States.   4. Family services—United States.   I. Title.

HQ778.63 .L66   2003
362.71'2'0973–dc21
                                                                            2002073201

To my family, for always having time to care,

    and

To all the parents and child-care providers
across the United States who get up every morning
and try to make it all work for children

Contents

Foreword

n the years immediately after World War II, just 12 percent of American women with children under six years of age were in the labor force. Over the next half-century, that share multiplied more than fivefold. At the same time, the labor-force participation of women with school-age children also soared, from just over one-quarter to slightly more than three-quarters.

The lion's share of those increases occurred during the past generation, but the trends have been evident for long enough that one might reasonably have expected the nation to have responded in significant ways to such a fundamental social transformation. As most other developed nations experienced comparable increases in the number of working mothers, they adopted a variety of public policies that enabled families to gain access to reliable child care. In the United States, however, the role of government at all levels with respect to child care has remained limited, fragmented, and underfunded for a number of reasons. Perhaps the most significant has been the long-standing and still politically potent ambivalence toward mothers in the workforce who have young children.

As a result of this passivity on the part of government, the market for child-care services in the United States leaves much to be desired, and the situation is much more difficult for low-income parents. Although child-care workers receive notoriously poor wages, the cost of care to very low-income parents averages almost one-quarter of their earnings. At a time when "market-based solutions" have gained political currency in addressing problems confronting the nation's health-care system, public education, and Social Security, its child-care system provides a sobering example of the consequences of minimal government involvement in the provision of a public good—something that benefits society at large as well as individuals.

Joan Lombardi presents an alternative vision for ensuring American families that their children will have access to high-quality, affordable child care. Formerly the director of the federal Child Care Bureau and deputy assistant secretary for policy and external affairs in the Administration for Children and Families in the U.S. Department of Health and Human Services during the Clinton administration, Lombardi examines effective local and state initiatives as well as the military child-care system. These models help to define policies that she believes would strengthen child care in the United States. In addition to describing new policies and programs, she pays close attention to formulating a political strategy for transforming the way we talk about child care in order to broaden support for a stronger public role.

Lombardi believes that one of the challenges facing those trying to elevate the importance of child care on the national agenda is to shift the perception of the issue as primarily one of parental responsibility to one of common concern as an educational priority. From World War II through the 1996 welfare reform act, child-care policy in the United States has been guided by the needs of adult workers. Child care first became part of the public agenda when the country needed women in the workforce to support domestic production after Pearl Harbor. The war's conclusion, and the return of men to the workforce and their wives to their homes, caused child-care funding to disappear almost immediately. Significant new federal assistance did not become available again until the passage of the Family Support Act in the late 1980s. Then, once more, the primary concern was to assist adults—this time to encourage them to work rather than remain on welfare. The welfare reform act also provided funding for child-care services to enable welfare recipients and low-income families to work but did not include adequate provisions related to the quality of the child care.

The obvious relationship between child care and the education of preschoolers has been neglected in part because of institutional disconnections, along with political and ideological predilections. While child care is primarily administered by human-service agencies, paid for primarily by parents, and provided by a range of institutions—including community-based organizations, churches, schools, and small, family-run programs—public schools are supervised by local boards under state oversight and financed mainly through local property taxes.

Lombardi argues that one catalyst for transforming child care into an educational issue may be recent neurobiological research that demonstrated the rapid pace of brain development in a child's early years. Because two out of three children under the age of six now spend at least part of their day in child care, the importance of making sure child-care providers are offering safe, clean, fully staffed services seems evident. Lombardi suggests that if child care came to be perceived as an educational priority and a family support, the public might not be as willing to accept the current market-based system. And while it is difficult to imagine the public school system rapidly subsuming child-care responsibilities, especially for children under four years of age, Lombardi believes that some features of the nation's public support for higher education may be adaptable to child care.

Over the years, as The Century Foundation supported work on inequality, poverty, and welfare, it became clear that the availability of adequate and affordable child care plays a critical role in finding solutions to these problems. The importance of child care to these issues was evident in such works as Blanche Bernstein's *Saving a Generation*, Robert Haveman's *Starting Even*, Richard Nathan's *Turning Promises into Performance*, and *Breaking Away: The Future of Cities*, a collection of essays edited by Julia Vitullo-Martin. Now the increasing information about the importance of early influences on children, particularly in terms of educational achievement, has created a strong interest in further exploration of this subject.

Many of our leaders have struggled for years to find ways of addressing the child-care difficulties that large numbers of their constituents confront. In this book, Joan Lombardi provides them with a road map for beginning the long-overdue process of reversing a history of neglectfulness.

Richard C. Leone, *President*
The Century Foundation

Preface

More than thirty years ago I stepped inside my first classroom and was greeted by a small group of wiggling three-year-olds. I knew right away, when I looked into their very young faces, that the time we spent together was important to their development. Those early experiences caring for young children grounded my conviction that child care is an educational opportunity. Yet it was not until I became a parent myself that I understood the emotions of the child-care issue. I remember how our young daughter would run to greet her father when he picked her up from child care. I remember beginning the search for part-time care for our eleven-month-old baby boy. Just thinking back to those days, recalling my worries and my joys, knowing that I was so much luckier than most, strengthened my resolve to help make child care a better place for all children and families.

It was from those two perspectives, as a provider and as a parent, that I moved on to the world of policy shaping and policy making. Along with many others, I spent hours and days, months and years writing reports, gathering statistics, listening to stories, rallying with fellow advocates, pursuing a common goal—real choices for parents in the care of their children. Along the way we increased resources and took some important policy steps forward. Unfortunately, the gaps are still very wide: between what we know and what we are able to do, between parents with resources and those on limited budgets, between rhetoric and real action.

By the mid-1990s, child care reached the national agenda, and I had the good fortune to represent the issue at the federal level. From that position I gained a deeper understanding of both the policy potential and the challenges. By the time my tenure in government came to a close, more and more people had come to see child care as an important work support. Yet many of us knew that child care as a work support was only half the picture: The real potential for child care is the enormous opportunity it provides to promote education and support families. Yet the United States still remains far behind other nations in recognizing the realities of the child-care issue.

This book has a straightforward message. In the twenty-first century we can no longer afford to ignore child care. Most children in the United States will spend time in non-parental care for part of the day on a regular basis during their childhood. Child care is a third setting—outside the time children spend with parents at home or with teachers at school—yet necessarily connected to both. It includes a continuum of care by family, friends, and neighbors; family child-care providers; and child-care centers. We need to redesign child care in the United States, taking advantage of the "opportunity time" children are in care to promote child and youth development, to reach out and support family life, and to help build the spirit of community. This calls for significant increases in public, private, and civic investment. To do less means abandoning the core values of equal opportunity and the importance of the family.

I started writing this book in 1999, a time when welfare-reform implementation was in full swing, the economy was booming, education reform was in the air, and an election was on the horizon. I worked on it when the election of the president remained undecided, when education moved to the top of the domestic agenda, when our world shook in terror and sadness on September 11, 2001, and when the debate over the reauthorization of child care and welfare began and a new interest in early education emerged. I completed my work before the final chapter was written in this Congress. Yet I remain sure that even if new resources are secured in this round, we still will have a very long road ahead. I have tried to look across the country and read the emerging signs that can provide a map for the journey we face.

Many people have contributed to this effort along the way. I am grateful to the parents and providers who have shared their stories with me and with others, helping to bring life to flat words and dry statistics. Early in the process, the editorial assistance of Laura Colker and Amy Dombro and the research assistance of Mary Bogle and Amy Cubbage helped me get started and keep going. Debra Al-Salam provided excellent research support, helping to track down and recheck the hundreds of references used in this book, and Nancy Davidson provided critical editorial support to complete this book. I extend my sincere appreciation to those who provided input and advice, including Mark Greenberg, Dick Clifford, Anne Mitchell, Helen Blank, Yasmina Vinci, Linda Smith, the anonymous reviewer, and the many, many colleagues who commented on specific chapters or sections. I would like to thank Nancy Steele, who polished the finished manuscript, and Janet Greenwood for her support during the publication process. I am grateful to The Century Foundation for its resources and technical support throughout the project, and especially to Greg Anrig, Beverly Goldberg, and Eric Rhodes. I am particularly grateful to Peter Wissoker and the staff of Temple University Press for giving me the opportunity to make this book a reality. And finally, I thank my husband, Neville, and my children, Nisha and Michael, for believing in my work and supporting me every step of the way.

1

Reframing Child Care

hether I was on a plane, attending an event in Washington, D.C., or visiting a welfare office, the stories were always the same, but always deeply personal. They came from fathers as well as mothers. They came from people who made minimum wage and people who worked at the highest rung on the corporate ladder. The words varied, but the message was usually the same: Can I talk to you about my child-care situation? Can you help me?

During the two years I served as the first director of the federal Child Care Bureau, I heard a range of questions and emotions about the care of children while their parents work. A father who called early one Monday morning could barely get the words out: "We just left the baby at the child-care center. How will I know she's really safe?" When we held a national child-care conference in a downtown hotel, we set up a resource room for experts who were attending from across the country. Throughout the meeting hotel employees kept stopping by, saying, "What is this about? Can I get some information, too? Can I tell you what happened the other day? Last year? With my toddler? With my teen?"

While I was having breakfast before an out-of-town meeting, I spoke with a waitress, a single mom who told me that she just could not get by. Her mother used to "watch the kids" until "they got to be too much for her." Then her sister took over, but now her sister wants to go back to work, too. Without a family member to help care for her children, and unable to pay for child care, she said that she may have to go back on welfare.

The questions kept coming. A woman called from the Midwest: "Just how old does a child have to be before you can leave her home alone?" A father from New York talked to me on the train. He had read all the studies and wanted to know about accreditation of child-care centers: What did I think? Was that the answer? A grandmother from California wrote to ask where she could get financial support because she was spending about a third of her wages on child care for her two grand-children. A friend of mine who had been home with her young daughter for thirteen months told me, "I've started to feel as if my brain is melting." The tension was affecting her marriage. She decided to go back to work part time, but she could not find good child care. She was angry.

By the time my own son turned twelve, he no longer wanted to go to his after-school program because there was not enough going on there to occupy him once he finished his homework. I kept thinking about what an opportunity all that valuable time provided, and I started to look at other programs. There were few choices for this age group; there were transportation issues, and then there would be the summer months. My husband and I were lucky that we had options. But it brought home to me once again, in a very personal way, how hard it is for working parents. Faced with these decisions, they feel very alone. Nothing seems to fit their reality. I wondered how long it would take to address this child-care crisis.

Acknowledging the Need

The influx of women into the workforce was one of the most signifi-cant social changes of the twentieth century. The number of women in the workforce who have preschool children has increased by more than five times, from 12 percent just after World War II to 64 percent in 1999; at the same time, labor-force participation of women with school-age children increased from 27 percent to 78 percent(see Figure 1).[1] Over the past twenty-five years, women with children of all ages have been returning to work, with significant increases in the number of working mothers who have very young children.[2]

Tragically, this social movement in the United States, in contrast to that in most other developed countries, took place without a corre-sponding effort to revolutionize the child-care system. A deep ambiva-

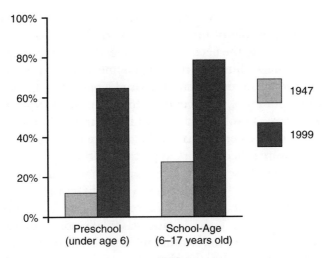

FIGURE 1. *Percentage of women in the labor force, by presence and age of youngest child: A comparison of the years 1947 and 1999.*

Included are women ages sixteen or older who work any number of hours for pay or profit, and those who work at least fifteen hours per week without pay for family enterprises.

Data for 1994 and later years are not directly comparable with data for 1993 and earlier years because of introduction of a major redesign in the Current Population Survey (household survey) questionnaire and collection methodology, and the introduction of 1990 census-based population controls, adjusted for estimated undercounts (Anne E. Polivka and Jennifer M. Rothgeb, *Monthly Labor Review*, September 1993, Vol. 116 [9], pp. 10–28).

Source: U.S. House of Representatives, Ways and Means Committee, "Background Material and Data on Programs within the Jurisdiction of the Committee on Ways and Means," *2000 Green Book*, 106th Cong., 2nd sess., *WMCP*: 106–14 (Washington, D.C.: Government Printing Office, 2000), Section 9, Table 9.1, pp. 571–73. Figure by Debra Al-Salam.

lence characterized the entrance of women into the labor force, causing the country to close its eyes to the fact that more children, at increasingly younger ages, were spending many hours in settings outside their homes. Despite widespread concern that poor child care might harm children, the public seemed uninterested in doing anything about it. It was as if recognizing the problem and supporting working parents would create a giant magnet, drawing women into the workforce, disarming their maternal instincts, and leaving their children neglected. Rather than responding by helping families and by providing a healthy environment for children to develop, for most of the century the United States tried to avoid the issue, as if hoping the need for child care would go away. But it did not.

Over the years, public policy toward child care has reflected deep feelings about the role of mothers and work. In the early 1900s, the country responded to the needs of poor widows by establishing pensions to support mothers while they remained home with their children. This was the forerunner to Aid to Families with Dependent Children (AFDC), and later Temporary Assistance to Needy Families (TANF), commonly known as welfare. Throughout most of the century, child-care support was provided only when it was needed on a temporary basis, such as when women were called to work as part of a national emergency. However, the expectations were always the same: that women would return home and that the need for child care would disappear.

Yet by the late 1960s, more and more women were steadily moving into the workforce. The United States was finally poised to make a serious investment in child care, as other industrialized countries had done. Once again, however, cultural ambivalence about working mothers created an obstacle. In 1971, after years of public debate, President Richard M. Nixon vetoed the Comprehensive Child Development Act, warning that child care would lead to communal child-rearing. This single action set the child-care agenda back for decades: While other countries moved ahead, the United States stood still.

In the meantime, the number of women moving into the workforce continued to grow. Former Labor Secretary Robert Reich notes, "Starting in the 1970s, the loss of manufacturing jobs required many women to work in order to maintain family incomes that previously had been sustained by one male worker."[3] At the same time, the lack of adequate child care and other factors contributed to an increase in the number of women on welfare. As working mothers with very young children became more commonplace, the expectation that the country would support poor women to stay home began to change. By the mid-1990s, a demand to "end welfare as we know it" led to the passage of the 1996 welfare-reform bill. Columnist Ellen Goodman called it "the end of a long cultural debate about motherhood as we knew it,"[4] since for the first time in modern history, the public expected mothers—at least very poor mothers—to work rather than to receive support to stay home. On the other hand, child care was finally beginning to be seen by some as an asset, an important work support for low-income families.

Outside the welfare context, however, poll after poll indicates that public ambivalence toward working mothers with young children continues.[5] Too often the child-care debate is reduced to the question:

Should mothers work or stay home? We have been forced to talk about work and family in black-and-white terms even though we know the situation is gray. Many women go in and out of the workforce. Sometimes they are home and other times they are working, depending on a number of life situations, including where they live, the ages of their children, the availability of care, and their family goals and needs at the time.

A second and related "either-or" question usually follows: Which has more impact on children, child care or family? As in the "stay at home or work" debate, many people are looking for black or white answers and find in the research whatever they want to see. Common sense tells us that in reality, both influences are important. Just as the quality of family life affects children, so does the place where they may spend twenty to thirty hours or more each week outside the home, especially when they are very young. In a study that asked children what they really think about working parents, Ellen Galinsky argues that it is time to move beyond the either-or debate.[6] The impact of work on children depends on how their parents feel about their work, whether it spills over into family life, what support is available along the way, and what happens at home when the parents are not working. Furthermore, much depends on the age of the child; yet the debate goes on as if children who are three months old will feel the same effects as children who are thirteen.

More recently, some have assumed that the answer to the child-care dilemma is for mothers to work from home. However, this is only a partial answer (and one often used to deny the realities of child care). As anyone with young children knows, there is only so much work one can sneak in during nap time. Beyond those hours, children need adult supervision and attention. And for many parents—especially for low-income parents—working at home is not an option.

Continuing the either-or debate sidesteps the realities facing most families and contributes to a sense of collective denial regarding the need for child care. A parent's decision to work is not static, and it does not result in hard-and-fast, wrong or right answers. Indeed, child care cannot be reduced to either-or questions. In the twenty-first century, most children in the United States will be in child care at some time in their lives, probably starting at a young age. Many mothers will work full time, for economic and personal reasons. Their children will need child care. Other mothers and fathers will be able to work part time and remain home for longer periods of time, depending on family needs and the flexibility of their employers. Yet they too will need child care, even if it is for fewer hours.

Finally, child care is not just an issue for working families. In 1999, about one-third of nonworking American mothers with children under age five used some type of non-parental care, on at least a part-time basis.[7] Moreover, while children may be in care for less time when they are young, this situation often changes; as they grow older and their mothers return to work, there is an increasing likelihood that children will need care in the afternoons and usually over the summer months.

Child care is here to stay. Some families may need less of it than others, but it is a service that will be used by most children in America. In a landmark study of the science of early childhood released in 2000, the National Research Council noted that it is in child care that "most children first learn to interact with other children on a regular basis, establish bonds with adults other than their parents, receive or fail to receive important inputs for early learning and language development, and experience their initial encounter with a school-like environment."[8] Acknowledging the need for child care is a first step toward making change. The next step is to understand how and why the current system is failing.

Recognizing that Market Forces Alone Will Not Work

While much of child care used to be provided free by family members, over the years it has increasingly become a paid service. According to The Urban Institute's 1997 data from the National Survey of American Families, 48 percent of working families with children under age thirteen had child-care expenses. Working families with younger children used paid care more often, with 60 percent paying for care.[9] Even when families rely upon relatives, friends, and neighbors, these providers often are paid. Historically, paying for child care has been seen as a private burden, not a public responsibility. It was assumed that market forces would produce what consumers need at a price they could pay if they had the right information to make informed choices. However, the reliance on market forces alone has failed children, families, and the providers who serve them.

A review of child care, conducted by Deborah Vandell and Barbara Wolfe and published in 2000 by the U.S. Department of Health and Human Services, describes market failure as "a situation in which a market left on its own fails to allocate resources efficiently." The report notes two causes of market failure in child care: parents' lack of information, and what economists call "externalities," which means that the benefits of quality care accrue not just to the parents and the child, but to society in general. If the benefits of a service are less apparent to the immediate consumer, there may be less demand for it.[10]

Even when families realize the benefits of good care, they often are not able to afford it. Vandell and Wolfe refer to child care as an "imperfect capital market" since "the parents of young children tend to have low incomes relative to their permanent incomes, and they may face borrowing constraints that reduce their ability to pay for high-quality care." The market failure perpetuates itself because the demand for high-quality care is too low; therefore compensation remains low, and the more qualified staff seek other jobs. This results in declining quality "unless intervention occurs." From this economic perspective, the clear evidence of market failure in quality child care indicates a need for public-sector intervention. Since the quality of child care affects school readiness and later school achievement, such intervention is justified as a means to ensure equal opportunity, particularly for low-income families.[11]

These economic forces in child care have been compared with a three-legged stool. The three legs—availability, affordability, and quality—are interrelated parts of the same system. Whether care is available depends on the supply of providers in a community, access to the care, and whether it is affordable. At the same time, whether families can afford child care depends on the cost of that care and the resources available to help families pay for it. In turn, the quality of care is highly dependent on the cost of providing the service and on what families are willing and able to pay.

The Supply of Child Care Is Not Adequate

Children are cared for in different ways when parents work. Some families manage to care for their children themselves, either by working split shifts or by bringing children to work with them. Yet most families make some non-parental arrangements for their children while they work. Some children are cared for by relatives, others by non-relatives.

Non-relative care can take place in the child's home by caregivers often referred to as "nannies," in other people's homes, often called family child care, and in facilities called child-care centers.

Today there are more than four hundred thousand licensed and regulated child-care centers and homes across the country. This includes more than 113,000 regulated child-care centers and more than three hundred thousand regulated family child-care homes.[12] Since 1991 the number of centers has increased by 24 percent and the number of child-care homes by 19 percent.[13]

Although the supply of child care has increased over the past three decades, the lack of availability of care is still a serious issue, particularly for low-income families. Relatives and friends who can provide child care may be less readily accessible to families than often assumed. One study found that more than 60 percent of welfare families had no friend or relative, inside or outside their immediate household, who could provide child care. Their access to child-care was limited not only by cost but also by transportation issues and lack of adequate supply.[14]

Although access to care for preschoolers has improved, there is still a shortage of high-quality child care, particularly for infants, children with special needs, school-age children, and children whose families work evenings, nights, and weekends. A 1997 study documented gaps between the supply and demand of care for infants and school-age children.[15] Schools in low-income communities are far less likely to offer extended-day services.[16] Moreover, two out of five employed Americans work mostly during the evenings or nights, on rotating shifts, or on weekends. Among the top ten occupations projected by the Bureau of Labor Statistics to experience the most growth from 1996 to 2006, most are service occupations, which employ a large percentage of their workforce in nonstandard hours.[17] The marketplace has not responded to these areas of need.

Good Care Often Is Not Affordable

Even when care is available, the question most families face is whether they can afford it. When young married couples start their new life together, they think about the expenses they will face when children come along. The cost of housing and food often top the list, and saving for a child's college education has become a top priority. Yet for more and more parents, the cost of child care takes a big bite out of family income.

The cost of raising children in the United States has risen in recent years, with a prime cause being the rising cost of child care. For example, child-care costs rose by 5 percent from 1998 to 1999.[18] Child-care costs already had increased by 44 percent between 1985 and 1995.[19] Families pay the lion's share of child-care costs, unlike many other services. Families contribute 60 percent of the total national expenditure for child care, with only 39 percent coming from the government and 1 percent from the private sector. Parent fees make up more than three-fourths of a child-care center's budget, while tuition covers only about one-third of a college's operating expenses.[20] The younger the child, the more expensive good child care can be. Yet parents with young children are most likely to be at the lowest point in their earning potential and often cannot afford good care, even when they know it matters and want their children to have the very best.

The cost of care varies by type of care, age of children, and geographic area. Generally, care for infants and toddlers costs more than care for preschoolers and older children. Furthermore, care in urban areas may be more expensive than care in rural communities. In 2000, child-care costs for a four-year-old ranged from $4,000 to $10,000 or more a year in urban child-care centers. For families in these areas, the average annual cost of child care exceeded the average annual tuition at a public college in almost every state.[21] The cost of care for a school-age child can be between $700 and $6,600 a year, depending on what costs must be assumed by the program and what in-kind resources are available.[22]

Low-income families often cannot afford even basic child care. According to 1995 Census Bureau data, working families paid an average of $85 per week for child care. Relatively fewer poor families pay for care. However, poor families who paid for care spent five times more of their income on child care than non-poor families, a gap that has persisted since 1987.[23] In the 1997 National Survey of American Families, The Urban Institute found that among working families who pay for care, 27 percent of low-earning families, compared with only 1 percent of higher-earning families, spend more than one-fifth of their earnings on child care. Very low-income families pay on average almost one-quarter of their earnings for child care (see Figure 2).[24]

In testimony before the U.S. Senate Finance Committee in March 2002, a thirty-year-old single mother from Florida described the child-care dilemma she was facing:

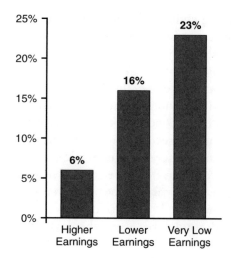

FIGURE 2. *Child-care expenses as a percentage of family earnings (among families who pay for care).*

"Higher Earnings" is more than 200 percent of poverty; "Lower Earnings" is less than 200 percent of poverty; and "Very Low Earnings" is less than the poverty level. Each percentage shown is the average of the percentage of earnings that each family in that group pays for care. This yields results different from the aggregate approach to computing percentages (aggregate expenses divided by aggregate earnings, or income across a group).

Source: Linda Giannarelli and James Barsimantov, "Child Care Expenses of America's Families," Occasional Paper No. 40, *Assessing the New Federalism* (Washington, D.C.: The Urban Institute, December 2000), pp. 7, 9, based on data from the 1997 National Survey of America's Families.

> I work very hard to provide a safe and stable environment for myself and my child while struggling to work and go to college.... Now I am confronted with a new obstacle.... My annual income is $13,500 per year ... my transitional child-care benefit ended ... my income still places me well within Florida's eligibility level for child-care assistance; ... however, due to lack of funds in Florida this year, my daughter and I have been placed on a waiting list (along with over 46,000 other families in the state).... I cannot afford to pay full child-care fees so that I can work, as my weekly child-care expenses total over 42 percent of my weekly take-home pay.[25]

This story reflects the dilemma of thousands of other families across the country. In 1997, U.S. Treasury Secretary Robert Rubin remarked, "In many states, a single parent leaving welfare to enter the workforce, after you take into account losing government benefits and the cost of child care, will see his or her income increase by less than fifty cents for each additional dollar earned."[26] Child-care expenses therefore may cause many families to remain in poverty. One estimate indicates that when income is adjusted for child-care expenses, 1.9 million additional persons—of whom more than one million are children—are "thrown into poverty."[27]

Moreover, child-care expenses remain an issue for families within a wide range of income levels—even families earning twice the minimum wage, with modest wages of $20,000 to $30,000 per year, face incredible challenges in paying for care, particularly if they have more than one child. For example, in California, the average cost of full-time care in a licensed center in 1999 for a child under two years of age was $7,020—almost one-quarter of the annual gross income of a family earning $30,000 a year, and 68 percent of a minimum-wage income. Similar costs were reported coast to coast, from Boston to Seattle.[28]

The Quality of Care Is Strained by Low Wages

The cost of care is directly related to its quality, and the key to quality is the staff. Yet for decades child care has been "subsidized" by an underpaid workforce. Now that workforce is shrinking dramatically. Directors of child-care centers across the country find themselves hiring from a pool of applicants whom they would have considered unqualified only a few years ago. Far too many programs are experiencing record turnover, while still others have been forced to close their doors because of their inability to hire staff.[29] Parents are having trouble finding home providers in their neighborhoods. This is not surprising, when child-care providers commonly earn half of what kindergarten teachers earn, even when they have the same credentials.

In 1999 only fifteen occupations had median wages lower than child-care workers; even service-station attendants, messengers, and food servers earned higher wages than child-care workers, who earned on average $7.42 an hour. Family child-care workers earned even less, about $4.82 an hour, in a typical fifty-five-hour week. Child-care workers classified as preschool teachers earned $9.43 an hour, but less than half a kindergarten teacher's average salary of $24.51 an hour (see Figure 3).[30] Low wages and limited health and retirement benefits have come to characterize child care throughout the United States.

Since compensation has not even kept up with inflation in many places, child-care providers are seeking other jobs. Low wages and poor job mobility serve to limit the number of people entering the child-care field. As communities struggle to find qualified teachers for public-

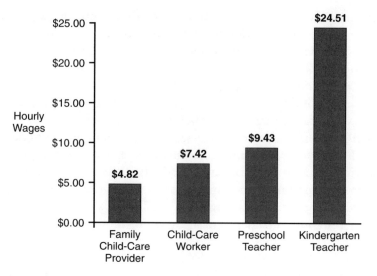

FIGURE 3. *Child-care workforce earnings in perspective: A comparison of mean hourly wages, by child-care job.*

The titles "child care workers" and "preschool teachers" are job titles defined by the Bureau of Labor Statistics.

The median weekly earnings for family child-care providers are $265.00, based on the Bureau of Labor Statistics' 2000 Current Population Survey (CPS). The hourly earnings of $4.82 reflects a fifty-five-hour week, the typical work week for family child-care providers. Because the sample size of family child-care providers in the CPS is small, an increase from year to year may reflect a change in the sample and not an actual increase in earnings.

Source: Center for the Child Care Workforce, *Current Data on Child Care Salaries and Benefits in the United States,* Washington, D.C., March 2001, based on 1999 data from the U.S. Department of Labor, Bureau of Labor Statistics.

school classrooms, where salaries far exceed child-care compensation levels, the issue of recruiting and retaining child-care staff has become a crisis. In a full-employment economy, women have many other career options. Directors of child-care programs struggle to increase wages, but they fear the increases will drive up prices and make services even less affordable.

The educational background of child-care teaching staff and the arrangements of their work environment are essential determinants of the quality of the services children receive. The most important predictor of the quality of care, in the adult work environment, is staff wages. A series of studies over the past two decades documents the crisis in child-care staffing. One study in the late 1980s found that wages were very low and that staff turnover had nearly tripled, from 15 percent in 1977 to 41 percent in 1988.[31] Six years later, a study of child care in four states reported that donations and "foregone earnings" accounted for more than one-fourth of the full cost of care. Higher-quality programs paid workers more than lower-quality programs, but even these still paid below market wages. Foregone earnings were even greater in programs serving infants. The study called for increased investments in child-care staff to assure a skilled and stable workforce.[32]

In 1998 another study found that child-care wages had remained stagnant over the past decade, and high turnover continued to threaten program quality. On average, the highest-paid teaching assistant in child care earned $12,250. Real wages improved little during the decade, and even the most highly paid teachers made only modest gains.[33] The study also found that more child-care centers received public dollars in 1997 than in 1988, allowing them to assist low-income families with child-care costs. However, because this increased public funding was spent to help families pay for care, and rarely targeted to improve quality or increase compensation, it has not resulted in better wages or lower staff turnover. In fact, centers paying the lowest wages were receiving the greatest increases in public subsidies. Furthermore, child-care centers continued to experience very high turnover of teaching staff, threatening their ability to offer good, consistent services to children. More than one-quarter of the child-care teachers, and more than one-third of the assistants, had left their jobs in the previous year—at a time when the demand for their services had grown dramatically.[34]

More recently, in 2001, the first large-scale longitudinal study, based on observations of quality in the same child-care centers over a period of six years, found that the workforce teaching in child care is alarmingly unstable. Seventy-six percent of all teaching staff employed in centers in 1996, and 82 percent of those in 1994, were no longer on the job in 2000. Directors reported having to fill positions with staff who were less qualified than in previous years. Teaching staff reported that high turnover among their colleagues harmed their ability to do their jobs.[35]

A Strong Infrastructure is Needed to Support Quality

Along with the need to improve compensation, investments are needed in such key elements of the child-care infrastructure as licensing and enforcement, consumer education, and professional preparation.

In a nation interested in consumer protections, there is not even a basic assurance of safety for all children in child care. Licensing has traditionally been a state and local function. Despite efforts during the 1970s, national standards have never been implemented, even for programs receiving federal money. As a result, there is wide variation in what state licensing of child care covers and how regulations are enforced. The purpose of child-care licensing is to protect the health, safety, and well-being of children receiving care away from their homes and families.[36] Although licensing is a basic element in structuring a high-quality system, it only serves as a floor.

State requirements for child care vary. For example, while some states regulate such key elements as group size or staff training, others have few, if any, such requirements. As of January 2002, more than half the states required no pre-service training for teachers in child care, and only a dozen states required pre-service training for family child-care providers. In fact, eleven states allowed directors who had no pre-service training to run child-care programs, even though they could be in charge of ensuring the well-being of dozens or hundreds of young children.[37] Some states do not even regulate basic safety issues such as background checks for staff. These minimum licensing requirements send the wrong message regarding the need for more qualified staff, and can have a chilling effect on efforts to improve the quality of child care.

Moreover, while recommended practice is to regulate all nonfamily providers who care for children outside the child's home, almost all states exempt some types of out-of-home providers from regulation. For example, some states exempt certain types of family child care, religious-based care, school-based care, or recreational care. Only two states regulate all of the provider types.[38] It has been estimated that between 82 and 90 percent of family child-care homes in the United States are unregulated, some legally and others illegally.[39] When using federal funds, states must apply some level of health and safety standards even for exempt care. However, more than 80 percent of the states rely on self-certification of health and safety standards for such exempt providers.[40]

Even when standards include all key elements and allow few exemptions, poor enforcement can undermine regulatory effort and threaten the health and safety of children. Proper enforcement requires not only sufficient numbers of competent, well-trained licensing staff who understand the principles of the regulatory system, but also strong administrative support and teamwork between licensing and legal staff.[41] The military child-care system, which has been hailed as a model for the country, specifies four unannounced visits by monitors each year. Although states have made improvements in the number of monitoring visits they make to child-care programs, many states monitor programs once a year or less.[42] No state appears to meet the military standard.

Inspectors who are responsible for monitoring child-care programs often have such heavy caseloads that they lack the time to probe for serious problems, to devise sensible solutions, or to take strong enforcement action. Furthermore, they often have little choice of intermediate action between the extremes of closing a program and just giving it a warning.[43] Finally, child-care inspectors may lack either the training or the time to provide the type of technical assistance or follow-up that programs may need to come into compliance. Only a handful of states follow the recommended practice of providing a minimum of twenty-four hours of training for licensing staff or maintaining caseloads at the recommended levels.[44]

Along with these licensing issues, the lack of consumer information and support continues to plague the child-care system and the families it serves. Good consumer information is critical to making the child-care market function effectively. Without adequate information, parents are not able to make informed choices, thereby limiting their access to the market. Lack of funding limits the support available to parents to help them make this important decision about their children.

Over the past few decades, more than eight hundred Child Care Resource and Referral (CCR&R) agencies have been established in communities across the country to provide consumer education to parents and overall support to the child-care community.[45] However, these agencies, like the rest of the child-care delivery system, have faced serious funding shortages. For example, forty-one states contracted with CCR&Rs in 1997 to provide some or all of the consumer education for parents using subsidies, yet they were insufficiently funded to provide consumer education to most families in need.[46] In addition to providing basic information to parents, most CCR&Rs make referrals, maintain databases, train providers, and help provide a range of other services to the community, yet often they are not fully supported to provide these services.

While some employers provide referrals for their employees, low-income families often have the least access to such services, particularly if they are not connected to the welfare system. These parents often do not have access to consumer education beyond a basic pamphlet. Furthermore, personal time constraints and transportation difficulties often limit parents' ability to visit child-care providers before making a choice.[47]

Finally, the United States does not have an adequate training system to prepare child-care providers or program administrators. Although literally hundreds of teacher-training programs exist in community colleges and higher-education institutions, collectively the country has been slow in responding to the diverse needs of child care such as specialized training for infant care, school-age care, family child care, and center directors. The system of early-childhood professional preparation is characterized by "fragmentation, a shortage of qualified personnel, inadequate career ladders, high turnover, too many barriers and too few incentives for training, and a lack of consumer demand for well-trained personnel."[48] Three-fourths of the early-childhood center directors profiled in one study indicated that they were not prepared for the kinds of issues they encountered when they first became directors.[49]

Other reports reflected similar findings. For example, the first national study of training and career development in early care and education found that there was no comprehensive system to train practitioners. Training was difficult to obtain and often did not provide college credit. The lack of a coherent system hindered career mobility. Furthermore, there was a lack of incentives for training, particularly funds for training and compensation and minimum standards for staffing.[50]

Despite some investments in recent years, support for a responsive professional development system continues to fall short. One study found that public schools allocate 9 percent of their professional-development funds for college coursework, compared with less than 1 percent allocated by child-care centers. Furthermore, child-care teachers spent a higher percentage of their salaries on professional development than their public-school peers.[51]

In summary, in the United States, unlike other industrialized countries, the public response to the need for child care has fallen short. Even though child-care assistance to low-income working families has more than doubled over the past five years, the vast majority of eligible families are still left out in the cold. Furthermore, middle-income families have been almost entirely ignored. Although a tax credit is available to all working families, it provides too little, too late. Families with incomes in the middle range, between approximately $17,000 and about $50,000, benefit little from child-care policies.

At the same time, investments in quality and infrastructure that could benefit all children or that could be targeted to those in greatest need have been minimal. The United States invests just pennies per child per day to ensure the quality of care for children. Most families go without consumer information. Most providers have limited access to good training. Most policy-makers have very little coordinated data to help them plan and build a system of care. Reliance on a market-based system of financing child care simply is not working.

Using Traditional Values to Make Change

In her review of social change and the family, research psychologist Arlene Skolnick notes that "as the world changes, prevailing cultural norms and understandings and practices are disrupted long before new ones have taken place." She discusses three stages of social and cultural transformation: In the first stage, individuals struggle with changes and experience personal and family stress. In the second stage, personal problems become public issues as society collectively struggles with issues brought about by these changes. Public discourse reflects a lack of consensus, and social and political conflicts arise surrounding the issues. Finally, a restabilization occurs in the third stage as a new consensus forms to reconcile older values with new realities.[52]

This theory of change can be applied to the child-care debate. For decades, individual families have been struggling to try to make ends meet. Women and men have been attempting to define themselves and their roles in the family and in society. This has caused tension in the family and pressure to cope with these changes. Over the years, public dialogue about these issues has escalated, with each side passionately holding to its position. In the meantime, public policies have not changed much. We appear to be stuck in stage two, not able to reconcile traditional values with new realities. One side argues that families have an obligation to care for their own children, and the other that society has an obligation to help families because of society's broad interest in raising good citizens. This has been referred to as a values gap.[53]

"Championing child care" has been like swimming upstream.[54] Anyone who has lived through the struggles to pass comprehensive child-care legislation has felt the strong current pulling in the opposite direction. Naturally, all social movements contain such a struggle. Yet I have often felt that something more is at play here, something that we should pay attention to: Throughout the child-care debate, a set of values that the country holds dear has been used to criticize child care and at other times has been largely ignored. Among others, these values include the importance of the family, a high regard for education, a goal of equality, and a commitment to citizenship. In reality, all of these values are inherent in good child care as well as essential to developing a good child-care system. It is time we put these values to work as instruments of change.

The Importance of Family

In the debate over child care, perhaps no word has been tossed around more than "family," especially when it is used to affirm the value of "mothering." Conservatives have claimed that child care is "anti-family." They ask mothers, "Would you rather work or have someone else raise your children?" The implication of this question is that if you work outside your home and use child care for part of the day, then somehow, someone else is raising your children. On the other hand, liberals have too often downplayed the importance and value of mothering in their quest to support mothers who choose to work.

We have to change this debate in three ways. First, we must be more direct in saying that good child care is good for families. We have equivocated too long on this point, worried that we play into the hands of critics who make us feel we are turning our children over to other people to raise or that we are saying that all families need to put their children in care. Neither statement is true. The truth is that good family-centered care promotes parenting. Child-care providers are not substitutes for parents; they are supplements—like extended family members. They can reinforce the bond between parents and children. Furthermore, good consistent care provides support for the family, alleviating stress and helping the family function as a team. Moreover, since child-care providers come into contact with families on a daily basis, they can provide a wealth of information on parenting—something that many liberals and conservatives agree is important.

One reason that many of us have been reluctant to say that child care can be good for families is that we are still struggling with how best to support the parental role. In their book, *Sharing the Caring*, Amy Dombro and Patty Bryan talk about the emotions surrounding child care.[55]

Parents who love and care for their children may find it difficult to "share" this sense of affection with others, particularly when children are very young and are in the care of strangers. On the other hand, child-care providers often develop deep feelings for the children in their care and may feel ambivalence about how parents are responding to their children's needs. Talking more openly about the goal of child care as a family support, rather than seeing it as a substitute, can contribute to change.

Second, we must stand up for the value of caring. In many ways the rhetoric around "family" has focused on mothering (although the fathers' movement has started to change this). Because many women have been afraid to be identified as mothers only, we have devalued the importance of the caring role. Instead we should view it as an important social value and public good. In her book *Care and Equality*, Mona Harrington argues that liberals should "embrace an ethic of care." Although she says that "it should be an ethic of care that does not unfairly burden women," it should be "an ethic that recognizes the moral values that motherhood has represented."[56] By valuing the caring role, we also can help move toward providing better support to others who are helping us care for our children.

Third, we must use the power of parenthood to help make change. A poll released in 2000 found that when parents step into the voting booth, they think of themselves as parents significantly more often than they view themselves as members of any other traditional political-interest group. Both mothers and fathers put "balancing work and family" at the top of their list.[57] Similarly, another poll the same year showed that the vast majority of women see balancing work and family as a critical concern.[58] In May 2000, the Million Mom March in Washington, D.C., gave mothers an opportunity to claim their right to stand up for their children. In one of the few such events since the women's movement began, women publicly acknowledged and used their "motherness" as an instrument for change. Rather than disassociating themselves from their motherhood in fear that it would be used as a stereotype to limit their options, they embraced it as a value.

Today, women can use their power as mothers to make change while not losing their sense of equality. Moreover, women do not have to do it alone. Increasingly, fathers are joining in as full partners in the care of their children, standing up for the important role of fatherhood. If our ambivalence about working mothers is driven by our concern that child care is not good, we have to work to make it better. We have to put an old tried-and-true value—our parental instincts—to work to fit the new realities and make child care the very best system it can become.

The High Regard for Education

The importance of education is a cornerstone of the American value system. Since colonial days, education has been seen as being in the best interest of the child and community. Public support for education became as American as apple pie. As the nation faced competition from other countries, the drumbeat for education reform grew. On the other hand, the care of children outside school remained a private issue. Despite the realities of modern America, the care and education of children remained separate and unrelated issues. The school bell rang, and children went home to empty houses. The summer began without fields to plow, but schools remained empty.

In part the disjuncture between child care and education grew out of the fact that public education began at a time when most mothers were home and before extended families spread across state lines. But the continued disconnection between care and education results largely from political and ideological biases. However, at the approach of the millennium there were some signs of change. The numbers of children in child care had swelled to the point where they no longer could be easily ignored. At the same time, public discussion of education intensified as test scores indicated that large numbers of children were not able to meet minimum standards of performance.

After-school programs and early education became popular issues, which coincided with increases in the numbers of children already enrolled in these programs because their mothers were working. Research on early education produced evidence that young children could spend time outside the home for part of the day without their development being harmed. Furthermore, this research opened a window on the potential benefits of out-of-home care for child development. Knowledge of how children learn demonstrated that for young children, caring and educating are inseparable.[59]

In recent years, data on the benefits of good child care have been mounting. While the debate about what the research actually says has not been free from controversy, for methodological and ideological reasons, by and large an increasing number of studies point to the fact that good care matters. Starting with a comprehensive study on early care launched by the National Institute of Child Health and Human Development (NICHD) in 1991,[60] research shows that child care in and of itself does not harm children. In fact, for low-income children especially, good care can be a benefit in the long run. Naturally, if the care is not good, and if the children are very young and in care for long hours, it can have an adverse effect. That is exactly why we need to make improvements, particularly when welfare reform in a number of states now requires women with children under age one to work.

The NICHD study and other studies indicate that the quality of care affects school readiness. One study released in 1999 found that children who attended higher-quality child care did better in math and language in elementary school.[61] Another study released in the same year found that children who had been in enriched child care did better in reading and math in the primary grades and into adulthood.[62] Moreover, other evidence, from scientific studies of the brain to high-level academic panels on precursors to literacy, all point to the importance of the early years and the quality of experiences both at home and in child care.

The evidence regarding the importance of school-age child-care programs to academic achievement is beginning to emerge.[63] New findings continue to document what most middle-class families, who ferry their children from music lessons to sporting events, always have known: A well-rounded education includes enriched activities after school.

Even without the benefit of research, it is clear that good places for children are essential to working families. If the research begins to indicate poor results from child care, than we have to use that research and the value we place on education to make things better for children. If the research shows no difference in the effects of child care, than we have to explore what we can do to take advantage of the opportunities that we have while children are in care. With or without the research, child care is where children will be spending their days while parents work. The question is no longer whether we should invest in child care, but rather under what conditions we can help children learn and grow.

The Assurance of Equal Access

The third value that the United States has strived to uphold is equality, particularly equal access to a good education. Because good child care is highly dependent on private means, families do not have equal access to high-quality child-care options for their children. For young children, the gap in access to good preschool services between families at higher and lower income levels means that inequality of education begins at an early age. At the same time, children in low-income neighborhoods do not have access to the same type of after-school opportunities that have always been open to upper-income families. This is particularly serious because art, music, and gym classes are diminishing in many public schools. Increasingly, a well-rounded education seems out of reach for the children of low-income working families.

For years, experts have been calling for increased public support of child care. A review of child-care coverage in U.S. newspapers found that the message "government should help pay for child care" was the most frequently used "frame" in substantive newspaper articles about child care published from 1994 to 1998.[64] Much less frequent were messages about the importance of the early years to child development and other education themes. Furthermore, equity of access to an educational opportunity was not even on the list of messages. Yet the goal of equity is an important value and one that is undermined by a reliance on market forces alone.

Equal access to a good education includes access to good child care before children enter school, after school, and during the summer. Children whose parents earn $15,000 a year cannot compete with children whose parents can afford to pay that same amount of money for the care of their children. Unlike public education, child care will continue to be delivered through a diverse set of private providers. However, additional public support is needed to balance a family's ability to pay with public investments in quality. Only such a third-party payment system will provide equal access to quality services for all families. The importance of equal access is an argument that should help support a shift from a private fee system to a system that offers more public support.

The Commitment to Citizenship

Fourth, we can help renew our communities through civic action on child-care issues. During the past decade there has been a growing concern about the state of democracy and the involvement of citizens at all levels. The National Commission on Civic Renewal notes that "too many of us have become passive and disengaged. Too many of us lack confidence in our capacity to make basic moral and civic judgments, to join with our neighbors to do the work of community."[65] More than 85 percent of all Americans believe that disconnection is at the heart of our most serious social problems.[66]

Citizenship is a value as old as America; it is the basis of self-government. When citizens take responsibility for improving the conditions of their lives, they strengthen their sense of power and their conviction that they can make a difference.[67] In a 1999 poll on civic action, 72 percent of the respondents stated that America's social problems are best addressed when government, religious, and charitable organizations collaborate.[68]

The good news is that there is a growing belief in community service and a renewed commitment to volunteering. More than half of the adult population volunteered nearly 20 billion hours in 1998. Many of those who currently volunteer indicate that they would be interested in becoming more involved. The participation of senior volunteers has gone up since 1995, a particularly promising trend given the aging population.[69] Furthermore, interviews commissioned by the League of Women Voters indicate that a focus on children and youth appears to be a motivating force to engage Americans in more community involvement.[70]

Civic action in child care is a rather recent trend. Although most funding for child care comes from the federal or state level, child care, like politics, is a very local issue since it is delivered in neighborhoods and towns. By promoting community service, business involvement, and parent and senior citizen participation in child care, we will be putting a traditional American value to work for change.

Putting It All Together: Promising Images for a New Era

Child care today is at an important crossroads. It took more than a century for child care to be recognized as a key support for America's poor working families. Yet it was only toward the end of the twentieth century that the potential of child care as an educational opportunity for children was beginning to be recognized. The future of child care rests on our ability to view it as a potential asset for children, families, and communities, rather than seeing it as a deficit. As the use of child care becomes a fact of life for more families, we need new ways of thinking to help us design child-care services that can respond to the needs of parents as well as children.

Over the past decade a new domestic-policy framework has been emerging, one that rests on the concept of "asset development" as a condition for economic security and opportunity for all.[71] Various types of assets provide opportunities in many ways. Assets provide financial or other resources needed to achieve a specific objective, such as to own a home, get a better job, or start a business. They also empower individuals by giving them hope, a goal to achieve, the impetus to plan and work toward a better future, and a sense of connection. Some assets affect the lives of individuals, and others the entire community or future generations.[72]

Child care is related to asset development in several ways. First, when the public assures affordable child care as a work support, it enables young working parents, particularly low-income parents, to get, keep, and even enhance what may be their most important asset, a secure means of income and benefits from a job. Without affordable child care, parents have little hope of building financial assets such as a rainy-day fund for an emergency or a down payment on a home, since child-care expenses are a significant drain on the family budget. In other words, when the public assures affordable child care, it removes a barrier to the accumulation of resources, which in turn leads to greater opportunities.

At the same time, by providing a good educational environment for children, child care helps build human capital. As increasing numbers of young children spend time in child care, these settings provide an opportunity to promote healthy child development and to reach out to parents with information and support. As more and more school-age children and young adolescents participate in programs after school, new opportunities open to promote healthy youth development. Such investments in human capital can grow over time and lead to improvements in the long-term economic prospects of children, particularly those from low-income communities. Finally, as more citizens help to develop and support a system of care in their communities, the improved and expanded child-care system itself becomes a community asset that supports economic development and civic involvement. It is against this positive framework that new images for child care can emerge.

I believe there are at least seven emerging principles that should shape our new image of child care.

First, child care is an opportunity. The reality is that children in the United States spend many hours in out-of-home settings. The argument for investing is straightforward. It is just plain common sense to take advantage of the opportunity that child care provides to promote education and to reach out to parents.

Second, regardless of the age of the child and the setting, child care is not exclusively a "home" nor a "school." Child care is a "third setting" that has value in and of itself. Since children spend long hours in care, it must reflect the comfort of home, yet it must include experiences to promote education. The educational experiences that children have in child care are not a substitute for school, but rather should complement and support the entrance into school or the regular school day. The goal of education in child care should be broadly defined, reflecting a developmental approach to learning that integrates the physical, social, emotional, and cognitive development of children at each stage of their lives.

Third, child care for young children is not the same as child care for school-age children. Like the little red schoolhouse, the term "child care" has been used to refer to services for children from birth through early adolescence. In the new era, we need to differentiate our image of child care for younger children from that for school-age children, since planning, staffing, and oversight differ among these developmental stages.

Fourth, the heart of any good child-care program is the relationship between the children and the provider, and the relationship between the provider and the parents. For young children as well as school-age children, child care must include supportive adults who help guide and mentor children while they learn. Providers themselves must be supported with adequate working conditions so that they in turn have the resources to nurture the development of children and support the family.

Fifth, child care is not an isolated service for children; rather it should be seen as a hub of support for families. Child-care providers cannot work in isolation from the families they serve nor from the communities where they live. Instead, child care can serve as a doorway for delivery of a range of services that families need. In addition, child care must reflect the diverse needs of families, which means that a range of good choices must be offered.

Sixth, child care is not a private responsibility, but must be a public service. Like any public utility, child care requires public financing to provide access to all families. It cannot continue to be funded by parents alone or financed on the backs of child-care providers. We need an infusion of public support to make it work.

Seventh, because child care supports children and families, it is everyone's business to get involved. Child care is a community-building endeavor that can help promote greater civic engagement and create stronger links between cultures and across the generations.

Based on these principles, three new images come to mind when I think of child care. I will refer to these as "a new beginning," "the new neighborhood," and "the caring community."

It is difficult for a single metaphor or any new term to capture what we really want child care for young children and families to look like. Old images and old words such as nursery school, preschool, or day care just do not seem to fit. Yet new words are still evolving. In the meantime, I use the image of a "good beginning" because I think that is what we are after. We are searching to design new settings and encourage relationships that blend caring, teaching, and nurturing. We want young children to get off to a good start with support from their family and other caregivers.

Traditionally, the neighborhood is a place where school-age children "hang out," socialize, and participate in activities that help round out their education. Sometimes these activities take place in the home, and other times in the school or the surrounding community. These activities include such things as music, art, and other lessons, clubs, sports, reading, playing games, and doing homework. In the old neighborhood there were always people around who cared: parents, grandparents, friends, and neighbors. The "new neighborhood" includes these influences, activities, and more.

The image of a "caring community" reflects the full range of supports—both formal and informal—that surround neighborhood programs. Every community needs a focal point of support services, such as information and referral for families. But services alone are not enough. Involved citizens, from parents to police to pediatricians, must be part of the process of making child care work. Furthermore, in years gone by, the old and the young came together naturally within families. In the "caring community" of the future, we have to recreate these linkages across the generations by engaging the elderly in the care of children.

This book is about values, possibilities, and the need for a national commitment. It is about reframing child care to incorporate these new principles and images. In Chapter 2, I look back to the twentieth century, tracing the history of child care as it evolved from being regarded as a deficit to being recognized as a potential asset, particularly as it became to be seen as an important work support for low-income families. In Chapters 3 and 4, I lay out a framework for redesigning child care as an educational opportunity and family support. I recommend building on existing services to create neighborhood early-learning and after-school programs. Such programs would be designed to promote child development while supporting working families. In Chapter 5, I turn to the community level, describing the network of activities that must be in place to provide a strong infrastructure to ensure quality, and examining the growing role of volunteerism and other civic actions on behalf of children in care. Using this framework, I describe some of the changes taking place across the country that seem to reflect pieces of this emerging vision.

In conclusion, in Chapter 6, I highlight the new thinking about financing child care and present six recommendations for increased public investment to achieve equal access to good early-education and after-school services. Rather than relying largely on parent fees and a marketplace approach, the United States must make a serious commitment to public financing of child care. A significant share of new public investments should take the form of "third-party payments" directly to programs and providers, supporting improvements in quality without raising fees to parents. Like higher education, transportation, and other public systems, the early-education and after-school system should include a mix of portable aid to families and quality assurances for programs and infrastructure. Financial assistance to families should include support to remain home with a newborn child, as well as expanded direct subsidy and tax support to pay for care. Direct support should be provided to improve programs, build infrastructure, and help prepare a workforce that will fit the new realities of child care.

There is a growing realization that the care of children outside the home is a fact of life for millions of children. For most mothers, the choice is no longer as simple as going to work or staying home. Most women go in and out of the workforce, with periods of part-time and full-time employment. Mothers and fathers often take turns, sharing responsibility, balancing work and family. However, most poor women have no choice, and they have very little flexibility either at home or at work. It is their children who are often at risk for educational failure, who suffer the most when child care is of poor quality, and who reap the greatest benefit when provided an enriched environment while their parents work.

The need for good child care is permanent. No end of poverty or end of war will make it go away. If we as a nation are concerned about the well-being of children, then we have to put that well-intentioned concern into action—by viewing child care not only as a work support but also as an opportunity that can enhance the health of children, improve their education, support their families, and help build a sense of community that will benefit us all.

The new framework for child care is not that of a crisis or a deficit, a problem or a safety hazard. Instead child care can be an asset that leads to new opportunities. It is time for policy-makers and the American public to embrace child care and allow it to become all it can be. It is time to allow parents the flexibility and resources they need to be successful at work and at home. The vast majority of children will spend at least some time in child care during their lifetimes. We all have to make sure it is time well spent.

2

Looking Back

*Child Care in the United States
in the Twentieth Century*

When Katherine and her husband, Jessie, had their first child, one issue became central in their lives: the need to find the highest-quality care for their son.[1] On October 23, 1997, Katherine stood in the East Room of the White House and told her story—a story repeated every day by millions of families across the country. For those of us sitting in the audience that day at the first White House Conference on Child Care, something had changed. This was not a mother leaning over the back fence sharing her story with a neighbor; this mother was talking into a microphone, and a nation was listening. Or so we hoped. Child care had made it from the backyard to the front page. It had been a very long journey.

From Charity to Work Support

It took more than a century for child care to gain any measure of public recognition in the United States. As the twentieth century began, few women were working, except for the poor. In those early days, most support of child care was philanthropic. Reflecting the value placed on "motherhood," public support eventually grew for helping very poor women remain home with their children. Although it was a transforming era for families, particularly for women and their children, for most of the century child care as an institution had a negative connotation, except in times of emergency. At best, child care was regarded as providing a safe haven while poor parents worked. Thus child care came to be seen as a targeted social service, rather than a larger public good.

In the last four decades of the twentieth century, child-care policy was driven primarily by efforts to reform welfare. Despite the rhetoric regarding the importance of family, public policy was influenced by another deep American value: the importance of work and the expectation of self-sufficiency. By the end of the millennium, child care reached a new stage. Just as welfare reform was sweeping the country, the concept of child care as a work support met education reform. The fact that millions of children were spending part of each day in care was difficult to ignore, particularly when many of these children were at risk for educational failure. Slowly, good care began to be seen as an educational experience for children.

Thus attitudes toward child care in the United States—although rarely favorable—did change somewhat to reflect changing values. The history of child care in this country can be divided into six phases, each reflecting a different view of child care: as a charity, as income support to poor mothers, as a response to emergencies, as an afterthought, as part of welfare, and as work support. Naturally, there was overlap among these phases. However, the most consistent theme driving child-care policy was the value that society placed on motherhood. This theme changed only toward the end of the century, when it was overcome by the expectation of self-sufficiency—directed primarily at poor women.

Child Care as Charity (1800s to Early 1900s)

For most of the 1800s, Americans viewed child care as an act of charity, aimed at rescuing the children of poor women forced to work in order to survive. According to historian Sonya Michel, the first institutional child care grew out of the charitable-reform movement and took the form of a nursery created as part of the Philadelphia House of Industry. Founded in 1798 by the Female Society for the Relief and Employment of the Poor, a group of female Quaker philanthropists, the House of Industry represented a departure from the practice of breaking up the family, which placed widows or other solo mothers in the almshouse and sent their children to orphanages. Instead it offered such women a way to support themselves and allowed them to keep their children with them.[2]

Unlike education, where the goal was to promote child development, the purpose of the day nurseries seemed to be to protect children from harm. The philosophy of the day nursery was basically hygienic: that is, to make sure that children were fed, kept clean, and protected from injury. Day nurseries were seen as a supplement to mothers, helping them avoid more serious disruption that could send their children away. By the late nineteenth century, dozens of day nurseries were operating across the country, through the efforts of both African-American and white female philanthropists. At the same time, networks of informal care, although less visible, also emerged.[3]

From these very early days, the basic characteristics of what we would come to call "child care" began to evolve. In her review of the history of early childhood education, Barbara Beatty points out that day nurseries were meant to be a temporary service, not permanent programs for working mothers. They were seen as a way to improve home-life rather than replace a child's "real home." Josephine Dodge, founder of the National Federation of Day Nurseries, was concerned that mothers might use day nurseries to "shirk the burden of child-rearing to earn money for the gratification of selfish ends."[4]

Although it is difficult to judge the quality and content of those early services, what does seem clear is that the "founding mothers" of the day-nursery movement believed that they could help improve the lives of children and support families. Gradually, however, attitudes toward child care appeared to deteriorate for several interrelated reasons. Child care took root during a time when charitable contributions to institutions that helped support the poor, particularly poor women with children, were still in favor. As attitudes toward the poor began to change, there was an increasing belief that the poor should be more self-sufficient and less reliant on institutions. Attention turned to helping poor women with parenting skills and homemaking.

Child Care as Income Support to Poor Mothers (Early 1900s to 1996)

Even the founding mothers of the day nurseries had viewed them as a last resort. Society reflected the belief that the only way a good mother could fulfill her role was to be home with her children. Early public policies in the United States were thus more oriented to providing income support for mothers to stay home than child-care support that would encourage mothers to work.

Nowhere was this more evident than at a conference in Washington, D.C., in 1909. Convened by President Theodore Roosevelt at the request of nine social workers and social reformers and attended by 200 child-welfare workers, this first White House Conference on Children produced a set of fifteen recommendations. In his landmark book documenting the history of child advocacy, Gilbert Steiner notes that the first of these recommendations addressed the question of child care, public and private charity, and the maintenance of the parent-child relationship:

> Home life is the highest and finest product of civilizations. It is the great molding force of mind and character. Children should not be deprived of it except for urgent and compelling reasons. Children of parents of worthy character, suffering from temporary misfortune, and children of reasonably efficient and deserving mothers who are without the support of the normal breadwinners, should as a rule be kept with their parents, such aid being given as necessary to maintain suitable homes for the rearing of children.[5]

The 1909 conference helped promote the notion of support for mothers' pensions, the precursor to Aid to Dependent Children. In 1911, the first state mothers' pension fund was enacted, and by 1920, the year women finally gained the right to vote, public assistance was available to poor mothers in more than three-fourths of the states. Although the exact provisions varied from state to state, they all provided some assistance to mothers of children under sixteen who had no male support. Such assistance usually was provided to widows, but some states also extended aid to women who had been deserted or divorced. Unfortunately, the mothers' pension programs were inadequately funded and had restrictive rules. Many mothers, particularly minority women, were specifically excluded from some programs.[6]

Where home care was not possible, the first White House Conference on Children, as well as the second, convened in 1919, called for higher standards for care out of the home.[7] However, the day-nursery movement began to wane, and the number of programs across the country eventually declined.[8] Sonya Michel notes that one of the main reasons the day-nursery movement declined was that as privately funded charity, they could not keep up with the need, and public funding was not forthcoming. Policymakers had switched their support to mothers' pensions, blocking the possibility of public funding for child care.[9]

Child Care as Temporary Response to National Emergencies (1930s to 1945)

Child care did not surface as a significant public-policy issue until the Great Depression, when once again a workforce need brought it to the attention of policy-makers. Responding to record unemployment that gripped the country, in 1933 President Franklin D. Roosevelt initiated the Works Progress Administration (WPA). For the first time, public funds were made available for out-of-home care and were used to provide child-care jobs for unemployed teachers, janitors, nurses, and cooks. Since these emergency nursery schools were employing teachers and most often were located in schools, they had a more educational orientation than the earlier day nurseries. While the WPA programs served mostly poor children, they emerged during a period of growing support for nursery school for middle-class children. Despite this increased focus on education, the programs still were seen as a temporary response to an emergency workforce issue, and support of the programs declined with the demise of the WPA.

Coming on the heels of the Great Depression, World War II caused another national workforce emergency that triggered another wave of public support for child care. In the early 1940s, the Lanham Act authorized federal expenditures for the operation of hospitals, schools, and child-care centers to meet the needs of those who worked in the defense industry. Picking up from many of the programs funded under the WPA, these child-care centers were not intended to provide services outside the defense needs of the country. In order to contribute to the war effort, $51 million was used to support some 3,000 day-care centers, serving at their peak a minimum of 105,000 preschool and school-age children.[10] Most of these centers were established in school buildings, and communities had to provide half of the funds. Some private businesses, such as the Kaiser Shipyards in Portland, Oregon, became active in the child-care issue for the first time. Using money from the U.S. Maritime Commission, Kaiser provided on-site child care for its employees.[11]

The Lanham Act centers were administered by the Federal Works Administration (FWA), which was not very sympathetic to the use of Lanham funds for child care. Although the Office of Education and the Children's Bureau attempted to influence the programs, and many programs focused on education services, these centers were primarily designed to help win the war,[12] supporting "Rosie the Riveter" on a temporary basis.

Beyond these national defense concerns, there continued to be very little public support for child care. Toward the end of the war, the FWA moved to terminate the programs despite appeals from the Congress of American Women, whose members called for continued federal support for child care. Although President Harry S Truman gave the Lanham-supported centers a six-month closeout period, this was intended to provide a transition rather than a signal of continued public support. After the war, widespread nostalgia arose for the "good old days" when mothers stayed at home to care for their children. With the exception of those in a few places such as California, New York, and Washington, D.C., many of the wartime centers were promptly closed.[13]

Child Care as an Afterthought (1945 to 1960)

Once the national emergencies were over, child care was put on the back burner of the national agenda. During the early and mid-1950s, as visions of mothers at home in aprons filled the expanding TV airwaves, child care received little public attention. Once again, a White House Conference on Children, this time held in 1950, reflected the mood of policy-makers as child care was omitted from the conference platform.[14] Although nursery school and kindergarten gained support during this period, child care continued to be seen as a temporary workforce need with a child-protection orientation. Ignoring the increasing participation of women in the workforce, policy-makers remained ambivalent about the role of public support for what was seen as a private family matter.

Ironically, despite the "Leave It to Beaver" image of the stay-at-home mom in postwar America, a quiet revolution was brewing. Two million more women were working after the war than before. In 1950, three times as many mothers were working outside the home as in the years leading up to the war.[15] Furthermore, the real legacy of women's participation in the war effort was that it served to legitimize work for women and gave millions their first opportunity in the workforce, helping to bring child care one step closer to the mainstream. Yet debates about the effect of women's work on children raged throughout the 1950s in professional journals and the popular press. The common thinking during these years was that dire consequences would result if mothers chose to work. A series of papers in the 1940s documented the devastating effects of poor institutional care on orphans, which was attributed to the children's lack of attachment to a specific caregiver. These findings were reflected in the popular literature and used to urge mothers to forgo employment during the preschool years for the sake of the children.[16] In the public dialogue, questions were raised about the motives behind women's decisions to work and the effects of those decisions on their family.

Meanwhile, the growing use of child care in communities across the country began to be documented, helping to dispel the myth that child care was needed only in times of emergency. In the early 1950s, an interagency federal committee (including the Women's Bureau, the Children's Bureau, the Office of Education, and the Bureaus of Employment Security and Public Assistance) was established to conduct research on the need for child care. In addition, the Women's Bureau conducted its own study in 1953, which highlighted the need for child care in twenty-eight cities in twelve states, documenting the fact that many women in the labor force had young children, yet facilities were "overcrowded, discriminatory, costly and uneven in quality."[17]

One of the early steps to address the ongoing needs of poor working families was taken in the 1950s. The role of government policy in child care became part of the larger tax discussions that were taking place in Congress at the time, and in 1954 a proposal emerged to create a tax deduction for child-care expenses. Since attitudes about maternal employment remained ambivalent, the debate focused on whether or not to impose an income cap on the deduction and what level of expenses should be allowed.[18] By limiting expenses and capping income, Congress gave a nod to the employment of low-income women while maintaining its distance from child care in general.

The child-care deduction was the first major public-policy step since the Lanham Act, and certainly the only significant action taken during the 1950s. Although the deduction clearly focused only on low-income families, it was significant because it provided ongoing support to working mothers, a departure from the policies that had provided income support for nonworking welfare mothers. Furthermore, the deduction was the forerunner of the dependent-care tax credit, which emerged in the 1970s and was expanded in the 1980s to allow a child-care credit to families at all income levels—to this day, one of the only universally available child care benefits ever enacted.

By the late 1950s, advocacy for child care was becoming stronger at the local and state levels, exemplified by Elinor Guggenheimer of New York. Through her efforts, and those of other child-welfare leaders, the Inter-City Committee for Day Care of Children, later named the National Committee on the Day Care of Children, was formed in 1958 to put child care on the national agenda.[19] Despite growing recognition of the need for child care, feelings continued to run deep that mothers should not choose to work for reasons other than financial. In

1960, two conferences were held in Washington, D.C.: the White House Conference on Children and Youth and the follow-up National Conference on the Day Care of Children. In her description of events leading up to the conferences, Sonya Michel quotes President Dwight D. Eisenhower, who attended the first planning committee meeting in December 1958. The president reflected the conservative opinion of the times when he stated:

> Today there are twenty-two million working women. Of that twenty-two million, seven and a half million are working mothers, and unquestionably a great number of [them] are working because they have to keep the wolf from the door. They work because they have to work. But if there is only a tiny percentage doing this because they prefer a career to an active career of real motherhood and care for the little child, I should think they would have to consider what is the price they are paying in terms of the opportunity that child has been denied. Certainly no one can do quite as much in modeling the child's habits of thinking and implanting certain standards as can the mother.[20]

This continued ambivalence about the role of mothers in the workforce stood in the way of significant progress on child care for decades. Over the years, advocates attempted to broaden the issue, particularly as more women chose to work outside the home. There were highs and lows in the debates over child care, with the issue gaining attention whenever a special event was held, a new piece of legislation was introduced, a forward-looking president was elected, or new research was released. Yet for a significant portion of the twentieth century, child care was an afterthought in domestic policy.

Child Care as Part of Welfare (1960 to 1989)

When reviewing child-care policies in the later part of the twentieth century, two trends become apparent. First, concern over the growing welfare rolls fueled interest in child care, which resulted in the incorporation of a number of child-care provisions into each successive wave of welfare reform that emerged from the 1960s through the 1990s. Second, efforts to move child-care policies beyond welfare, and to see it as an ongoing need of average working families, were met with continued resistance. Although some progress was made through tax policy, significant levels of direct assistance to working families outside the welfare system did not emerge until the last decade of the twentieth century.

In 1967, amendments to the Social Security Act established the Work Incentive Program, which required parents on welfare, except those with young children, to register in work and training programs. These new amendments also required states to provide child-care services to families who participated in such programs. Until the early 1980s, the primary mechanism within the welfare system for encouraging work was a set of incentives that allowed recipients to keep a portion of their earnings without a reduction in their welfare benefits.[21]

Debate over public assistance continued throughout the 1970s and may have been one of the reasons that President Nixon showed at least some early interest in the child-care issue. A significant effort was underway in the late 1960s to move the child-care issue forward in a broader context, detaching it from welfare policy and focusing on comprehensive legislation. Like many other industrialized countries, the United States was poised in the early 1970s to develop a more integrated system of child-development programs that would respond to the needs of working parents and promote good services for children. With the unique backing of a broad-based coalition of diverse groups, and after a vigorous debate in Congress, the Comprehensive Child Development Act of 1971 passed both the Senate and the House, only to be vetoed by President Nixon.

The Nixon veto was one of the biggest setbacks in the twentieth century for working families and their children. Edward Zigler, who served as the first director of the Office of Child Development within the Department of Health, Education and Welfare, later wrote that the bill "embodied my greatest hopes, but also led to my greatest disappointment."[22] The legislation would have developed a network of child-care programs, ensured federal standards, and provided funds to train caregivers and purchase facilities. The $2-billion authorization, although far less than needed, would have provided support on a sliding scale to hundreds of thousands of low-income working families.[23]

The failure to enact the Comprehensive Child Development Act is most often remembered by the language that Nixon used vetoing the bill. In his review of the history of the bill, Steiner notes that the Nixon veto reflected the words of a widely quoted article by James J. Kilpatrick which called the bill "the boldest and most far reaching scheme ever advanced for the Sovietization of American Youth."[24] Nixon's statement argued that "for the Federal Government to plunge headlong financially into supporting child development would commit the vast moral authority of the National Government to the side of communal approaches to child rearing over (and) against the family-centered approach."[25]

The message was clear: Child care was once again seen as contrary to good mothering and something to be avoided for the good of children and the country.

Not only did the veto play into the traditional ambivalence toward working mothers, but it also disrupted the momentum of advocates to pass significant legislation despite repeated attempts throughout the 1970s. Moreover, it shattered for decades to come the hope of merging child care with a child-development approach. From this point on, Head Start and other preschool programs, which were always seen as child-development programs, and child care, which historically had been seen as a temporary custodial service for working parents, continued to move along separate tracks.

Despite the cultural signals that women should remain home, throughout the 1970s and 1980s women continued to enter and remain in the workforce. Federal policy did not keep pace with this change; rather it appeared to take several steps backward as child care suffered through deep cuts in social services. Alfred Kahn and Sheila Kamerman characterize the 1980s as a period when "decentralization, deregulation, and privatization became the guiding principles in federal child-care policy."[26] Efforts to implement federal child-care standards came to a halt. Cuts in social-service programs limited the growth of federal spending on child care. The focus turned away from the federal government and toward a greater role for the states and the private sector.

By the middle to late 1980s, the child-care debates intensified—and the ambivalence surrounding working women persisted. A 1984 cover story in *Newsweek* reflected the thinking of the times: "Many Americans have ambivalent feelings about day care. In a society that claims to put the family first, child care outside the home may appear to be, at best, a necessary evil."[27] The article, like many others that appeared throughout the 1980s, described the quality and affordability issues that families were facing as they made tough decisions in balancing work and family.

Once again, this debate attached itself to welfare legislation. This time, however, the federal government went one step beyond child care for welfare recipients. The Family Support Act of 1989 not only guaranteed child-care assistance for welfare families but also provided an entitlement of up to one year of child-care assistance for families who were leaving the welfare rolls. This was an important step forward in extending child care beyond welfare as a support for working poor families.

Child Care as Work Support (1990 to Present)

Throughout the 1980s, many groups representing children and women's issues continued to focus on promoting public policies to support child care. While real progress had been made in securing the child-care entitlements as part of welfare reform in 1989, only minimal support was available to low-income working families who had never been on welfare and for families a year after leaving public assistance. For many women, lack of affordable child care was a primary reason for remaining on welfare or for returning to it. A series of studies in the late 1980s documented the need for child-care assistance and the growing concern with quality. Two events took place between 1990 and 1996 that finally tied child care more directly to ongoing work support: the passage of the Child Care and Development Block Grant (CCDBG) in 1990 and the passage of welfare reform legislation in 1996.

The Child Care and Development Block Grant of 1990. With the needs of working families growing, a broad-based coalition, the Alliance for Better Child Care, spearheaded by the Children's Defense Fund, came together in the late 1980s to help pass the first significant child-care legislation in two decades. The debate over passage of CCDBG reflected the emotions and ambivalence that had surrounded the child-care issue throughout the century. While coalition members fought hard to convey the needs of working mothers and their children, the opposition pictured child care as "antifamily," arguing once again that providing child care would encourage women to work, undermining motherhood and putting their children at risk. The deliberations also reflected old debates over the role of various agencies and levels of government in the management and administration of child-care resources as well as the role of the federal government in protecting and supporting quality. Successful passage of the bill appeared to stall many times throughout 1990, as various counter- provisions were debated.

Nothing provoked more passion in the debate than the role of parental choice, and more specifically the role of "certificates" or vouchers in the delivery of child-care assistance. The voucher issue caused tension, sending traditional allies into opposite camps. As in the voucher debate in public education today, opponents of the provision were concerned about a market-based approach to child care and the possibility that church-state issues could surface if public funds were used for sectarian child care.

Proponents argued that parents needed maximum flexibility in order to choose an appropriate provider for their children and that, in fact, unlike public education, most children were already cared for outside any public system, including facilities that included churches and the homes of relatives and friends. The Bush administration, although under political pressure to oppose any new child-care legislation, also recognized the opportunity to move the "parental choice" issue forward. The Children's Defense Fund and other coalition members had been working on child-care legislation for decades and tasted victory on a major children's issue affecting millions of working families. A well-organized grassroots network lobbied effectively for final passage. Despite serious concerns over the voucher provisions raised by several members of the coalition, including many influential national organizations, the Child Care and Development Block Grant passed both houses of Congress as part of the reconciliation act and became law in November, 1990.[28]

In addition to CCDBG, Congress established a new capped entitlement, the At-Risk Child Care Program, for families who were "at risk" of going on welfare.

Enactment of CCDBG was significant because it was the first major child-care legislation since the vetoed Comprehensive Child Development Act to provide resources for low-income working families beyond those who had been receiving welfare. Yet unlike the 1970 proposal, which would have sent funds directly to programs, CCDBG funding went primarily to parents through vouchers. Furthermore, since it was the first block grant specifically focused on child care, it galvanized a series of public and private activities in the states. For the first time in the history of the country, every state was required to develop a child-care plan for working families.

Despite this leap forward, CCDBG had serious limitations. First, the funds authorized were only half the amount that would have been provided under the Comprehensive Child Development Act some twenty years earlier. Although the states could establish eligibility for families earning up to 75 percent of median income, discretionary resources remained limited, and most states were forced to target resources to very low-income families. Furthermore, CCDBG added another set of policies to the child-care landscape, which was already replete with complex rules governing the child-care policies set in motion by the 1989 Family Support Act.

One of the most serious limitations of CCDBG was its lack of attention to quality. Despite the words "child development" in its title, CCDBG was more focused on providing work support to as many families as possible rather than ensuring the quality of services to children. Although one goal was to improve the quality of care, the vast majority of the funds were to be used to provide direct services through a system that offered parents a choice of providers. Standards were left up to the states, with only minimum protection for health and safety. While one-quarter of the funds could be spent on improving the quality and availability of child care, only 5 percent of the funds were actually targeted to quality improvements.[29]

The Personal Responsibility and Work Opportunity Reconciliation Act of 1996. The second event that linked child care to work was the passage of the welfare reform bill of 1996. As the debate over welfare heated up in the early 1990s, once again child care became a key issue. At that time federal child-care assistance included two entitlements: a guarantee of child care for families on welfare, and a guarantee for families up to one year after leaving welfare. In addition, states received more than $1 billion through a combination of the Child Care and Development Block Grant and the At-Risk Child Care Program. Both of these federal programs served similar populations, primarily low-income working families. There was a growing consensus that the complex set of child-care programs and policies needed to be simplified; however, there was much to be debated. Issues surfaced regarding the level of support needed, the continuation of the guarantee for child-care assistance for families required to work, and the quality assurance needed for children.

In 1992, as the first wave of CCDBG funding was being spent in the states, Bill Clinton was elected president with a campaign promise that called for "ending welfare as we know it." Under the leadership of Mary Jo Bane and David Ellwood, two of the most prominent scholars on the subject of welfare policy, the new administration began crafting welfare legislation, including new provisions to expand child-care assistance to working poor families. Despite renewed attention to addressing quality issues, child care still was seen largely as a workforce issue.

The welfare legislation proposed by the administration would have continued the guarantee for both welfare and child-care assistance. However, it also would have focused more attention and resources on work support by significantly expanding child care for working poor families and providing new training opportunities. Furthermore, it would have ensured some additional funds targeted to improving quality. But the congressional elections of 1994, in which Republicans gained control of both the House and the Senate, changed everything, and the administration's proposal never received serious consideration.

Despite this setback, in the continuing debate over welfare reform, the administration and some members of Congress did stake out a strong position that argued for dedicating significant new resources to child care. In the end, they won an increase of $4 billion in child-care funding over a period of five years. New funding levels were consolidated into a block grant to states that became part of the final welfare bill, the Personal Responsibility and Work Opportunity Reconciliation Act of 1996. However, it was clear from the start that the funds fell far short of the child-care support that would be needed to serve working families beyond the welfare population. In partial response to the concern over child-care funding, a provision was added to the bill that would allow states to transfer up to 30 percent of their traditional welfare funds (now called Temporary Assistance to Needy Families, or TANF), to child care. The new consolidated child-care program took the name of the original block grant, Child Care and Development Block Grant. The administration later referred to it as the Child Care and Development Fund (CCDF), since it brought together both discretionary and mandatory funding.

While Congress and the popular press covering welfare reform focused primarily on the debate over the guarantee of income support, there was relatively little attention to the child-care entitlements. In the end, the most controversial provision in the welfare bill was the elimination of the entitlement for cash assistance to families and the establishment of time limits for receiving welfare benefits. In one stroke, Congress and the administration ended an important income support that had been in place for decades. Just as poor women lost this important guarantee, they received another blow: the loss of their entitlement to child care.

It is difficult to speculate why there was not more debate on the loss of the child-care entitlement. At least two possible explanations come to mind. First, the whole notion of ending entitlements of any kind permeated the welfare debate. In this sense, the child-care guarantees were swept away with the tide. Second, the child-care provisions had become very complex over the years. There was some opinion that a more simplified block grant, with adequate funds, might be able to protect welfare families and, at the same time, streamline the administration of child-care assistance.

Although simplification of the system was a welcome relief to some, the immediate consequences of losing the child-care guarantees were a serious concern to many others. The only minimum child-care protection that remained in the final bill was an assurance that states could not impose sanctions on women with children under age six who were unable to work due to the lack of "appropriate" child care. However, this provision had serious limitations. Not only did the states retain the authority to define what was "appropriate," but for women who remained on public assistance, claiming lack of child care as a reason not to work, the clock continued to tick as they moved one step closer to the time when the welfare checks would stop.

The establishment of a fixed amount for child care and the loss of guaranteed child care for welfare families had an impact on how the states approached child-care assistance. Faced with the immediate need to move families from welfare to work, and lacking assurance that additional federal funds would be forthcoming in future appropriations, some states initially targeted welfare families at the expense of working families. Furthermore, given the need to move quickly, several states continued complex child-care policies such as maintaining multiple child-care programs and conflicting rules, rather than moving to a more simplified system. Other states, however, such as Illinois and Wisconsin, moved to an income-based system of child-care eligibility, rather than a welfare-related system, forging new ground in the effort to serve low-income working families.

While most of the debate about child care revolved around the level of funding, serious concerns surrounded the quality provisions. Although attempts were made to ensure that additional funds were set aside for quality, the final bill required states to set aside only 4 percent for such activities. The new law thus eliminated the CCDBG requirement that states set aside 25 percent of the funds to expand availability and to improve quality. Some states were using the funds set aside for availability to increase the supply of quality programs. Therefore, although the new 4 percent targeted for quality was to be funded from a larger pool of money, it still represented less than the states were spending in 1995 for quality activities through CCDBG.

Other provisions in the new law ran counter to ensuring quality care for children. First, the law eliminated the CCDBG requirements that payment rates take into account variations in the costs of providing child care to children of different ages in different settings, and the additional costs of providing child care for children with special needs. Furthermore, states no longer were required to determine and pay reimbursement rates at the 75th percentile of the market, a provision that emerged in the child care regulations of the 1989 Family Support Act. Finally, health and safety standards remained minimal. Although welfare-related child care did not have the same level of health and safety standards as CCDBG, the new law extended the CCDBG provisions to all care funded in the consolidated program. However, language elsewhere in the bill actually gave states more flexibility on health and safety issues.[30]

At a Crossroads: Child Care as Education (1995 to 2002)

As the millennium approached, interest and activity around child-care issues grew. As I have described, child-care assistance became associated with an important American value: the work ethic. Welfare reform had helped transform public attitudes toward child care, at least for the poor. There was increased recognition that if low-income parents were required to work, they needed child-care assistance.

Along the way, something else was changing. Child care appeared to be at a crossroads. Not only was it being linked to work, but child care also had begun to be seen as an environment that could promote positive child and youth development. While traditionally child care had been considered separate from education, now it began to be seen as part of the education-reform agenda. Although it is impossible to point to any one incident that signaled a new direction in the long journey for child care to be recognized as an educational opportunity for children, over the years several research and policy reports began to link the quality of care to educational outcomes (see Chapters 3 and 4). Together, these reports sent a clear message that the early years are important and that where children spend them, whether at home or in child care, matters to their overall development. While reinforcing the importance of the family, these reports increasingly recognized the growing influence of quality child care on children, particularly low-income children. After decades of viewing child care as separate from education, a transformation began.

A Turning Point (1995 to 2000)

Slowly, improving child care and reforming education appeared to be two sides of the same coin. Policies at the state and local level began to reflect this changing view. While most policy-makers continued to see child care only as a work support, more and more people were talking about the dual nature of care and the importance of promoting education. This changing attitude was reflected in a number of events that took place at the federal level during the Clinton administration, including the establishment of the Child Care Bureau in 1995, the White House Conference on Child Care in 1997, and the President's Child Care Initiative of 1998. Some of the policies set forward during this period represent a clear departure from the old vision of child care solely as a work support, thus providing another signal that child care was moving in a new direction.

The Establishment of the Child Care Bureau. At the federal, state, and local levels, there was a new receptivity to pulling together the many aspects of child care and developing new, coordinated structures that would reflect the dual goals of child care as a children's service as well as a work support. In early 1994, while the administration worked on a welfare bill, a decision was made within the Department of Health and Human Services to streamline the administration of child-care assistance and to create a strong focal point for this ever-growing and important issue.

Historically, federal child-care assistance had been administered in at least two places. By 1994 the Child Care and Development Block Grant was under the direction of the Children's Bureau, the part of the Administration for Children, Youth and Families that was traditionally responsible for child-welfare services. On the other hand, child-care entitlements were administered by the Office of Family Assistance, the home of cash assistance. Unlike Head Start, which was seen as a child-development program with its own bureau, child care had been seen as a welfare support on one hand and a child-welfare service on the other. Although child-care units or task forces had existed within the federal government at various points in history, they were most often small, under-funded, and scattered among various agencies.

From the onset of the planning process, the goal was to create a new home for child care that would help streamline and consolidate policies. This was particularly important in an era favoring smaller and more efficient government. The new bureau was to be established within the Administration for Children, Youth and Families. By placing child care in a children's agency, and outside a purely welfare or social-welfare orientation, a new direction was set. Child care was to be seen as a two-generation program: It was considered a service to children as well as a work support for their parents.

The Child Care Bureau began official operations in January 1995. Its mission statement describes the bureau as dedicated to enhancing the quality, affordability, and supply of child care for all families. The bureau's two-generation focus was designed to promote healthy child development and family self-sufficiency. Quality services were to include safe and healthy learning environments, parent involvement, training and support for providers, and continuity of services. Linkages to health, family support, and other community agencies were part of the vision. Finally, consumer education, public awareness, and outreach to the private sector and community services also were included in its mission.[31] Although legislative authority did not yet allow this new mission statement to drive resources, the Child Care Bureau did provide critical leadership to steer the issue in a new direction, particularly to link child care to health and family support and to cooperate with the Head Start Bureau to encourage greater collaboration among programs to improve services for children in child care (see Chapter 3).

The 1997 White House Conference. While the Child Care Bureau was getting underway, a wave of interest in brain research and early education began to grow. *Starting Points*, the Carnegie Corporation's landmark report on the importance of the first three years of life, set off a national dialogue that brought renewed attention to parenting, children's health, and the quality of early-childhood experiences. A White House Conference on Early Childhood Development was planned, and a special issue of *Newsweek* focused on the early years. The deep interest and energy of actor Rob Reiner in promoting the implications of brain research for child development helped fuel the "I Am Your Child Campaign," a national public-awareness campaign that brought a message about the importance of early brain development to parents, child-care providers, and policy-makers across the country. Although some questioned the interpretation of the new research,[32] a higher level of awareness toward the early years was achieved, and another link was formed between education and high-quality child care.

In the spring of 1997, planning for the White House Conference on Early Childhood Development was in high gear. Although the logistics, speaker selection, and the politics of the invitation list seem to rule any White House conference at times, it is the formulation of policy announcements that is central to the delivery of a meaningful event. Policy announced at the White House can either chart a new course or can be largely ceremonial with little long-term impact. Each agency had labored for weeks with its list of accomplishments and ideas, hoping to get visibility for emerging initiatives. One year after welfare reform, many people within the Department of Health and Human Services, from the secretary on down, wanted to see something about child care announced and discussed at the conference to "keep it on the agenda." There was a strong belief that to make welfare really work for children and families, child care for low-income working families would have to continue to expand, and significant investments would be needed to improve quality. The night before the conference, HHS officials received good news: Although the president would not be announcing a major new child-care initiative, he would talk about child care, point to the military child-care system as a model, and announce a separate conference on child care to be held that fall.

For those who had been toiling away at child care for years, the announcement of a White House conference on the topic of child care was a hopeful sign. Child-care advocates had been working to bring the issue back onto the national stage since the veto of the Comprehensive Child Development Act in 1971. Although passage of the Child Care and Development Act in 1990 was an important part of this history, there was so much more to be done. The fact that the announcement about the White House Conference on Child Care grew out of an early-education forum was a new perspective on an old issue: that child care was about the education of children as well as a support for working parents.

For the next six months, many meetings were held to help plan the White House Conference on Child Care and to gather ideas for policy initiatives. White House staff met with a wide variety of advocates and other leaders, seeking recommendations on themes and goals for the conference. Top agency officials were asked to participate. By

October 23, 1997, thousands of people across the country were linked by satellite to this national event. With presentations by the president, the vice president, the First Lady and three cabinet secretaries, including Health and Human Services, Education, and Treasury, child care took its place on the national agenda.

Throughout the day it was clear that child care was being seen not only as a workforce issue and a business issue, but an education issue as well. Speaker after speaker spoke of the importance of good care to healthy child development. The military child-care system, which had invested heavily in quality improvement, was held up as a model. Secretary of Education Richard Riley described the importance of child care this way:

> What happens during the school day is only part of the solution. What goes on in a child's life before and after school . . . are crucial ingredients. . . . Our young people need and deserve more than an afternoon spent alone in a house, sitting alone in front of a television. . . . We need to focus on creating positive alternatives . . . positive place(s) where they can go before and after school.[33]

The stage was being set for an important new policy direction.

President Clinton had campaigned in 1992 on a promise to create a network of child-care programs as important as the public schools.[34] Kicking off the White House conference, he recalled a series of speeches he had given as a candidate about what the country should look like in the twenty-first century. The president put it this way:

> [We have] to make sure we live by what we believe when we say that all parents should be able to succeed at home and at work and that every child counts. No parent should ever have to choose between work and family, between earning a decent wage and caring for a child.[35]

By emphasizing child care as both a work support and a children's issue, the president himself reinforced the two-generation focus that was emerging around child care. He went on to say that "affordable, accessible and safe child care" was "America's next great frontier in strengthening our families and our future." No longer was child care something that would weaken the family; rather, good care could strengthen families. This was a far cry from the message that had emerged about child care throughout the history of the country. Things appeared to be changing. As then HHS secretary Donna Shalala, ever a sports enthusiast, put it in her remarks that day, "I see us in a seventh- inning stretch; we know we are doing better, but not as well as we should."[36]

The 1998 Child Care Initiative. At the White House conference, the president announced that the administration would develop a plan to improve access to affordable care that he would unveil in his upcoming State of the Union address. When the bright lights dimmed for the day and the last person had left the conference, the difficult task of putting together a policy agenda had just begun. From late October until January, a series of high-level meetings were held with the domestic policy staff to craft a child-care initiative. The messages from the White House conference had been clear: Despite the gains made by child care through the 1996 bill, affordability and quality remained serious issues.

The Child Care Initiative was unveiled by the president in January 1998. The proposal called for an increase of $21 billion. I believe what came out of this planning process held great promise for establishing an important foundation for sound child-care policy. The key elements of the plan included expanded financial assistance, after-school programs, direct support for early-childhood programs, and improvements in infrastructure, licensing, and professional development. Specifically, the proposal included:[37]

- *Child-care support to parents.* To make child care affordable for more parents, the proposal provided $7.5 billion to expand CCDBG and $5.2 billion to expand the dependent-care tax credit both over five years.
- *After-school programs.* An $800 million increase over five years for the 21st Century Community Learning Centers. At the time, this was a small federal program that was funded under the community-school provisions of the Elementary and Secondary Education Act. This program clearly promoted the use of after-school time to help improve the academic achievement of school-age children.
- *Investment in early education.* HHS also had developed a new proposal for younger children. Along with a significant expansion of Head Start ($3.5 billion), the department called for the establishment of an Early Learning Fund to be supported at $600 million a year for five years—an investment of $3 billion—to improve the quality of child care for children from birth to age five. Modeled on North Carolina's Smart Start initiative, the Early Learning Fund would provide resources to states for a range of activities and set in motion a community-planning process to improve the quality of care. Similar initiatives had been introduced in Congress in recent years.

- *Infrastructure improvement.* The administration also requested $500 million to improve licensing, $250 million for a professional-development fund to improve the training of child-care teachers, and $150 million for research, all over five years.

The 1998 Child Care Initiative was announced with much fanfare and great expectations, and many advocates expected immediate results. Yet it took three years to make any real progress, and some of the improvements were not realized. For several reasons, the administration was not successful in its attempts to substantially increase funding in 1998. First, funding was tied closely to tobacco legislation, which would have provided additional resources, so when this failed, money was not available to fully fund the child-care proposals. Furthermore, there was a growing sense in Congress that the states had enough money to cover child-care needs. Although the states were fully utilizing CCDBG funds made available in 1997, declining caseloads had resulted in surpluses in the new TANF block grant. Because states could by law transfer funds from TANF to child care, many members of Congress believed additional child-care resources were not necessary, despite the fact that most states still were serving only a small percentage of eligible families. Finally, other personal and political distractions facing the administration and Congress affected this issue as well as others during this period.

Although substantial increases were not forthcoming in 1998 or 1999, the administration did secure some of the funding that was more closely linked to education, namely additional funds for 21st Century Community Learning Centers, an increase in Head Start, a doubling of the quality funds in CCDBG, and a $10 million set-aside for research. Furthermore, determined to push forward on child care, in the early months of 2000, the administration once again requested substantial child care funding, including a request of more than $800 million for expansion of CCDBG and an expansion of the child care tax credit. Moreover, they proposed an additional $1 billion for Head Start, the establishment of the Early Learning Fund, and additional funds to bring funding for the 21st Century Community Learning Centers up to $1 billion a year.

In the fall of 2000, after the close of the fractious presidential campaign, and with only a few months remaining in the Clinton presidency, the administration finally succeeded in obtaining the biggest increases in history in both child care ($817 million) and Head Start ($933 million). Moreover, funding for 21st Century Community Learning Centers also increased by more than $300 million that year. In addition, in the final hours of budget negotiations, Senators Ted Stevens and Edward M. Kennedy managed to win approval of a bipartisan provision in the appropriation authorizing the Early Learning Opportunities Act.

The Promise of Education (2000 to 2002)

While child care began to meet education in the closing years of last century, the child-care story still is evolving. As the Bush administration took office, education reform took top billing on the domestic agenda. Most of the administration's focus on early childhood was on curriculum and assessment, with a strong interest in promoting literacy. In July 2001, during the first year of the new administration, First Lady Laura Bush also held a White House conference, this one on early-childhood cognitive development. While this high-level interest in early learning was welcomed by the early-childhood community, it still was not clear whether this interest in education would translate to better child care. While the president requested new funds for an early reading program, the overall budget requests that year did not reflect an interest in promoting improved or expanded child-care services.

As the second year of the administration opened, signs of interest in early childhood continued. In January 2002, Mrs. Bush testified before the Senate Health, Education, Labor and Pensions Committee. Her testimony that morning reflected a commitment to helping young children succeed. Thinking back on what she had seen over the years, she said: "I realized that, for many children, being left behind did not begin in elementary school—it began in the years between diapers and their first backpacks." She went on to say that she had convened the White House summit the previous summer to "develop a clear understanding of what parents, grandparents, early childhood teachers, child care providers, and other caregivers can systematically do to provide children with rich and rewarding early experiences during this period of development that is marked by extraordinary growth and change."[38]

During the early months of 2002, the president focused much attention on education by signing an important bipartisan education bill, the No Child Left Behind Act. New provisions in the law provided for $75 million for literacy programs in early childhood. Moreover, in his State of the Union speech delivered on January 29, 2002, the president indicated that despite the passage of the landmark bill, there was more to do. He went on to say, "We need to prepare our children to read and succeed in school with improved Head Start and early childhood development programs."[39]

In the winter of 2002, the child-care community continued to wait for signals that child care, both for younger children and for school-age children, would be seen as an important part of the domestic agenda. Tax cuts and budget constraints threatened the momentum that had been growing in the closing years of the century. When the Bush administration unveiled its plans to reauthorize welfare, those hoping to continue to expand and improve child care were disappointed. Although the administration proposed to increase the work requirements for families, no new funding for child care was offered.[40]

In February 2002 the Senate Committee on Health, Education, Labor and Pensions held a hearing on early education. Dr. Jack Shonkoff from Brandeis University, who had chaired the National Research Council Committee on Integrating the Science of Early Childhood Development, spoke about the importance of early child care to education. In his testimony he posed an important question:

> How can the recently enacted No Child Left Behind Act of 2001 emphasize the need for stronger performance standards and financial incentives to attract bright and highly motivated teachers, while we simultaneously tolerate large percentages of inadequately trained and poorly compensated providers of early child care and education who have an important influence on the foundations of school readiness?[41]

While child-care advocates continued to argue for more child-care assistance to support working families, they also called for increasing investments in the quality of services. They hoped that the administration's interest in literacy, character education, and other important values could be promoted outside school through child care. In April 2002, the president announced an early-education initiative. While it called for states to develop professional development plans and voluntary early learning guidelines, and to promote better coordination, all very important goals, it did not include any new resources to make the needed improvements once the planning was complete.[42]

Several weeks before the president's announcement, Senator Kennedy and others on Capitol Hill began a series of discussions with White House officials regarding early-childhood issues.[43]

On the same day the president made his announcement, Senator Kennedy announced that he would be working with Senator George

Voinovich and others to introduce a new $5 billion, bipartisan early-education initiative that would include incentive grants to states to create a seamless system of high-quality early-education and support activities.[44] On May 23, 2002, Senator Kennedy, together with Republicans as well as other Democrats, introduced the Early Care and Education Act.[45]

Would the administration and Congress view child care as a potential asset to build upon to promote education? Would working families be provided the supports they need to really " make work pay?" Would early education begin to receive the attention it deserved? Would these two tracks begin to merge? These and other important questions would surface during the debate in the spring and summer of 2002 during the reauthorization of child care and the emergence of new provisions to address the school readiness of young children.

Across a century of child-care policy, the United States has moved from perceiving child care as charity, to providing income support to poor mothers, to offering temporary child-care support during times of emergency, to offering a guarantee for child-care assistance as mothers move off welfare, to providing work support for low-income families. Finally, during the very last years of the century, child care reached a crossroads. Now we are poised to enter a new era, one that again reflects the values so important to this country. Traditional values—family, education, equality of opportunity, and citizenship—can provide the fuel to light a new fire under the movement to improve access to high-quality services for all children and their families.

3

A Good Beginning

Redesigning Child Care as Early Education and Family Support

Second only to the immediate family, child care is the context in which early development unfolds, starting in infancy and continuing through school entry, for the vast majority of young children in the United States.

—National Research Council and Institute of Medicine, *From Neurons to Neighborhoods*

When I first taught in a child-care program for young children in Washington, D.C., Karen was one of the four-year-olds in my class. Her mother, a single parent, lived and worked only minutes from the Capitol. Karen and a group of eighteen to twenty other children spent their days with me and a teaching assistant. The center was where Karen ate breakfast and lunch, listened to stories, explored new interests, made first friends, and learned to write her name. She came to the center early in the morning and often stayed until closing.

This center, not the kindergarten classroom, was Karen's first formal educational experience. This was a place that could leave an impression, that could make a difference in her readiness for school. It was a place to share information about parenting and good health care, a place that could provide support for parents in their everyday struggles to balance work and family.

54

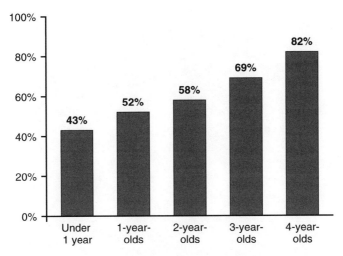

FIGURE 4. *Percentage of children under age five in non-parental care on a regular basis, by age, in 1999.*
 Source: Tabulations generated by Donald J. Yarosz, National Institute for Early Education Research, Rutgers University, based on data from the U.S. Department of Education, National Center for Education Statistics, National Household Survey, 1999, Parent Interviews.

Yet despite these opportunities, the program was strained. Teachers came and went, lured by higher-paying jobs and better opportunities. Although the rooms were bright and sunny, equipment was limited: The playground equipment was broken, and even the eating utensils were in short supply. Few special services were available to families. Yet the parents that I greeted every day were some of the most needy that I have ever seen, struggling with low wages, high housing costs, long working hours, and a host of health and family issues.

More than two decades have passed. Karen must be a grown woman by now, with young children of her own. I hope they have better care than we were able to offer her mother. Unfortunately, I know that even today, in the earliest years of the twenty-first century, in one of the richest nations in the world, I still could find far too many examples of care for young children that is less than optimal.

In 1999, 61 percent of young children spent time in non-parental care, regardless of whether their mothers were employed.[1] In the same year, more than 50 percent of one-year-olds were in non-parental care on a regular basis (see Figure 4).[2] Among children from birth to four whose parents were employed, The Urban Institute's National Survey

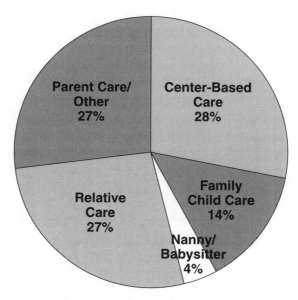

FIGURE 5. *Primary child-care arrangements of preschool children from birth to age four who have an employed parent, 1999.*

Source: Sonenstein et al., "Primary Child Care Arrangements of Employed Parents: Findings from the 1999 National Survey of America's Families," Occasional Paper No. 59, *Assessing the New Federalism* (Washington, D.C.: The Urban Institute, June 2002), p. 4.

of American Families found that about half were cared for by parents and relatives, and about half in centers, family child care, or "in their own home" with a nanny (see Figure 5). A significant number of children of working families are in care for more than thirty-five hours a week (see Table 1).[3]

Regardless of the setting, we need to see all those hours and days in care as opportunities to help young children grow and develop and to help their families thrive. We should redesign child care for young children to develop an early-learning system that includes a more cohesive and better financed network of neighborhood-based services.

The Evolution of Early Education in the United States

In the late 1800s there were about three thousand public and private kindergartens serving some two hundred thousand children. By the early

TABLE 1. *Hours that Children with Employed Mothers Spend in Child Care*

Hours	Percentage of children
No hours	22
1 to 14 hours	15
15 to 34 hours	24
35 or more hours	39

Source: Urban Institute, National Survey of America's Families, 1999.

part of the twentieth century, middle- and upper-class mothers already had recognized the benefits of early-childhood education. The National Kindergarten Association, begun in 1909, had a goal of kindergarten for all children, and although federal legislation for universal kindergarten never passed, advocates were successful in establishing a Kindergarten Bureau within the Department of Education as early as 1913 and in expanding kindergarten through state and local action throughout the 1940s and 1950s. By 1954, more than one million children were enrolled in public kindergarten, a 300 percent increase from 1910.[4]

At the same time, nursery schools, growing out of the progressive era of the 1920s and 1930s, were established as part of child-study programs at several universities. Primarily serving the children of educated women, nursery schools were seen as child-centered supplements to the home. The spread of nursery schools reflected a better understanding of the importance of the early years and the growth of the "science" of child development. Furthermore, research conducted during the late 1950s and early 1960s, most notably the work of J. McVicker Hunt and Benjamin Bloom, suggested that early experiences have an important effect on overall development.[5]

The concept of Head Start as a federal child-development program grew out of the increasing recognition of the early years. Research began to document the importance of the early years to later development, and experimental parent-education and home-visiting programs held early promise to change behavior and foster child development. Spurred on by the civil rights movement of the late 1950s and early 1960s, and in the wake of national interest that followed the launching of Sputnik by the Soviets in 1959, Head Start emerged as a strategy to fight poverty and equalize educational opportunity. From its beginning in 1965 as a summer program for poor children before they entered school, Head Start grew to serve more than 800,000 children by the end of the century.

As Head Start and other model preschool programs continued to grow, new studies emerged that confirmed the benefits of investing in early childhood. In 1978 a collaborative effort of twelve research groups conducting longitudinal studies on the outcomes of early education reported on the positive effects of preschool. These researchers found that early-education programs had lasting effects that could be measured by achievement scores, assignment to special education, retention in grade, and other child-development measures.[6] Throughout the 1980s and 1990s, additional results from these and other studies continued to reinforce earlier findings. A cost-benefit analysis of the Perry Preschool Program and a later analysis by Rand helped persuade policy-makers that investments in early education had a significant positive return.[7]

In large part as a result of these promising studies, funding for Head Start as well as state preschools continued to grow. However, the same research had relatively little effect on the quality of child care. Most studies were conducted on model programs. Because the early preschools began during a time when most mothers were home, they were designed as part-day programs. In 1960, when model preschools were being conceptualized, only 19 percent of children under age six had two employed parents or a single working parent.[8] Since these programs were seen as providing model services focused on child development, it was difficult to persuade policy-makers that they could have implications for child care in general. In contrast, most early research on child care was focused on whether it would harm children, rather than what benefits it could provide, once again reflecting the dichotomy between care and education.

As the 1980s came to an end, early childhood reached a new level of recognition. President George Bush and the fifty governors announced new national-education goals following the 1989 Education Summit Conference at Charlottesville, Virginia. The first goal—that by the year 2000, all children in America would start school ready to learn—was supported by political leaders of both parties and the public, putting early childhood on the agenda as a serious education issue. However, early education and child care remained separate. The readiness goal practically ignored child care. In fact, ironically, these goals were supported by many policy-makers who at the same time were arguing against standards and quality provisions in the pending child-care legislation.

In the winter of 1995, the Packard Foundation's Center for the Future of Children released a report documenting decades of research regarding the long-term outcomes of early-childhood programs. The report noted that two types of programs for children were running on parallel tracks: publicly supported, part-day preschools intended to promote children's learning, and full-day child-care programs that offered care for the hours needed by parents and that were largely reliant on parent fees. The report acknowledged, "In too many families, the parent's need to work means their children cannot access those enriched early-childhood programs."[9]

Just a few months before that report was issued, the Carnegie Corporation of New York released a landmark report that brought widespread attention to the vulnerability of children during their early years and the importance of research on brain development. The report provided evidence that brain development which takes place before age one is more rapid and extensive, and also is much more vulnerable to environmental influence, than previously realized. The influence of early environments on brain development is long-lasting and affects not only the number of brain cells and the number of connections among them, but also the way these connections are "wired." The Carnegie report discussed a number of important protective factors in the early years that interact and largely influence children's development. These include the child's temperament, perinatal factors (such as full-term birth and normal birth weight), dependable caregivers, and community supports. Finally, the report noted that there is new scientific evidence for the harmful effects of early stress on brain function. Along with a call for the promotion of responsible parenthood and improved health services for pregnant women and young children, the report included a set of recommendations to guarantee high-quality child-care choices.[10]

As the early years began to gain more and more attention, research on child care began to increase. One of the most significant steps was taken in 1989, when the National Institute of Child Health and Human Development (NICHD) set out to develop a comprehensive longitudinal study about the relationship between the child-care experiences of children and their development. The study was launched during a period of intense interest in the issue by Congress and the public. Designed and implemented by a group of researchers working cooperatively, the study included more than thirteen hundred children and their families, from diverse economic and ethnic backgrounds in ten locations across the country, who were enrolled in the study in 1991.[11]

The NICHD study has continued to follow most of these children and their families, and the findings have received widespread attention. Given the interest and emotion surrounding the child-care issue, some of the earlier findings of the NICHD study were the subject of talk shows and newspaper articles across the nation. The research team found that child care itself neither adversely affects nor promotes the security of infants' attachment to their mothers at the fifteen-month point. The researchers did find that certain child-care conditions (poorer quality of care, more than ten hours of care per week, or more than one child-care setting within the first fifteen months of life), in combination with certain home environments (such as mothers who were less sensitive to their infants), did increase the probability that infants would be insecurely attached to their mothers.[12]

Although these and later findings have been used to make arguments both for and against child care, the study's findings were instrumental in demonstrating the complexity of the issue and providing some of the first evidence that child care in and of itself does not harm children's relationship with their mothers. This had been, and still remains, one of the driving issues behind public ambivalence toward working mothers. These and other findings of the NICHD study also helped broaden the discussion of child care. Issues surrounding the effects of child care began to be seen in the context of what else was going on in the family as well as the quality and length of time in care.

Along with the NICHD study, a series of reports appeared in the mid-1990s that raised concern about the quality of care in both centers and homes. Of particular concern was a comprehensive 1995 study of center-based child care in four states, *Cost, Quality, and Child Outcomes*, which found that child care in most centers was poor to mediocre, with only one in seven centers providing a level of quality that promoted healthy development.[13] Similarly, a study of children in family child care and relative care found that fewer than 10 percent of the homes were providing care of good quality.[14]

Some studies led to follow-up research that explored the effect of such care on development. These were particularly important because they clearly made the link between child care and its effects on educational outcomes. The findings from three studies are significant. The continued findings of the NICHD study, released in 1999, found that the quality of care affected school readiness. For example, children in better care scored higher in their ability to express and comprehend language.[15] Similarly, the follow-up to the 1995 study of child care in four states found that children who attended child care with better classroom practices had better language and math skills from the preschool years into elementary school. Furthermore, children who had closer teacher-child relationships in child care had better classroom social skills, thinking skills, language ability, and math skills, from preschool to elementary school.[16]

In the final months of 1999, the report of the Carolina Abecedarian Project was released. Although many earlier studies had been conducted on half-day model preschools for children who were typically four years old, the Abecedarian Intervention focused on low-income children receiving full-time, high-quality educational intervention in a child-care setting from infancy through age five. The study therefore provided important information regarding whether enriched child-care environments could benefit at-risk children. Each child had an individualized prescription of educational activities. Children's progress was monitored over time with follow-up studies conducted through age twenty-one. The results were impressive.

Children who participated in this enriched child-care experience had higher cognitive test scores than their counterparts, from the toddler years to age twenty-one. Academic achievement in both reading and math was higher, from the primary grades through young adulthood. Participating children completed more years of education and were more likely to attend a four-year college. Enhanced language development appears to have facilitated cognitive test scores.[17]

The research findings released on child care and early education throughout the 1990s paint an emerging picture that clearly links the quality of care to educational outcomes for children. The question was no longer whether child care would harm children, but rather under what conditions child care could promote healthy child development.

Bringing a Vision into Focus

Despite the emergence of research linking care to education, the public continued to see them as separate. One of the key challenges to improving child care is that many decision-makers still do not have a picture of the goals. If a program has the "child care" label, many people automatically assume that it is not an educational setting. People's image of child care appears to reflect the memory of a teenager who would come over on a Saturday night to "watch" the children while parents went out to a movie. The babysitter would play a few games with the children, watch television with them, and make mounds of popcorn along the way. Since many people, particularly policy-makers, have no experience with out-of-home environments, these old images remain. To move child care forward, we need a new vision.

Since child care takes place in centers and in homes, the new vision should capture the best of both worlds. I like to think of child care for young children as a hybrid between a school and a home—a third type of setting—that has value in and of itself. We need a new metaphor that incorporates the images of warmth and comfort found in a home and the images of learning in a school. Naturally, a center will feel more like a school, and a family child-care home will feel more like a child's own home. However, when you combine these two images, they represent an environment for children that feels natural, yet allows everyday moments as well as planned activities to focus on the child's development and learning. A sense of comfort is important for children who are very young. The attention to learning is important for the same reasons, and because of the opportunity that child care offers to promote curiosity, cognitive and social skills, and a sense of confidence and motivation.

Regardless of where children are cared for, the setting should be seen as an educational environment. The central question is what this care for young children should look like; what are the goals? To answer this I draw on three experiences: my perspective as a parent, what we know about child development, and the lessons we have learned from Head Start, the Military Child Development Program, and from other nations.

A Parent's View

Choice in the care of our children is an important value, particularly while they are young. Despite the diversity of our child-care system, many families do not feel they have real choice among quality options. Too often we look at the type of care that parents are using, and assume that the care chosen reflects their preference, rather than what is convenient and what they can afford. Moreover, the availability of certain types of care, changing work schedules, and a mother's level of trust and education all influence child-care choices. Yet regardless of the type of setting that parents use, all parents want good care for their children.

As I was struggling to define good care, a friend asked me, "What did you need from your child care when your children were young? What did you want your child-care provider to do?" Naturally, there is no easy answer since the early years are so variable. What we want for a very young infant often is very different from what we need for that very precocious four-year-old. Despite this challenge, I found myself responding with a three-part answer:

First, I wanted my young children to be safe. Most parents respond that way. But there was more. I wanted to know that my children were eating well and were treated well, hugs and all, particularly when they were very young. Their nutritional and mental-health needs seemed as important as their safety. I wanted them to have a good relationship with the people who cared for them. I wanted them to care for each other, to be friends, to feel like family. I wanted the child-care provider to appreciate the uniqueness of my children, what made them special, not just to me but also to the world. These feelings run very deep when our children are young.

Second, I wanted my children exposed to many interesting ideas and experiences. I wanted to make sure people were talking to and listening to them. They needed attention and good conversation, toys and books, and lots of experiences to help them gain a sense of wonder, new skills, and a love of learning.

Finally, I wanted to be listened to as a parent, to have my opinions and my concerns valued. I wanted to be kept informed, to hear on a daily basis, what had gone on that day, particularly with my baby. Although I enjoyed my work, I really did not want to miss a thing that was going on with my children. I was dependent on the provider to keep me posted. I savored those special times when we exchanged stories about the children, laughing and sharing the care.

In many ways this answer represents the goals and expectations of many parents I have talked with over the years. At the same time, this three-part answer responds to what we know young children need for healthy development. These same themes are encapsulated in the three objectives of the readiness goal outlined in 1990 by the nation's governors: In order for children to be "ready for school," we must promote good health, ensure supportive parents, and provide access to high-quality education during the early years. This same basic wisdom was reflected by the founders of Head Start. They called it a comprehensive approach: Ensure health, involve and support families, and provide good educational services.

Not all children will need the same intensity of services reflected in this trilogy; however, these key "domains" of development need to be addressed for all children. Yet in the past, the vision of child care has not provided the essential ingredients to ensure that the hours and days expended in child care were used to promote health and early development or to support families. But in the child care of tomorrow, promoting the optimal development of children must be the goal.

A Child-Development Approach

More than ten years ago, the National Commission on Children reminded the country that "development during the early years has important implications for children's later success in school. When a young child's needs for affection, basic health care, adequate nutrition, safe environments, and intellectual and social stimulation are met in the early years, the child is more likely to develop the skills, habits, and attitudes necessary to succeed in school. On the other hand, young children who are put at risk through poor health, unsafe environments, or inadequate stimulation often experience . . . early academic failure."[18]

It is in the early years that children experience rapid growth in physical, intellectual, linguistic, social, and emotional development. During this critical period they learn to depend on, respond to, and trust adults in their world. Children begin to master motor skills, take in more and more of their world through their senses, gain a sense of self-worth, take part in early social exchanges, and learn to communicate through gestures, sounds, and then words. If these experiences are positive, children gain a sense of confidence that forms the foundation for later success.

The National Association for the Education of Young Children, the largest professional organization in the United States representing the interests of young children, has outlined a number of principles of child development and learning to inform practice. They include among others:

- Children's physical, social, emotional, and cognitive development are closely related. Development in one area influences and is influenced by development in the other areas.
- Development occurs in a relatively orderly sequence, with later abilities, skills, and knowledge building on those already acquired.

Yet development is individual and may occur at different rates from child to child.

• Development and learning result from interaction of biological maturation and the environment. Children develop and learn best in a community where they are safe and valued, where their physical needs are met, and where they feel psychologically secure.

• Children have different modes of learning, and they need varied experiences to help stimulate their development. Children need lots of time and opportunities to practice their emerging skills, to try out new combinations.[19]

Translating these principles of development into programs for young children is the challenge. As early-childhood programs have grown, there has been ongoing debate about what children should learn and how they should be taught. The debate often swings from stressing social and emotional development to emphasizing the learning of specific cognitive skills. Like so many educational debates today, both sides are right, yet neither has the only answer. Child care must be used to promote emerging skills, but it should be done in a way that reflects a more relaxed environment—one that not only fits the needs of younger children but also responds to the long hours that children are in child-care settings. This is very different from designing a two- or three-hour preschool.

For young children, the acquisition of knowledge and skills cannot be separated from how they feel about themselves. A "heart" start and a "head" start go together. Ten years after the National Commission on Children reminded the country of the importance of the early years, The National Research Council released another landmark report, reinforcing the fact that elements of early-intervention programs that enhance social and emotional development are just as important as the components that enhance cognitive and linguistic competence. Based on what science has revealed about the early years, the report strongly recommends that public policy and practices be better aligned with what is known about development.[20]

Lessons from Head Start and the Military

The United States has two national child-care efforts that we can turn to with pride: Head Start and the military Child Development Programs. Both of these systems provide important lessons for redesigning child care. After three decades of experience, we now have a better understanding of the key ingredients in good care: high expectations, skilled providers, and an infrastructure of support.

Finding a Vision in Head Start. In celebration of the thirty-fifth anniversary of Head Start, a report released by a blue-ribbon panel of the National Head Start Association called Head Start "a promise" the country made to its most vulnerable low-income children, a promise to provide quality comprehensive services—education, health, nutrition, family support, and parent involvement in order to give them a head start in school."[21] Anyone who has worked with Head Start knows the magic that it holds: the passion of the staff, the commitment of its parents, and the deep respect for diversity, community, and families.

More than twenty million children have benefited from Head Start since its inception in 1965. Head Start has been a national laboratory of innovation for the entire early-childhood field. Its overall goal is to promote "social competence," which is defined as everyday effectiveness in dealing with both the present environment and later responsibilities in school and life. The program promotes school readiness by addressing the three interrelated issues of early-childhood development, health, and family services. Just as Head Start has served as a model for early education for preschool children, Early Head Start, started in 1995, now serves as a national laboratory for services for children from birth through age three.

Head Start gives us a vision: Good child care is not just another service in a list of what families need. Instead it can be the hub of services for the children of working families. For example, if we are concerned with reaching out to families with a new health-insurance program or improved dental care, we can do this outreach through child care. If we want to deliver a message to parents about the importance of "buckling up for safety" in cars, we can reach them through child care. If we are concerned about the reading levels of children when they reach fourth grade, we can start by ensuring that there are books and well-trained staff to nurture emergent literacy while children are in child care.

From Head Start we know that ensuring children's health means not only screening but also follow-up. It means helping parents make sure that their well-baby visits and immunizations are up-to-date and their families are connected to medical resources that will provide treatment and follow-up. It means promoting good nutrition and helping to address mental-health needs. Children in child care from middle- and high-income families may be able to obtain these services, yet increasingly many low-income working families cannot. They need the extra support that linkages between child care and health can provide.

Head Start has excelled in achieving the respect and involvement of families. In a family-centered early-childhood program, there is ongoing communication between staff and parents. Parents are always welcome to drop by, to ask questions, to suggest activities. The room and the staff reflect the culture and languages of the home and community. Parents help make key decisions, they help interview staff, they suggest activities, and they volunteer to help. The program may help them address issues that are affecting their family and can connect them to other community services. These important aspects of Head Start exemplify best practice and can provide a model for the field of early education.

On a daily basis, it is the education component of Head Start that promotes language, numeracy, curiosity, and motivation to learn. The teachers help guide children, recognizing their uniqueness and promoting new skills. They help children feel confident. A curriculum, a set of activities, and a philosophy helps guide the daily routine. Every program has an education coordinator, and supervision of teachers is an important part of the educational services.

Before the passage of the Americans with Disabilities Act, Head Start recognized the importance of including children with special needs. By law, at least 10 percent of the children enrolled in any Head Start program must be children who have a diagnosed disability. This requirement has helped open opportunities for thousands of children with a range of special needs, from speech and language issues to more severe disabilities. Moreover, Head Start provides support to the staff and the providers to help make the inclusion of children with special needs successful.

Together with a vision for good early education, Head Start provides three lessons for redesigning the child-care system: Resources should be tied to a set of performance standards with a monitoring and enforcement system; a commitment should be made to professional development, including adequate compensation and supervision of staff; and an infrastructure of resources and support (either directly or through linkages) should be made available to promote core services.

Head Start has long been the leader in providing early-childhood program standards. In response to quality issues, Head Start established performance standards in the mid-1970s to help define program operations. The program standards and other policies are established at the national level and are monitored by a network of regional offices across the country. Revised by law in the 1990s, the Head Start performance standards set forth the requirements for comprehensive Head Start services. The standards cover preschool programs as well as programs serving infants, toddlers, and their families. Monitoring includes regular visits and in-depth assessment. In more recent years, Head Start also has moved to a more results-based system, establishing a set of performance measures to track progress. In child care, programs have been guided by basic regulations rather than program standards or results-based accountability. However, new efforts are beginning to link new resources to better standards and higher expectations.

What has kept Head Start in the vanguard of early-childhood programs has been a commitment to staff training and support. These two key elements have been missing in child care. Since its inception, Head Start has invested in the professional development of its staff; 2 percent of all funds are set aside for an extensive training and technical-assistance network. The 1990 legislation reauthorizing Head Start included a 10 percent set-aside for quality and a 25 percent set-aside in any additional funding, with half of this amount targeted to salary increases. This quality set-aside was maintained in the 1994 reauthorization and increased in 1998.

Finally, Head Start has established an infrastructure of support to ensure comprehensive services, including education, family support, health, and services to children with special needs. Program coordinators for each of these key components spend considerable time working with community resources to make sure that their families have full access and information. Although it would be difficult to recreate such an infrastructure in every child-care program, promising initiatives are emerging across the country to ensure that such services are available on a community-wide basis, particularly through local child-care resource and referral agencies.

Borrowing a Plan from the Military. Head Start provides a vision and long-standing strategies to promote child development. With adequate resources and a strategic plan, even a failed child-care system can be turned around, using similar strategies. We have a model of success from a most unlikely place: the United States military. The Department of Defense (DOD) child-care system is the largest employer-sponsored child-care program in the world, serving more than two hundred thousand children from birth to age twelve daily at more than three hundred locations worldwide. Known as the Child Development Program, in 2000 it included more than eight hundred child-development centers and more than nine thousand family child-care homes.[22]

In the 1980s, the U.S. military child-care system suffered from a series of problems similar to those currently reflected in civilian life. Tens of thousands of children were on waiting lists, facilities often were unsuitable, there were no comprehensive standards or a rigorous inspection system, and, most notably, caregivers lacked training and were poorly paid, earning less than the people who stocked the commissary.[23]

Then the situation changed dramatically. Spurred by a series of reports and congressional hearings, Congress enacted the Military Child Care Act of 1989, mandating improvements in military child care. In the same year, the Department of Defense inspector general made fifty-three recommendations for improving the program. The military took action, putting in place a comprehensive improvement plan to provide high-quality affordable care.[24] Nearly ten years later, a study conducted by the Rand National Defense Research Institute examined the implementation and outcomes of the military efforts and found significant improvements.[25] The military has important lessons to share with the rest of the nation on how to improve the quality of child care for all children.

As was true in Head Start, at least three essential ingredients have helped improve the quality of the military child-care system: standards and enforcement, training and compensation, and an infrastructure of support. A critical element of the effort to improve the quality of programs was the adoption of a set of measures to hold child-care providers accountable. First, DOD established uniform certification standards that all the child-development centers and family child-care homes were required to meet. Next they developed mechanisms to determine whether these standards were in fact met and enforced sanctions for failure to meet them. The enforcement process includes unannounced visits at least four times a year. Standards established by DOD govern facility requirements, staff/child ratios, staff training and qualifications, child-abuse prevention procedures, funding, parent participation, and health and sanitation. Third, the military required that programs go through a national accreditation system.[26] Along with improving standards, DOD increased staff training and compensation. One of the main reasons the military was able to implement these changes was the increased use of appropriated dollars that helped keep programs afford-able to families while improving quality. DOD implemented a comprehensive training program. New hires working in centers, family child-care homes, and school-age programs are required to undergo an orientation before they work with children. The orientation includes such topics as child-abuse identification and reporting, first aid and CPR, health and sanitation procedures, and parent and family relations. Once they begin work, center and family child-care providers must complete fifteen competency-based training modules within two years of being hired. Furthermore, all staff must participate in twenty-four hours of training annually.[27]

This training system is tied to improved wages and promotions. DOD requires that center caregivers complete all training modules to remain employed and to receive the highest hourly wages available to DOD caregivers. Both full- and part-time staff receive life insurance, health insurance, sick leave, and retirement benefits, generally providing an additional value equal to 22 percent of their salaries. The military wage policy increased incentives to complete training, improved wages, and reduced turnover. Staff turnover, which had been as high as 300 percent at some bases, in 2000 was below 30 percent annually.[28]

Like Head Start, the military Child Development Program also includes an infrastructure of support for the programs, including a "single point of entry" (or a primary contact) at each installation. Although its exact location may vary across the services, this single point of entry helps bring cohesion, information, and support to the programs. For example, DOD is required by law to ensure that every child-development center employs a training and curriculum specialist who is a professionally qualified early-childhood educator.[29] Furthermore, family child-care providers benefit from being part of a network that provides ongoing training, visits, and support. The single point of entry helps bring together these resources for the individual programs.[30]

Lessons from Other Nations

While we can learn much from the military and Head Start about how to design good services, a critically important lesson about public investment in the early years comes from other nations. In recent years, there has been a growing interest in the United States in international early-childhood issues. An increasing number of study tours to France, Italy, and other European countries are underway. The United States participated with the Organization for Economic Co-operation and Development (OECD) in its recent field review of early childhood in a number of countries, and several international conferences on early childhood have been held, both for policy-makers and for practitioners.

In most other developed countries, public investment in families with young children and early education has become the norm. Dr. Sheila Kamerman, who has been carrying out international research on child and family policies for more than twenty-five years, spoke about this support when she testified before the Senate Committee on Health, Education, Labor and Pensions in March 2001. She said:

> Early childhood education and care (ECEC) is high on the child and family policy agenda for all advanced industrialized countries today and many developing countries as well. . . . In more and more countries, young children are spending two or three or even four years in these programs before entering primary school. In some countries, access to these programs is a legal right— at age one in most of the Nordic countries, at age two in France, and age three in most of the other continental European countries, such as Belgium, Germany and Italy.[31]

Several lessons emerge when we look at child and family policy in other developed countries. First, unlike the United States, most countries ground their approach to the early years by providing paid leave and other family-support policies. As discussed in Chapter 6, the United States must begin to address child-care issues first by providing more choice for parents with very young children, including the choice to remain at home with their infants. Second, early-education policies in other developed countries include substantial public investment and assure universal access.

As we have seen in Head Start and the military model, other countries also are continuing to focus on quality improvements and are placing an increasing emphasis on staff qualifications and training. There appears to be a consensus that staff require specialized training and that compensation should be equitable across early-childhood education and care programs. Furthermore, there is beginning to be some recognition, in some countries, of the importance of staffing that reflects the ethnic and racial diversity of the children served.[32]

Central to the approach of other countries is the integration of child care and education. Kamerman describes three major "models" of early-childhood care and education in the industrialized countries: The first model is designed to respond to the needs of working parents as well as children, covers the normal working day, and serves children for a period from the end of a paid leave and lasting for one to three years, depending on the country. Demark and Sweden have such programs. The second model includes preschool for children ages two or three to compulsory school entry (typically age six), covers the school day and year, and provides supplemental services for the parents' work day. It also may include a second program for children under age three that begins when the country's paid parental leave ends. Italy and France are examples of this model.[33] In both of these models, the needs of working families, as well as the developmental needs of children, are integrated into the system.

In contrast, a third model has grown up in some of the English-speaking countries, where, as we have seen, care and education have been on parallel tracks, with little integration. Yet this has begun to change in Britain, New Zealand, and the United States, where the role of education is increasing. As we will explore later in this chapter, new strategies are emerging to bring the needed resources and standards into child care, and therefore improve the education component. These strategies vary among the states, with some states taking an approach that integrates education into child-care services for children from infancy through the preschool years, and other states taking the approach of integrating a preschool program for children three or four into child care.

Finally, while the United States has invested more than other countries in research on early education, a review of long-term outcomes of early-childhood programs in other nations provides important lessons. "Research from several nations at different levels of economic development consistently indicate that attendance at high-quality preschool programs is positively associated with children's cognitive and socio-emotional development and their success in school." Some of the best evidence of these outcomes is found in studies from Western European nations with highly developed early-education programs, including studies of the French *ecole maternelle* and the Swedish child-care system.[34]

Pulling Together the Pieces

When we consider what parents want, what we know about child development, and lessons from successful programs in the United States, as well as in other countries, it becomes clear that we need to redesign our child-care system for young children in two fundamental ways. First, we need to clearly establish a network of early-learning programs that parents can choose from to provide developmental services to children from birth through age five. Such programs should receive direct funding to ensure a floor of quality and should be held accountable for meeting program standards. The standards should include requirements for staffing, curriculum, and parent involvement.

Second, we need to provide community-wide supports to the various neighborhood providers through a more clearly defined infrastructure that would be publicly funded. Both the military child-care system and Head Start have such support. This support would be similar to the district-level support for neighborhood K–12 schools. Such a focal point could be housed in one agency, such as a child-care resource and referral agency, or could be more like a "virtual" network, perhaps with one agency coordinating and connecting a wide variety of agencies and supports to families, providers, and the larger community. This system of community supports is discussed in Chapter 5. First, however, let us turn to the key components of a good early-learning program and review some of the emerging strategies to fund such efforts.

The Early Learning Program

Child care for children under age five is being redesigned. While the United Sates should build on its diverse delivery system, there is a strong movement to ensure that the places where children spend their days are promoting healthy child development. I envision a network of early-learning programs serving working and non-working families in a community. The early-learning program would provide services to children either in a center, or through a combination of a center with a system of satellite family child-care homes around it. Parents might choose a program near work or near home, depending on their needs. In order to receive funding and support, programs would need to agree to maintain six key elements.

- basic health and safety standards
- program standards
- staff qualifications
- curriculum and school linkages
- parent involvement and family support
- family child-care networks

Basic Health and Safety Standards

At a minimum, the licensing system should ensure basic health and safety protections for children in care. This is the most basic element of an early-learning program. As such, licensing forms the floor of a regulatory approach. Gwen Morgan, a leading authority on regulatory issues in child care, reminds us that "licensing is not a definition of quality, it is a threshold defined by the state to reduce the risk of harm."[35] As the military program has shown, such standards must be accompanied by a comprehensive enforcement system. The United States has not been successful in requiring even basic health and safety protections from the national level. Moreover, as discussed in Chapter 1, state child-care licensing provisions and enforcement still remain grossly inadequate, despite recent investments of CCDBG funds by some states to improve the capacity to monitor programs. However, efforts to ensure better health and safety in child care have been advanced by a set of national guidelines and recommendations.

In 1987 the American Public Health Association and the American Academy of Pediatrics, with the support of the Maternal and Child Health Bureau of the U.S. Department of Health and Human Services, took a big step forward when they began to develop guidelines for out-of-home care. After five years of development, the National Health and Safety Performance Standards were published in 1992. This was a critically important step for child care since the standards set forth recommendations, guidelines, and regulations for the care of young children in centers and family child care. Although the standards were not mandated by federal law, they provided a model of good practice in key areas such as staffing; program activities for the promotion of healthy development; nutrition and food service; facilities, equipment and transportation; and control of infectious diseases.[36]

Since that time, a number of states have used the standards to review their licensing provisions and make improvements. This should be done in every state. In 1997 HHS published the particular standards most needed to prevent injury, morbidity, and mortality in child-care settings.[37] All states should include these critical provisions in their licensing regulations. The Maternal and Child Health Bureau has funded a National Resource Center for Health and Safety in Child Care, which tracks child-care licensing standards across the country and provides technical assistance and support to improve child-care standards.

Every child-care center and family child-care home, without exception, should be licensed and should be required to meet basic health and safety standards. Furthermore, at least the same number of unannounced visits should be made to programs in the civilian sector as in the military. The standards recommended by the Maternal and Child Health Bureau should form the basis for the basic standards used to guide all early-education programs.

Program Standards

Basic health and safety licensing standards alone are not enough to guarantee quality. Program standards must be put in place to ensure a higher level of quality and accountability, particularly when public funds are spent. Both Head Start and the military program have not only basic protections but also standards. In the case of Head Start, programs are required to meet federal performance standards; in the case of the military, all centers have to become accredited. However, since child care has not been seen as an "educational setting," program standards have not been incorporated into public policy. This is beginning to change as the concept of child care evolves.

Over the years there has been some debate regarding which key elements to include in program standards to ensure quality. In her review of the research, Alison Clarke-Stewart outlines what she calls "our best clues" to the indexes of quality child care. Some of the key elements are "structural" features, including adequate child-staff ratios, appropriate group size, and a consistent caregiver who has a balance of training in child development and some professional experience. Together these elements often lead to processes that improve the quality of care. For example, she notes that a quality program is one in which "the child's interaction with the caregiver is frequent, verbal, and educational, rather than custodial and controlling."[38] Achieving such interactions is dependent on maintaining small groups and a sufficient number of well-trained staff. More recently, *Eager to Learn*, a report on early-childhood pedagogy by the National Research Council, noted similar components in its list of key ingredients to quality, including, among others, responsive interpersonal relations between child and teacher, a curriculum that is integrated across domains, and professional development and supervision of teachers.[39]

Several important steps have been taken over the past decade to move beyond basic health and safety standards in licensing and to promote higher program standards. The development of voluntary standards and accreditation has expanded rapidly. As discussed later in this chapter, there also has been a movement to link higher standards to additional resources, either by reimbursing accredited programs at higher rates or through the integration of Head Start and publicly supported preschool standards and resources into child care.

While the health community was developing health and safety standards during the 1980s and early 1990s, a movement to develop a system of voluntary standards and accreditation emerged from professional organizations representing the child-care and early-childhood communities. In recent years, states have begun to develop policies that support accreditation through a variety of incentives. By 1999, thirty-five states had policies that support accreditation using three primary approaches: quality-enhancement grants, technical assistance, and training to help providers to become accredited; recognition of accreditation; and establishment of higher payment levels for accredited care.[40]

The National Association for the Education of Young Children (NAEYC) began developing accreditation criteria in 1981. After three years of development and extensive comments, the accreditation system was put into place in the mid-1980s. Criteria were revised again in 1991. NAEYC defines a high-quality early-childhood program as one that meets the needs of and promotes the physical, social, emotional, and cognitive development of the children and adults—parents, staff, and administrators—who are involved in the program.[41] The accreditation criteria include ten important components of group programs for young children, including interactions among teachers and caregivers, curriculum, staffing, and other key issues. The accreditation process includes a self-study, a validation visit, and a decision regarding accreditation made by an expert commission. Although accreditation has grown over the past few years, in the year 2000 only about 5 percent of the centers in the United States had earned NAEYC accreditation.[42]

Research on accreditation has shown promising results in providing higher than average quality services for children. However, alone it is not a guarantee of excellence. Further research is needed to explore the relationship between accreditation and other key variables such as stability of staff, compensation, and continuity of care.[43] Higher wages and retention of skilled teachers are key factors that, in combination with accreditation, may be the best predictors of quality.

While NAEYC and other organizations accredit centers, the National Association of Family Child Care (NAFCC) has developed a system of accreditation for family child care. Kathy Modigliani, a long-time advocate in efforts to improve home-based child care, notes that "family child care is surely one of the oldest occupations" but that "it has been nearly invisible, woven into the fabric of every neighborhood."[44] Until recently, there had been little attention to defining best practices in family child care or research and policy development that would support those practices. In 1988 things began to change when NAFCC, a national membership organization working with more than 400 state and local family child-care provider associations across the country, began to develop its first voluntary accreditation system. Following this initial effort, in 1994 NAFCC began a major initiative to develop a new accreditation system. Field-tested in 1998, the new accreditation system began national operation in 1999. It covers the content areas of relationships, environment, activities, developmental learning goals, safety and health, and professional and business practices. A 1995 study conducted by the Families and Work Institute confirmed that accreditation increases the professionalism, self-esteem, and leadership skills of family child-care providers and improves the quality of care.[45]

Staff Qualifications

While standards have received increased attention, the most important variable in quality remains the caregiver. The National Research Council's report, *From Neurons to Neighborhood,* states that "parents and other regular caregivers in children's lives are active ingredients of environmental influence during the early childhood period."[46] J. Ronald Lally, a pioneer in the field of child care, has observed that good care for infants and toddlers is a blend of science and art. The science includes knowledge of health and safety, understanding of the developmental stages in the first years of life, and familiarity with the temperaments and other individual characteristics of the children. The art of child care is the ability to respond to a child—and a group of children—in a moment that will support development and learning.[47] Knowing both the science and the art of caring takes special training. All early-learning programs should have staff with specialized training and credentials.

There are many challenges to providing qualified staff in early childhood. First, child-care providers are a very diverse group: Some work in homes, some work in centers, some work with infants, some work with preschoolers, some work in schools, and some work in community-based organizations. It is difficult to decide what to call people who work with young children: The nomenclature of the profession includes words such as teachers, providers, workers, and staff. Second, state child-care and preschool regulations vary widely regarding the qualifications for a person who works directly with children, in a center or in a family child-care home. The National Health and Safety Performance Standards recommend that centers employ licensed or certified teaching staff for direct work with children.[48] Similarly, the report of the Quality 2000 Initiative, an extensive effort to develop a set of recommendations for creating an early-care and education system, recommends that by the year 2010 states should require all providers responsible for children in centers and family child-care homes to hold individual licenses. To obtain such a license an individual working in a center with preschool children would need at least an associate's or bachelor's degree in early-childhood education or child development from an accredited institution; practical experience with the age group with which they would work; certification in pediatric first aid; and demonstrated competence in working with children and families.[49] The National Research Council's Committee on Pedagogy recommended that each group of children in early-childhood and care programs should be assigned a teacher who has a bachelor's degree with specialized education related to early childhood.[50] Such credentials offer the benefit of increasing the recognition and, hopefully, the rewards of early-childhood staff and encouraging career mobility.

Central to the challenge of requiring specific qualifications is the need to improve the compensation and overall working conditions of the child-care workforce. The adult work environment—both the physical setting and the working conditions—affect the living conditions of the children. If providers feel frustrated by low wages and a lack of benefits, that frustration can affect the children in their care, either through poor job performance or turnover.

States and communities have begun to address the compensation issue in two ways. First, some programs are receiving additional resources to meet certain program standards that often include specific staffing requirements. Although there is little documented evidence that this is actually raising salaries, one can at least assume that standards and additional resources are beneficial in recruiting and retaining more qualified staff. Second, as described in Chapter 6, some states and communities have launched specific compensation initiatives that provide salary and benefit enhancement directly to providers. This allows compensation funds to flow to both center-based and home-based providers.

Curriculum and School Linkages

Throughout the early-childhood field today, there is much debate and discussion, not only about staff qualifications, but also about what children should know and learn to do and how they should be taught. Lilian Katz, director of the ERIC Clearinghouse on Elementary and Early Childhood Education, outlines four categories of learning that are relevant to all levels of education, but especially to the education of young children. These include:

- Knowledge, which includes facts, concepts, ideas, vocabulary, stories, and aspects of children's culture. Children acquire such knowledge from a range of experiences, including hearing answers and explanations to their questions, descriptions and accounts of events as well as active processes, and direct observations.
- Skills, including physical, social, verbal, counting, and drawing skills, which can be learned from direct instruction or imitated and improved with guidance and practice.
- Dispositions, which can be thought of as habits or tendencies to respond a certain way and which include such behavior as curiosity, friendliness, generosity, and curiosity.
- Feelings, some of which can be learned such as confidence, competence, belonging, and security.[51]

The teacher or family child-care provider must have the necessary training and support to help design the environment in a way that provides ample opportunity for young children to enhance their knowledge, skills, dispositions, and feelings. Content—such as language and literacy, mathematics, science, social studies, the arts, and technology—must be integrated into a range of activities that occur throughout the day. The philosophy, goals, objectives, and daily activities of a child-care program often are defined by the curriculum it chooses. Preschool teachers are constantly making decisions about the well-being and education of the children in their care.[52] A curriculum is what pulls all the pieces together and allows teachers to make consistent decisions that support children's learning.[53] It is the relationship that the provider has with the children which makes the curriculum come alive.

Unfortunately, curriculum in child care has been largely neglected. For example, state licensing, with its emphasis on basic health and safety, rarely puts any emphasis on curriculum. Furthermore, even federally supported child care, which serves more than one million low-income preschoolers a year, has no requirements or support for curriculum or supervision. These factors, coupled with the lack of attention to professional development, must change if child-care programs are to become educational environments.

Fortunately, interest in early-childhood curriculum has been growing. The national voluntary accreditation systems have helped focus attention on curriculum issues. For example, the NAEYC accreditation criteria include these provisions, among others:

- The program has a written statement of its philosophy and goals for children that is available to all staff and families.
- The program has written curriculum plans based on knowledge of child development and learning and assessment of individual needs and interests. The learning environment and activities for children reflect the program's philosophy and goals.
- Teachers have clearly defined goals for individual children that guide curriculum planning.[54]

The National Research Council (NRC) report on early-childhood pedagogy reinforced the importance of curriculum. It found that "while no single curriculum or pedagogical approach can be identified as best, children who attend well-planned, high-quality early-childhood programs in which curriculum aims are specified and integrated across domains tend to learn more and are better prepared to successfully master the complex demands of formal schooling."[55] In Head Start, while no specific curriculum is required, every program must have a curriculum and a system to assess children's progress. Similarly, while no state pre-kindergarten program requires a single curriculum, almost all states provide some general guidelines on curriculum as part of their pre-kindergarten initiative, offering models or examples that programs may follow.[56]

Yet providing a good educational program is more than just having a curriculum. The NRC's report also notes that "programs found to be highly effective in the United States and exemplary programs abroad actively engage teachers and provide high-quality supervision."[57] Supervision of child-care staff can include in-service training and ongoing observation and feedback by a qualified professional. DOD provides at least one training and curriculum specialist in every military child-development center. These specialists usually do not have responsibility for administration or caring for children, and therefore are free to focus on the teaching staff and the curriculum. The specialists help improve curriculum design and staff training, advise and encourage caregivers to obtain their credentials, and help facilitate the accreditation process.[58] Similarly, in Head Start, every program has an education coordinator or supervisor (whose title and responsibilities may vary) who provides supervision and support to the staff working directly with children. An extensive technical-assistance network supports these activities, and special efforts are made to promote such skill areas as literacy. If we are to take advantage of the educational opportunities in child care, these types of support must be made more widely available.

A growing interest in curriculum should help build bridges between public schools and the child-care community serving children under age five. While schools will continue to be among the providers of early-childhood services, most children under age five will continue to be served in the community-based child-care system. More and more states are beginning to develop content standards that address the preschool years and provide continuity with goals and content standards for grades K–12. In Maryland and other places across the country, center-based staff and family child-care providers are being trained in curriculum through new partnerships with public-education departments. These initiatives are bringing a fresh view of the potential of school linkages into the child-care picture.

Parent Involvement and Family Support

A good early-childhood program is founded on strong principles of parent involvement and family support. I remember applying for my first early-childhood job, a position as an assistant teacher in a full-day Head Start class in Boston. What stands out about the interview was the fact that it was conducted by parents as well as agency staff. The parents, speaking both English and Spanish, asked me about my background, why I wanted the job, and what I thought I could bring to the children *and* their families. The interview sent a message: This was a place that respected the parents, a program that considered parents as partners in the education of their children. I was impressed. I also was lucky to get both the job and the message.

After years of research, few people doubt the important role that parents play in the education of their children. Traditionally, parent involvement in education has meant volunteering in a classroom or helping out at a bake sale and attending the annual parent-teacher conferences. Yet a family-centered approach to child care goes far beyond these traditional images. It is based on a set of guiding principles or values about the role of the family.

The first principle of a family-centered approach is that the family is the most important influence in a child's life. Child care is not a substitute for parents, but rather should reinforce the parent-child bond. The family is the center of a child's life, and child care should support and promote the secure attachment of children to their parents. Child care also should empower parents with information. The most important contacts between providers and parents happen every day, when parents drop off and pick up their children. It is during those all-too-often brief and hurried moments when provider and parents can connect—when the world of home and the world of child care come together for the child. Parents need to feel welcomed; providers need to feel respected. It is this mutuality that leads to ongoing communication on behalf of the children.

Second, each family is unique and has strengths that should be respected. These strengths include language, culture, and values. Services should be built on the strengths of each family, and parents should be encouraged to be involved in a variety of ways. Staff of child-care programs should reflect the cultures and languages of the families they serve.

Third, parents and staff work as a team in a relationship based on equality and respect. Many early-childhood programs have been pioneers in generating innovative ways to work with families. A view of "parents as learners" that was prevalent through the 1950s, and which continues in some parts of the field today, began to shift in the 1960s to a view of parents as partners with educators.[59] This means that parents and providers have something to learn from each other: While providers bring information to parents about child development and about their experiences with many children, families provide information about the individual child, across time and in a variety of settings. Both these perspectives are important.

Fourth, families today may need extra support. Families experience multiple demands, and they may need support to help them fulfill their important role in the lives of their children. Child care, and other agencies that support child care, can serve as a central point of contact for delivering a range of services to families, including parent education and information about community resources.

In recent years, there has been a growing focus on fathers' involvement in child care and other family-support programs. A growing body of research documents commonsense knowledge: Children benefit from positive relationships with their fathers, and a father's parenting style affects his child's well-being.[60] A number of fatherhood initiatives have documented and shared promising practices and models for reaching out to fathers through Head Start and child-care programs. Through materials, training, and technical assistance, they have helped programs across the country to create a father-friendly environment, recruit men into their programs, develop new activities and special events, form men's groups, and help expand and sustain father involvement in their programs.[61]

Historically, the family-centered approach to child care has had very limited support. Services to help parents find good care and to build supply often are limited; professional preparation of teaching staff too often overlooks the important role of working with parents; and resources are rarely available for programs to hire the staff needed to focus more directly on the needs of families. In addition, community services for children are too often separate and distinct from those offering overall support to families. As discussed in Chapter 5, community-wide supports for some of these important functions are starting to emerge, but they still are very limited.

Research is beginning to document the benefits of teaming early-childhood services with parent education and family support. For example, while many parents use child care and other preschool programs, the state of Missouri also has invested in the Parents as Teachers Program, an innovative program of education for parents of children from birth to age five. In 1999 the state released the findings of the Missouri School Entry Project, a comprehensive early-childhood effort designed to gather information about the preschool experiences and school readiness of children as they enter kindergarten. The study found that the highest-performing children attended a preschool or child-care center and had parents who participated in the Parents as Teachers Program. This was true for children in both high-poverty and low-poverty schools.[62] Recent evaluation data from Starting Early, Starting Smart, an integrated system of child-centered, family-focused, and community-based services designed to serve at-risk children, found that this two-generation approach strengthened positive parent-child interactions and the development of young children.[63] These findings have important implications for the need to team child care with parent education and support.

Family Child-Care Networks

Since many families may prefer home-based settings, particularly for their youngest children, early-learning programs should develop family child-care networks around center-based services. The military child-care system has a long history of support for such networks. Moreover, as Head Start serves more and more children under age three, family child-care networks offer new opportunities for expansion.

The U.S. Department of Defense supports family child care because it offers needed flexibility. As part of the system, family child-care providers receive training comparable to child-development center staff training, and the same inspection process and frequency of inspections is applied to both family child care and center-based programs.[64]

Head Start has only recently become more active in family child care. Although some programs were using a family child-care model in the 1980s, in 1992 the Administration for Children, Youth and Families funded eighteen Head Start family child-care demonstration projects for a three-year period. By recruiting family child-care providers to work with Head Start programs, families can receive full-day services and their children can receive comprehensive services. Participating providers also receive benefits from the affiliation with Head Start, including ongoing support and training. Results from the demonstration effort indicated that Head Start services could be successfully delivered through a family child-care network.[65]

Many family child-care networks are emerging through state action or community-wide initiatives growing out of centers, resource-and-referral agencies, family child-care associations, and a wide variety of other mechanisms. These networks are discussed in Chapter 5.

Emerging Strategies to Fund Early Learning in Child Care

The vision of an early-learning program is emerging across the country. Yet the key components cannot be financed solely through parent fees. We must begin to drive additional resources directly into programs, holding the programs accountable through standards and outcomes. States and communities have been using different strategies that put additional dollars into the system. First, some states have increased efforts to *pay higher rates for better-quality care*, with these higher rates usually tied to accreditation. While this is a promising strategy, it does not ensure significant improvements for programs serving a limited number of subsidized children. In other places, *the move to expand preschool* and Head Start programs has driven resources into child care, since these services must now meet the full-day needs of working families. While this has been an important step forward, since most preschool programs serve children ages three to five, this strategy does not significantly reach children under age three. Finally, an increasing number of states *distribute funds to local communities to improve services* in several key areas, again providing resources and support directly to providers for training, compensation, accreditation, and health outreach. While this strategy allows communities to target resources to local needs, it does not necessarily ensure that all key elements of quality are in place in every program it affects. Despite these limitations, the growth in additional resources provided directly to programs can only help improve the quality of care.

Higher Rates Tied to Higher Standards

In a growing number of states, voluntary accreditation has helped to define a higher-quality program. Slowly, funding decisions are beginning to be tied to quality improvements. More states are starting to differentiate their licensing standards, creating several levels or tiers. Increases in public funding are then tied to whether programs can reach the higher standards of quality. States may pay a higher reimbursement rate for this higher-quality care or may provide direct grants or contracts to programs that agree to meet these standards.

Establishing higher standards of quality also can be used as a way to help parents recognize good care. For example, New Mexico has instituted a three-tiered system: The state identifies programs that meet basic licensing standards with a bronze star; those that meet more stringent state-developed requirements are recognized with a silver star, and those that are accredited by a nationally recognized accrediting body with gold. In Oklahoma, the Reaching for the Stars program is a tiered reimbursement-rate system based on training, compensation, and accreditation.[66]

Along with differential rates based on a tiered licensing system or other criteria, states can move to establish programmatic criteria in their contracted system. For example, a state or community may decide to develop a network of early-childhood programs that would receive direct support based on a set of standards or criteria. This is most often the case when a state develops a pre-kindergarten program that is delivered through community-based organizations such as child-care programs. As discussed below, Head Start and pre-kindergarten initiatives are guided by a set of program requirements that go beyond basic health and safety standards. These standards are mandatory and serve to guide funding decisions. As Head Start and pre-kindergarten programs are integrated into child care, these higher standards should apply, and the quality of care should improve.

Pre-kindergarten Partnerships

As more states move to provide preschool programs, many have begun to use a more collaborative model to deliver services. Rather than delivering the program only in the schools (which was typical some years ago), a state can choose to require or recommend that local schools contract with local child-care providers to provide preschool programs, or a state can contract directly with child-care providers. A child-care center then has to meet a set of standards that may include requirements for staff training, curriculum, child-staff ratio, group size, parent involvement, and other elements of quality.

State leadership has been evident in emerging efforts to provide pre-kindergarten services through child care. For example, in 1995, with support from state lottery funds, Georgia expanded its preschool program, opening it up to all four-year-olds in the state, without regard to income. Subsequently Georgia became the first state in the nation to offer universal pre-kindergarten. Through a competitive process, Georgia awards grants for pre-kindergarten services to a wide range of agencies across the state, including public schools, child-care providers (both for-profit and nonprofit), Head Start, universities, and churches. Each program receiving funds must meet requirements outlined by the state regarding child-staff ratio, group size, staffing, and curriculum.[67] In this way, the overall quality of child care, at least in those classrooms with four-year-olds, can be improved. Moreover, the state also has provided enhancement grants to programs with pre-kindergarten classrooms that also have infant rooms in order to enhance the quality of services for babies and toddlers. Although the pre-kindergarten program is not designed for younger children, the development of the pre-kindergarten program has brought renewed attention to the quality of care for all young children.

Like Georgia, New York has taken important steps to expand pre-school and to integrate early learning into child-care settings. In 1997, the New York state legislature enacted a package of education reforms that included a commitment to fund pre-kindergarten for four-year-olds, beginning in the 1998–99 school year. Funding is administered by the state's education department as grants to local school districts, allocated based on need and the number of eligible four-year-olds. Each school district must appoint a Universal Pre-K Policy Advisory Board that includes teachers, parents, community leaders, and representatives of early-childhood programs to recommend whether the district should implement pre-kindergarten programs and to create a plan for implementation. At least 10 percent of the funding must be used for collaborative, universal pre-K services arranged through contracts between school districts and a range of eligible community-based agencies, including child-care agencies. All participants must meet state program standards, and teachers must be certified in early childhood. The proportion of pre-K delivered in non-school settings steadily increased from 35 percent in the 1998–99 school year to 51 percent the next year. By 2000–01, it was estimated that more than 60 percent of the funds were supporting pre-K in non-school settings.[68]

Head Start Partnerships

As more families have made the transition to move off welfare, Head Start has been faced with the need to move from a predominantly half-day program to a full-day program. New partnerships have emerged between Head Start and community-based child-care providers that are helping to ensure more full-day services. While many of these collaborations have been stimulated by action at the program, community, or state level, several national initiatives also have contributed to greater

collaboration. In the 1990s, Head Start legislation focused greater attention on linkages with other organizations and established Head Start
collaboration offices in all fifty states. More recent Head Start expan-
sions strongly encouraged links with existing community-based
providers, and a national technical-assistance effort was launched to
help share promising practices emerging in programs across the country.

As we have seen in pre-K partnerships, a Head Start program may
contract with a child-care center to deliver Head Start services in that
setting. The center must agree to meet the Head Start performance
standards, and in turn it receives supplemental funds for the Head Start
children it serves. Such a center also receives additional training and
technical-assistance support that is typically available only to Head Start.
The Head Start agency might provide the comprehensive services
(health and family support) or may contract all services to the child-care
agency. A liaison (or a coordinator) from the Head Start agency usually
works with the child-care center or group of family child-care providers.

Given the strong need for high-quality services for infants and toddlers, a collaborative approach also has been used extensively by Early
Head Start programs. Launched in 1995 to serve children under age
three from low-income families, Early Head Start is based on the comprehensive model of service delivery that has proven so successful in the
Head Start program serving children ages three to five. Early Head Start
is designed to enhance children's physical, social, emotional, and cognitive development; to enable parents to be better caregivers and teachers for their children; and to help parents meet their own goals, including improving their own education and economic self-sufficiency.[69]
Since the program was established at a time when many low-income
families were working or leaving welfare, planners recommended that
programs should meet the needs and schedules of working parents.[70]

Some states have launched statewide partnerships with Head Start,
including Ohio, which focuses on preschool children, and Kansas, which
expanded Early Head Start. However, most partnerships grow through
community efforts. One of the earliest Head Start partnerships was
launched by Dwayne Crompton, the enterprising director of the KCMC
Child Development Corporation in Kansas City, Missouri. KCMC was
established in the 1970s to provide high-quality child-care services in
inner-city neighborhoods. Over time it expanded its scope and now
offers a broad range of services, including Head Start and Early Head
Start. In 1993, KCMC launched its Full Start program, which uses Head

Start funds to purchase services for eligible Head Start children who need full-day, full-year care not available in traditional Head Start centers. It requires that participating centers meet all Head Start performance standards, including the provision of comprehensive health and social services. Based on an independent review of the Full Start program after only three and one-half years of experience, this collaborative initiative showed promising results.[71]

Community Partnerships

Unlike integrating a specific program into a child-care setting, the community-partnership model is a strategy that focuses on improving the quality of care in an entire community. Resources are driven by a menu of allowable activities, a set of expected outcomes, or both. A local council or board is established to administer the funds and to help in the planning process. Funds may be provided to the community through a state funding source or through city or county revenue. In recent years, the private sector also has taken an interest in this community-wide approach to quality improvements. If the initiative is statewide, the state may establish specific benchmarks or outcome measures to help guide the distribution of the funding.

Statewide community-partnership models are implemented in a variety of ways. For example, some states administer an initiative through a state agency, while others establish a nongovernmental structure. Each state sets guidelines for representation of agencies and constituencies on local councils, but the number and composition of these vary. Some states appropriate new funding for local councils that may include prekindergarten or child-care dollars, while other states use local councils to implement plans to redistribute existing funds. In most states, the councils are charged with the task of assessing existing services and needs and developing a plan to address the gap that exists. Although program goals may vary, they usually focus on improving the quality of care and promoting school readiness.

One of the most celebrated examples of community partnership is North Carolina's pioneering Smart Start initiative. Launched by Governor Jim Hunt in 1993, Smart Start is a comprehensive public-private partnership to help all children in the state enter school healthy and ready to succeed. Smart Start programs and services provide children from birth to age five with access to high-quality and affordable child care, health care, and other family support. Over the years, the Smart

Start budget has grown significantly. The program now covers all of the one hundred counties in the state. North Carolina has one of the highest percentages of working mothers in the country, with more than two hundred thousand young children enrolled in regulated child care.[72]

Local partnerships have been established, covering one or more counties, to administer the Smart Start program at the community level. These local partnerships include representatives of both the public and private sectors, including health and human-service agencies, child-care providers, county and municipal governments, local education agencies, and families. Each local partnership must assess community needs and develop a plan to use Smart Start funds in its community. At least 30 percent of the funds must be used for child-care subsidies. Local partnerships must work toward measurable outcomes. The North Carolina Partnership for Children provides statewide oversight to the local partnerships, serves as their fiscal agent, reviews local plans, provides technical assistance, helps with fund-raising, and manages various aspects of the program.[73]

Smart Start can provide a range of supportive services to child care and can target specific quality improvements. Approximately one-fourth of the Smart Start funding (averaged across all counties) is being spent to improve the quality of child care. These improvements are paying off. A six-county study of the effects of Smart Start child care on kindergarten-entry skills was released in 1999: Children from centers that had received funds directly related to improving quality through Smart Start had better cognitive and language skills than their counterparts when they entered kindergarten. In addition, fewer children from these programs were rated by kindergarten teachers as having behavior problems.[74]

Another community-wide, rather than program-specific, approach to delivering early-childhood services is the Massachusetts Community Partnership for Children (CPC). Growing out of pre-existing preschool and special-education initiatives, CPC was established by the state legislature in 1993 as a response to a renewed focus on education reform and is targeted at three- and four-year-olds. CPC has grown dramatically, and in fiscal year 2000 had a budget of more than $100 million. CPC has five main goals, including increasing affordability and accessibility; providing high-quality early-childhood services; providing comprehensive social services such as health, nutrition, family education, and family literacy; conducting community outreach; and enhancing collaboration among families, business and community programs, and services serving children and families.

Interested communities must form a planning and policy-making council to select a lead agency, assess community needs, and submit a plan to the state to meet these priorities. Educational services may be delivered in public schools, Head Start, child-care centers, and family child-care settings. Participating programs must meet certain standards, depending on the type of provider, including specific provisions for staff-child ratio and group size. In addition, all programs must agree to become accredited. The first evaluation of CPC, conducted in 1996 by Tufts University, found that CPC had increased collaboration, affordability, availability, quality, and comprehensiveness of early care and education in the communities, despite challenges such as turf issues, limited resources, and time constraints.[75]

Since the pioneering efforts of North Carolina and Massachusetts, several states have initiated similar community-partnership efforts. For example, in 1999, South Carolina launched a First Steps initiative, modeled after Smart Start, which provided some $20 million to community partnerships throughout the state to promote school readiness. In California, the Children and Families First Act of 1998 (Proposition 10) took effect in January 1999, adding a fifty-cent-per-pack surcharge on cigarettes to raise new funds for early-childhood services and for smoking-prevention programs. Eighty percent of the funds are to be spent by county commissions created by the initiative to implement plans for improving early-childhood development programs in the counties. In 1998, Iowa established the Community Empowerment Initiative in an effort to create a partnership between communities and state government with an initial emphasis to improve the well-being of young children. The initiative called for the creation of community empowerment areas statewide.[76]

Along with the investment of public dollars in community collaborations, the private sector also has shown increasing interest in investing in this approach. One of the first efforts to focus on a community planning approach, Success By 6®, was started in Minneapolis in 1988 through the leadership of the United Way, a corporate executive, the mayor, and the superintendent of schools. In more than three hundred communities across the country, United Way now convenes community leaders to coordinate the efforts of business, government, labor, education, and health and human-service providers to raise awareness of early-childhood development, to improve access to critical health and human services, and to advocate improved policies affecting children.[77]

Considering all of the collaborative activities going on across the country—some initiated in a single area, others statewide, some paid for with public dollars, others with a combination of public and private resources—more child-care settings are integrating key components of good early-childhood programming. Furthermore, although data on the outcomes of these initiatives are just emerging, taken together, "devolution" of activity from the federal to the state and local level has created a groundswell of activity and civic involvement at the grassroots level, including more involvement of parents and community leaders, which can only lead to increased public awareness and investments in the care of young children.

A Good Beginning: Still Emerging

Although we now have a much better vision of what good early-childhood programs should look like, we still are missing essential ingredients to make the child-care system really work. While we have more agreement on the key elements of good program standards, we still lack both the resources and the support needed to put them in place on a large scale. The examples of emerging strategies to fund early learning in a range of settings are laying the foundation for more systemic changes within the child-care community; however, these efforts still are not reaching the majority of children in care. Furthermore, while we now realize the importance of a trained and stable workforce, we lack both an appropriate higher-education system to prepare those who care for young children and the resources to adequately compensate them once they are trained. Finally, while we know that all three components of good early-childhood programs—health, parent involvement, and education—need an infrastructure to support them, few centralized resources are in place in communities and states to pull together the pieces for providers and parents. These missing pieces not only make it difficult for working families to obtain good care, but they also threaten to undermine the healthy development of children. The future viability of child care as a support for early education depends on connecting the dots and using public resources to create a network of early-learning programs out of a disconnected array of child-care services. There are pieces in place, but we lack the whole picture.

Someone once asked a longtime child-care director, Douglas Baird, president and CEO of Associated Early Care and Education in Boston, to describe how he would characterize the last few decades if he were looking back a hundred years from now. Reflecting on our recent progress, he said, "We'll note that parents and their real needs were way ahead of public policy; that research had confirmed the value of high-quality education programs; and that by early in the twenty-first century, we had come to realize that providing early education for children was not a threat to family life, but rather a life gift to children and an essential resource to their families."[78] It is time to make this life gift a reality.

4

The New Neighborhood
Redefining Education After School

Our society can raise the chances that millions of ordinary children, growing up in circumstances that make them vulnerable, will develop into healthy and productive adults.
—Lisbeth B. Schorr, *Within Our Reach: Breaking the Cycle of Disadvantage*

t was the summer of 1975. I had been hired to help set up five child-care centers in Montgomery County, Maryland. Four of the centers were to be after-school programs. Walking into one of the empty rooms in a community center, I felt a sense of excitement, but I also felt very alone. I wondered where to start. There were few places to look for guidance on how to do this, few other programs to visit, few experts to turn to; there was no easy formula, no system of support.

That hot summer day came back to me in a flash twenty-five years later. On the last day of July 2000 I walked into another room, but it was hardly empty. Nearly a thousand professionals from across the country were sitting in a large ballroom of a hotel near Washington, D.C., waiting for the start of a national conference on after-school programs. So many people were interested in the event that organizers had to hold the meeting in shifts over the course of the week to accommodate everyone.

The previous autumn, a *Washington Post* article had noted that "Americans—in astonishingly high proportions—are

94

telling Democratic and GOP pollsters that they want more and better after-school care."[1] More and more candidates running for office across the country from both parties began to talk about after-school issues, pledged to expand services, or featured promising programs in their communities. That summer a record number of children were attending summer school and youth programs, and, plans were underway to mount a major national public-awareness campaign to promote after-school programs for all children.

Together with the advent of the Internet, cell phones, and video games, something had happened along the road that stretched between those two summers, something that would have great importance for children and their families. Michelle Seligson, founder of the National Institute on Out-of-School Time, referred to it as a "sea change," noting, "it isn't just a small band of advocates, parents, teachers and researchers who are speaking out about the importance of discretionary time, [but] policy-makers, funders, government officials and—even the president of the United States."[2] Adriana deKanter, then serving as a special adviser to the secretary of the U.S. Department of Education, called the burgeoning interest in after-school programs a "silent revolution."[3]

Decades after I walked into that empty room, a paradigm shift has occurred. The country appears poised to take what then seemed like an uncommon step—developing after-school programs—and turn it into a common expectation. Five bipartisan national polls on voter attitudes toward after-school have been conducted since 1998. Unlike public ambivalence about out-of-home care for young children, public support for after-school programs is clear. The most recent poll, released by the After School Alliance in 2001, found that more than 90 percent of registered voters believe that there is a need for some type of organized activity or place where children can go after school every day and where they have opportunities to learn. Eight out of ten voters believe that after-school programs are a necessity in their community. This strong support crosses all racial, ethnic, geographic, and partisan lines. The intensity of the support has lasted over several years (see Figure 6).[4]

Children spend only 20 percent of their waking time in school, since most schools are open six hours a day, 180 weekdays a year. This leaves 185 full days and many hours each day free, a time of both risk and opportunity.[5] Non-school hours represent the largest block of time in the lives of American children and youth.[6] Writing in the *New York*

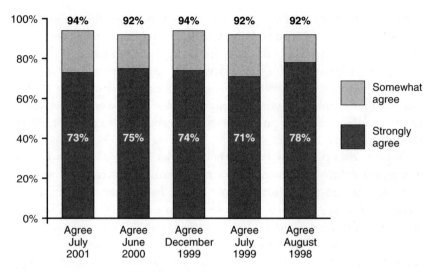

FIGURE 6. *Support for after-school activities.*

This figure is based on the responses to the question: "Do you agree or disagree that there should be some type of organized activity or place for children and teens to go after school every day that provides opportunities for them to learn?" (In 1998 and 1999 the words "that provides opportunities for them to learn" were omitted; also, in 1998, the words "every day" were omitted.)

The findings are based on a nationwide survey of eight hundred adults, eighteen years of age or older, who are registered voters. The data is from the polling firms of Lake Snell Perry and Associates and The Tarrance Group. The margin of error for this poll is ± 3.5 percent.

Source: Afterschool Alert Poll Report, Afterschool Alliance (Washington, D.C.: July/August 2001), p. 1.

Times Magazine in January 2000, James Traub noted that "a child living in an inner city is in school for only so many hours. It's the rest of the day—as well as the rest of the neighborhood—that's the big influence, and the problem."[7]

Today, too many children are spending time without adequate adult supervision and productive activities after school and during the summer months. In 1997 overall, more than twenty-eight million school-age children had parents who worked outside the home.[8] It has been estimated that on any given day, anywhere from five million to seven million of these children, and perhaps as many as fifteen million, spend time unsupervised after school.[9] According to a 1997 study by The Urban Institute, 5 percent of children ages six to nine and 24 percent of children ages ten to twelve are in non-supervised settings. Another

40 percent of children ages six to twelve were not reported in any child care—supervised or non-supervised—while their mothers were working.[10] Although The Urban Institute study did not look at families with children over age twelve, the number of young teens without adult supervision may be almost double that of younger children.[11]

The number of children in unsupervised settings may be significantly underestimated. It is difficult to explain exactly where the 40 percent of the children who are reported in "no care" might be spending their days. One could speculate that parents either may be arranging their schedules around the school day or that the children are attending non-child-care activities such as lessons or sporting events. However, many of these children could be in unsupervised settings for at least part of the time, since worried parents probably would not admit to a stranger conducting a telephone survey that their children are home alone. Even if parents are able to arrange to work part time while children are in school, providing adequate supervision during the summer months can be even more challenging.

A book that has become a classic for after-school staff quotes an eleven-year-old girl describing how she feels being home alone after school: "I am in the house alone at times; sometimes I feel like crying because if something happens there is no one to turn to. [I] Sit and watch TV with the phone next to me. Yes, I am afraid, just being there alone. [I] Sit there and don't say a word."[12]

The authors pose an important question for the nation: Will the time after school be "wisely used" or "wasted hours?" In this chapter, I present some of the essential ingredients to help make sure the time after school is well spent.

The Growth of School-Age Programs

As interest in preschool education was emerging, the launching of Sputnik set off new efforts to improve curriculum and other aspects of public schooling. However, like child care for younger children, the care of children after school was not seen as part of the education agenda, despite the fact that millions of women with school-age children were moving into the workforce. After-school programs had received support during World War II, and later through the Social Security amendments that provided child-care assistance for welfare families. However, in 1972 a special Interagency School-Age Day Care Task Force found that there was a lack of school-age programs nationally and little research on the topic.[13]

In the 1970s, new efforts to integrate community services into schools began to gain attention. In 1978, amendments to the Elementary and Secondary Education Act included language that addressed the potential involvement of schools in community activities. Title VIII, the Community Education Act, allowed the use of schools for various activities in collaboration with the community. Some states began to pass legislation allowing school districts to use their buildings for child care. Articles on school-age care started to appear in education magazines and journals. The trade-offs of providing school-age care in schools were debated.[14] Yet at this point few people made the clear link between after-school programs and education reform.

In 1983, the same year that the landmark report, *A Nation at Risk*, documented the growing dissatisfaction with American education, one of the first national policy reports on school-age care also was released. This report highlighted the inadequacy of the available research on school-age children. Although several studies had been conducted on the effects of maternal employment, they often seemed to ignore the effects of differing forms of care on children. Unlike preschool studies, for which long-term data began to emerge in the late 1970s, research on the effects of care for school-age children lagged behind. Most research was focused on the effects of maternal employment on children, without regard to the type of care available. Although early-education studies were documenting the beneficial effects of preschool on later achievement, no parallel studies were designed to discover if participation in some type of organized school-age activity can act as a preventive strategy. Nor was there any national agenda to promote child or youth development through school-age programs.[15]

During the 1980s the school-age movement gained momentum. In 1984, the First National Conference on Latchkey Children was held with the National Committee on the Prevention of Child Abuse.[16] By the mid-1980s, the Dependent Care Block Grant provided new funds to start after-school programs and to network and train after-school staff. This small funding stream brought new momentum to the field of after-school care. In 1987, school-age child-care providers and advocates from across the country came together to form the National School Age Care Alliance.[17] In the same year, when a Harris opinion poll asked teachers to rank seven possible causes of student difficulty in school, 51 percent of the respondents listed the number-one factor as children being left alone after school. The following year, in a survey conducted by the National Association of Elementary School Principals (NAESP), 84 percent of the responding principals said children in their communities need supervision before and after school, and two-thirds felt that public schools should provide the care. A few years later, NAESP, in collaboration with the School-Age Child Care project, published one of the first sets of standards for quality school-age care.[18]

The big change that has occurred over the past decade is that after-school programs have become central to overall school reform. In the 1990s, this link between education and after-school time began to emerge. In 1992 the Carnegie Council on Adolescent Development released a report outlining the risk and opportunity in the out-of-school hours for early adolescents, ages ten-to fifteen. Children in this age range spend a significant amount of their time out of school. The report noted that many of these children are home alone after school and therefore at serious risk for substance abuse, crime, violence, and sexual activity leading to unwanted pregnancies and sexually transmitted diseases. The report called for more positive youth-development activities, including partnerships between schools and community groups to expand services after school and in the summer months.[19]

At the same time, a number of other foundations and some states and communities were beginning to invest in the development of after-school programs, particularly in low-income neighborhoods. Despite this increasing activity, there was still a severe shortage of high-quality care for low-income children and youth. In 1993 the National Study of Before and After-School Programs was released. The study found that nearly fifty thousand after-school programs were operating in the country; yet a pattern of findings indicated that participation even in publicly sponsored before- and after-school programs was limited largely to families who could afford to pay full fees.[20]

In 1995 the U.S. Department of Health and Human Services held a national conference to help draw attention to the issue and convened a series of meetings to bring together school officials and community-based providers to plan for high-quality after-school activities. In 1998 the Department of Education and the Department of Justice issued a joint report entitled *Safe and Smart*, which focused on making the after-school hours work for children. The report cited FBI data from the early 1990s indicating that violent juvenile crime increases when school is out.

Like the Carnegie report before it, this report noted the risk factors involved in unsupervised out-of-school time. What was so significant about this new report was the emphasis it placed on the potential of after-school programs in three key areas: providing supervision, offering enriching experiences and positive social interaction, and improving academic achievement. The report noted that "more and more practitioners and parents are turning to after-school programs as an opportunity to prevent risky behaviors in children and youth and to improve student learning."[21]

In 1998, members of the National Governors' Association (NGA) began to focus attention on what they called "extra learning opportunities." Indiana Governor Frank O'Bannon, who served as co-chair of the special NGA task force, summarized the importance of school-community partnerships when he said, "Children and young people have a natural thirst for learning that does not confine itself to the typical school day, week or year—or for that matter, to the classroom."[22] From a developmental point of view, what is important is that there are connections across the day for children and families. The school hours and the after-school hours can complement each other. Staff on each side of the three P.M. hour should take time to meet with each other to plan a more integrated day that will help children develop competence and confidence. Such an integrated approach sets the stage to look at the total school environment.

This growing interest in after-school programs as a vehicle for school reform also was reflected in federal policy. In 1998, the Clinton administration began to build on the provisions in the Elementary and Secondary Education Act (ESEA) that allowed for the funding of community school activities, including after-school. As part of ESEA, Congress established the 21st Century Community Learning Center program to award grants to public schools and consortia of such schools to enable them to plan, implement, or expand projects that benefit the education, health, social services, culture, and recreation needs of the community. The law required that schools collaborate with other public and non-profit community agencies and organizations, local businesses, and other educational and human-service organizations.[23] Funding for 21st Century Community Learning Centers grew from $40 million in 1998 to $1 billion in 2002. Despite these increases, funds could not keep up with demand; only a small fraction of the requests could be filled due to limited resources.[24]

In addition, several states had begun to invest in after-school programs. For example: In 1998, the California legislature created the After School Learning and Safe Neighborhoods Partnerships program. This statewide program allocates annual grants to school-community partnerships that provide after-school, academic and literacy supports, and other constructive alternatives to elementary and middle school children. Maryland created the After-School Opportunity Fund to bring together interested stakeholders to assess needs and develop comprehensive planning. Funds are provided to expand programs and for training and evaluation. By the end of the 1990s, a number of similar efforts were spreading across the country.[25]

In the closing months of the century, The David and Lucile Packard Foundation released a report, *When School Is Out*. Cautioning that data were still limited and most programs voluntary, the report did find early evidence that after-school programs can have a positive impact on participants, particularly low-income children.[26] Like preschool education, after-school programming was beginning to be seen as a key element in an education reform agenda. In January 2001, reports began to appear that schools were beginning to extend the day and year. The mayor of New York called for a sixth day of school for some struggling students, and the governor of California asked the state to extend the school year by thirty days for some children in middle school who needed extra time.[27]

While after-school programs began to be seen as a way to close the gap in academic achievement, debates emerged regarding a number of issues: the goal and content of after-school programs, the appropriate role of the school and community-based organizations, the challenge of staffing, and accountability. It was not enough to extend the day; something new had to be created, a new vision of after-school programming.

Crafting a Vision for After-School Learning

Things used to be simple after school. Children came home, had milk and cookies and did their homework, went to a Scout meeting, played some ball, climbed trees. Or at least this is the image that many people conjure up when they nostalgically think back to their own childhood. Whether those images are true or not, they do appear to reflect something we want for our children. One of the central challenges of the next ten years is how best to design after-school programs to reinforce our key values: keeping children safe, providing them with leisure activities, ensuring educational equity for children, and supporting their families.

Policy-makers and other decision-makers too often have the wrong images of what is meant by after-school programs; they may picture a schoolroom where everyone sits quietly for hours doing homework, or they may imagine a large gym with dozens of children and a few basketballs. Neither is correct.

To begin to craft a vision for after-school learning, we must consider at least three important sources of information. First, we have to recognize what parents want and need for their children; their perspectives count. Second, we must ground our thinking about after-school in what is best for children, and what we know about how they grow and develop. Third, in designing after-school programs, we have to build on the years of experience gained from those running such programs, whether those programs have been called child care, or youth clubs and sports, or extended learning. The after-school system of the twenty-first century must incorporate all of these perspectives: parents' opinions, knowledge of youth development, and lessons learned from years of experience.

A Parent's View

A prominent researcher once wrote:

> When my son started kindergarten, more than a decade ago, I had a surprise. During earlier struggles to find dependable, high quality child care, I had assumed (naively) that my child care worries would be over once my son began elementary school. Wrong. Collin's school day was considerably shorter than my full-time workday. When school holidays, teacher in-service days, and summer vacations were added to the mix, we had at least one child-care crisis a month.[28]

Parents often are surprised by the extent to which child-care issues linger, even when children reach school age. The march into the school building serves as a rite of passage, and parents expect that they will leave behind the issues that they faced in the preschool years. Yet the need for child care goes on and may be even more difficult due to complicated schedules and lack of services. So what do parents look for?

First and foremost, parents are concerned about the safety of their children. Hanging out after school at the coffee shop, the 1990s version of the "soda shop," does not seem as safe as it appeared to be in those old movies. Parents want to know where their children are—and do not want just to rely on "e-care." I have talked with many parents over the years who have encouraged their children to go home directly after school because at least then they will know where they are. Parents worry about what can happen when their children are home alone, but they often worry more about dangerous neighborhoods and what children can "get into" on their way home.

Along with keeping them safe, parents want their children to be busy with many things after school: homework, music lessons, sports, clubs. They don't want their children to miss out on these things because they are working. Parents seem to want a range of activities, not one single type of program. In a national opinion poll, most parents indicated that they wanted several types of activities for their children, including technology and computers, art, music, drama, and basic skills.[29]

The real challenge is that parents need after-school services that are accessible, affordable, and conveniently located. For low-income families, services for school-age children can easily fall outside a tight family budget. In a study of out-of-school time in three low-income communities, parents reported that they would like to enroll their children in lessons and other organized activities but were prevented from doing so by prohibitive cost, transportation difficulties, worries about neighborhood safety, and a shortage of options.[30]

Going home after school, even to an empty house, is at least free. Moreover, most parents cannot rearrange their schedules at three P.M. to drive children to various activities. Although images of "soccer moms" might have dominated the news a few years ago, I have always thought the better image was the "cell phone mom," constantly making arrangements and managing logistics for the family. While many moms and dads are lucky enough to be able to squeeze in those late-afternoon "pick-up and drop-offs," it is becoming harder to balance it all.

Increasingly, parents want these activities to be on or near the school grounds. Over the years, the idea of using schools to deliver a range of services has been debated in the child-care community. Some argue that schools are not equipped to provide the balance of activities that children need in the after-school hours, and they don't want to see just an extension of the school day. Others are concerned about supplanting traditional community-based agencies that have been working for years with children and youth after school.

As a former after-school provider, I am sensitive to the debate. However, as a parent, I think the dialogue often sounds like some insider game. The truth of the matter is that as parents we want it all: We want the convenience of children being in or near their school so we don't have to worry about transportation, but we also want our children to enjoy and learn at the same time. We know that if a program feels, looks, and smells too much like what has gone on before three P.M., and attendance is optional, children, particularly as they grow older, will "vote with their feet" and not participate. It is important that children enjoy and look forward to their after-school program. Hearing their child say, "I just don't want to go to that place any more" makes parents worry and feel guilty and contributes to family stress.

In short, parents want schools and community groups to work together. As our children might say, we just want them "to work it out." It seems like common sense to maximize the use of the resources that are already in schools, particularly space and equipment. At the same time, schools can't stand alone. Schools must work with parents and community groups if educational competence and positive child and youth development are the ultimate goals. What parents want is not pieces of an education patched together to meet the needs of their whole child. Their work schedules and the development of their children call for a more integrated day.

I think the best image of what we want for after-school was provided by Tracey Ballas, past president of the National School-Age Care Alliance, who referred to after-school programs as "the new neighborhood."[31] To me this means a place that lets our children have what some of us were able to experience in the old neighborhood: games to play, balls to throw, books to read, nutritious things to eat, good friends, a person to listen, some leisure time, and some new challenges. Yet the new neighborhood brings some assets not found in the old one: It often reflects more diversity and may provide more productive activities. From a parent's point of view, creating a new neighborhood means being able to count on someone to support you, to provide the same schedule every day; believing that your child is engaged in enriching activities; and knowing that at least there has been a good start on the homework before you leave work, stop at the store, and start dinner. These are the simple pleasures that really make families work and children thrive.

A Youth-Development Approach

How many of us can recall our elementary school years? For some they were carefree, with lots of time to linger; for others they were jam-packed with activities and work to get done. For most, they included a combination of awkward days, endless attempts to either fit in or stand out, and probably some combination of tender moments and tough times with friends and family. The years from six through adolescence are years of great change: a time when we hope children develop a sense of confidence; a time when children seek to know who they are; a time marked by dramatic changes in their physical, social, emotional, and cognitive development.

In the discussion of young children in Chapter 3, I described the importance of grounding the design of early educational services for children from birth through age five in a developmental perspective. The same is true when planning after-school programs. Historically there has been much less emphasis on developmental principles when discussing school-age services, particularly when they are linked to education. Teacher training, school curriculum, and high-stakes testing often do not encourage us to think broadly about development. Instead traditional "education" too often splits the cognitive area from biological, sociological, and affective domains. However, while we want after-school programs to be seen as part of education, the approach must be developmental, putting more attention on the needs of the whole child.

In her review of the developmental stages of children ages six to fourteen, Jacquelynne Eccles writes that "it is during these years that children make strides toward adulthood by becoming competent, independent, self-aware and involved in the world beyond their families." These years include two broad periods: middle childhood (ages six to ten) and early adolescence (approximately ages eleven to fourteen). Middle childhood has not received as much attention as other developmental stages. Erik Erickson viewed this period as the time when children learn to be competent and productive or are left to feel inferior and unable to do anything well. It is during this period when children learn and refine fundamental skills and develop more self-awareness. They develop the ability to find information—to "learn how to learn"— to plan, and to understand that there are other perspectives in the world, different points of view. As children reach adolescence, their exposure to the outside world grows and they begin to search for their own identities. They experience tremendous physical change as they reach puberty. Relationships with peers seem to rule as they gain more autonomy from family. Cognitively, children in this age group begin to think more abstractly.[32]

Understanding these and many other concepts of youth development is the first step in designing after-school programs. I use the term "youth development" when referring to school-age children, although one may argue that someone does not become a youth until reaching the age of ten or twelve.[33] It does not appear that there is one hard-and-fast rule about what age group should be included in the term "youth."

By using the term "youth" I do not assume that younger school-age children should be treated the same as young teens. Quite the contrary; it is critically important that after-school programs design their activities in a way that reflects those developmental differences. For example, younger children may need more help organizing their activities, may demand less autonomy, and may be satisfied with many of the traditional games that are the staple of schoolyards and Saturday afternoons. Older children, on the other hand, usually need to feel that programs are responding to their growing independence, providing more opportunities to try new things, to "act older" (within reason). We can mentor and guide these older children, but they certainly would not like it if we referred to their after-school programs as "child care."

The main reason to use the term "youth development" is that it is starting to really mean something. Over the last decade, there has been a surge of interest in better understanding this developmental period, to define a set of expected outcomes, and to retool the approach to service delivery. A number of special commissions sponsored by national foundations, including the Carnegie Council on Adolescent Development, issued reports in the late 1980s and early 1990s that brought renewed attention to this age group. More recently, the National Research Council and Institute of Medicine continued this focus on youth development, providing increased visibility to developmental stages during this period as well as implications for the design and evaluation of community-level programs.[34]

The National Collaboration for Youth, a coalition of leading youth-development organizations in the country, has developed a position statement that is helping to define positive youth development: "Positive youth development is a process which prepares young people to meet the challenges of adolescence and adulthood through a coordinated, progressive series of activities and experiences which help them to become socially, morally, emotionally, physically and cognitively competent."[35]

Such an approach is preventive; it addresses a broad set of developmental needs rather than focusing solely on deficits or problems that may arise. Simply stated, positive youth development is an asset-based approach that encourages success and builds on the resources that youth themselves bring to the table. In its recent report, *Community Programs to Promote Youth Development*, The National Research Council and Institute of Medicine outlined the personal and social assets that facilitate positive youth development (see Figure 7). It concludes that "having more assets is better than having few. Although strong assets in one

Physical Development

- Good health habits
- Good health risk-management skills

Intellectual Development

- Knowledge of essential life skills
- Knowledge of essential vocational skills
- School success
- Rational habits of mind—critical thinking and reasoning skills
- In-depth knowledge of more than one culture
- Good decision-making skills
- Knowledge of skills needed to navigate through multiple cultural contexts

Psychological and Emotional Development

- Good mental health, including positive self-regard
- Good emotional self-regulation skills
- Good coping skills
- Good conflict-resolution skills
- Mastery motivation and positive-achievement motivation
- Confidence in one's personal efficacy
- "Planfulness"—planning for the future and future life events
- Sense of personal autonomy; responsibility for self
- Optimism coupled with realism
- Coherent and positive personal and social identity
- Prosocial and culturally sensitive values
- Spirituality, or a sense of a "larger" purpose in life
- Strong moral character
- A commitment to good use of time

Social Development

- Connectedness—perceived good relationships and trust with parents, peers, and some other adults
- Sense of social place/integration—being connected and valued by larger social networks
- Attachment to prosocial/conventional institutions, such as school, church, and nonschool youth programs
- Ability to navigate in multiple cultural contexts
- Commitment to civic engagement

FIGURE 7. *Personal and social assets that facilitate positive youth development.*

Source: National Research Council and Institute of Medicine, *Community Programs to Promote Youth Development, Committee on Community-Level Programs for Youth,* Jacquelynne Eccles and Jennifer A. Gootman, eds., Board on Children, Youth, and Families, Division of Behavioral and Social Sciences and Education (Washington, D.C.: National Academy Press, 2002), pp. 6–7.

category can offset weak assets in another category, life is easier to manage if one has assets in all four domains [physical, social, psychological and emotional, and social development]."[36]

Merging Three Perspectives: Care, Education, Youth

Faced with designing a whole new generation of after-school programs, we must remember that we are not starting from scratch. Programs for school-age children have been operating in communities for many years. The challenge is that they often are separate circles of influence with differing philosophies or approaches to working with children and families. Effective programs no longer can be thought of as "just a safe place to go," or "just a place to play," or "just more school." The vision for a "new-age" after-school program transcends all of these static models. The new image must grow out of a combination of three overlapping circles of information: experiences with community-based child care, youth programs, and school-based after-school programs. These intersecting circles overlap at the point where after-school learning begins (see Figure 8).[37]

Years of providing community-based child care for children have shown how important after-school care is to supporting families and how the resources of an entire community can be brought to bear on the activities of school-age children. Moreover, we have known for years that children learn as much outside school as they do within. For decades, school-age child-care programs have been trying to provide both a good influence for children while their parents are working and a prevention against the risks too often found in the surrounding neighborhood.

Yet when school-age children grow older, particularly when they reach early adolescence, many move on to a local youth program, if they are lucky enough to live in communities that have such services. A patchwork of community organizations attempts to provide services to youth, providing opportunities for older children to stay productively involved with their communities and with their peers. Youth programs, with their focus on mentoring and helping children develop their skills and talents, provide an important approach for all after-school programs.

Finally, the involvement of public schools, the "newer" player on the after-school block, brings a legitimacy to after-school programming, making it part of a larger system of support for children that is seen as a public responsibility. Although schools provided child-care services as far back as World War II, it is only in more recent years that their

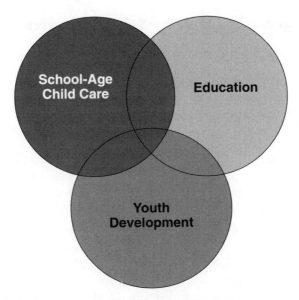

FIGURE 8. *After-school programs: Merging three perspectives.*
Source: Beth M. Miller, "Power of the Hours: The Changing Context of After School,"
School-Age Review, The Journal of the National School-Age Care Alliance, 2 (Fall 2000), p. 20.

involvement has significantly grown. After-school programming can help provide more equity in the educational system by extending the learning time and reinforcing what goes on before three P.M.

However, not any one of these perspectives, nor any single location—be it a community-based child-care or youth program or a public or private school—can go it alone. Children are exposed to a range of ideas and settings, and they learn and grow from multiple perspectives. It is how we put it all together that matters. After-school programs are very diverse: They serve primary-age children, middle-school children, early adolescents, or a mixture of ages. This makes it difficult to create one simple image, one single type of program, or one overarching goal.

Despite the need to reflect this diversity, after-school programs provide an opportunity not only to promote education in the traditional sense, but also to help children have a broad range of experiences. We want safe children, smart children, and caring children. The best way to reach that goal is to learn from the multiple perspectives that have contributed to the evolution of school-age services.

The Neighborhood After-School Program

If you walk into a good after-school program, you might find a group of children doing their homework at a table or eating a healthy snack; others could be using computers or listening to music. Some children might be volunteering to clean up an empty lot on a corner as part of a community-service project, reading to a group of younger children, going out for a spirited game of baseball, or preparing for the peacefulness of a yoga class. There might be a large art project that has been in progress for several weeks to serve as the backdrop for a play in the making. There might be gardens and young gardeners, clubs and group games, and solitary reading. This is the new neighborhood in action.

The world of after-school services is being redefined. While programs for school-age children remain diverse, certain key elements should be part of any after-school program: a goal that leads to a well-rounded education; partnerships between the school, parents, and community-based organizations; well-trained and supported staff; and standards and accountability. Regardless of where the program is located, what goes on after school should be related or connected in some meaningful way to what goes on during school. This does not mean that the after-school program should duplicate what goes on in school. Quite the opposite; activities after school should complement, not substitute, schoolwork. Furthermore, just as in early-childhood programs, the central ingredient in quality is staff. After-school providers must be well prepared and well compensated in order to have the resources to support the children in their care. Finally, programs must meet specially designed standards in order to be accountable for the increasing amount of public investment.

Promoting a Well-Rounded Education

The Carnegie Task Force on the Education of Young Adolescents described a successful fifteen-year-old as "an intellectually reflective person, a person en route to a lifetime of meaningful work, a good citizen, a caring and ethical individual, and a healthy person."[38] Such a person used to be described as "well rounded." Young adolescents do not acquire these characteristics overnight; they evolve over time. Helping a school-age child become such a person by adolescence means providing structured activities, meaningful relationships, and a wide variety of opportunities to explore new ideas at home, at school, and in the hours in between.

We all can remember classmates who were considered "well rounded." They could tackle just about any task, get along with everyone, do well academically, excel in sports, and play in the orchestra. They were resilient and self-assured, social, and comfortable with themselves. A well-rounded education is grounded in what Howard Gardner has called "multiple intelligence." Gardner developed the concept that children have a number of different capacities, such as linguistic, musical, logical-mathematical, spatial, bodily-kinesthetic, and personal intelligences.[39] Observant parents and teachers know that each child is unique and has different talents and ways of learning. During the school-age years, it is critically important to expose children to a wide range of activities to allow them to meet their full potential. While the school day may be focused on one type of learning style, a good after-school program offers the opportunity for children to experiment with a range of activities, exposing them to new ideas and reinforcing emerging skills in a way that fits a child's strengths.

Too often the debate about what activities should go on after school seems to be reduced to whether the focus should be on sports, art, and music *or* on homework and tutoring that supports reading, writing, and math. This either-or-approach is not helpful to children. If the staff of an after-school program truly understands development, they will appreciate the fact that they must promote children's self-confidence by helping them do well in their schoolwork. Children who cannot read do not feel good about themselves; one area of development affects the other. At the same time, after-school programs often have the luxury of a more relaxed setting, which allows them to reinforce skills with a more creative approach.

Good after-school programs include health, nutrition, and physical activities, the promotion of literacy (both reading and computer knowledge), the arts (music, art, drama), nature, the immediate community, and the larger world. These content areas, along with the overall goals, make up the emerging curriculum in after-school programs. Unlike the curriculum of the regular school day, these content areas are not "subjects" or skills, but rather are interrelated areas of interest that can promote development and learning. One review of research on after-school practices found strong support for flexible programming that established and maintained a favorable emotional climate and provided a sufficient variety of activities.[40]

Health, nutrition, and physical activity have not been afforded the attention they deserve in discussions regarding the education of children.

Yet there is nothing more important, or the subject of more attention among school-age children, than what they eat and how they look and feel. After-school programs have to start with a strong commitment to health and nutrition. Every parent knows how hungry their children are after school. Children don't need chips and soda from a vending machine that makes money for some school project; they need nutritious snacks that can help them thrive. Obesity has already sapped the self-confidence from an increasing number of school-age children. Approximately 25 percent of children and adolescents are overweight, a figure that has doubled in thirty years.[41] Not only should every after-school program provide physical activities, but health-education programs in schools should be linked to health promotion after school. The improvements in the federal Child and Adult Care Food Program, which expanded access to snacks and meals, is a big step forward in efforts to ensure adequate nutrition for children in after-school care.

At the same time, after-school programs must be part of the solution to help all children read. A high percentage of the nation's fourth-graders read below grade level, and we must work to change this. Literacy activities—book clubs, libraries, tutoring, leisure reading—all are part of the after-school scene. Moreover, rather than taking time away from basic skills, music, art, and drama actually complement and enhance academic competence. Finally, literacy in a new era cannot be confined to print: Computer literacy is critical for all children. After-school programs are essential to the effort to close the digital divide that too often isolates children of low-income families. Just as a bank of computers is now available in every library, after-school programs should have access to up-to-date computer equipment and trained staff. In fact, nearly 70 percent of 21st Century Community Learning Center programs offer technology-related activities, ranging from intergenerational computer mentoring to Web site design to literacy programs.[42]

While the need to improve literacy and computer access has received much attention, there has been less focus on bringing the natural world back into the lives of children. Video games and other multimedia experiences have replaced tree-climbing and outdoor play. Since computers and video games easily attract children, it takes special effort to steer them toward outdoor experiences. Finally, the after-school program, like public education, can expose children to a wide range of activities and cultural experiences in their communities. It can provide the time needed to learn a second language or get to know something about how others live, both in the community and in the global village.

But we must be cautious in talking about the content of after-school programs. It is not just what is taught, but the way these activities take place, the atmosphere of the program, the relationships that develop between the children and the staff and among the children themselves, that lead to the achievement of these important goals. After-school programs provide new opportunities for children to experience and learn from each other and practice cooperation and problem-solving. Social competency is linked to success in school and later in life. The middle childhood and early adolescent years are critically important times for nurturing friendships and developing interpersonal skills.

Karen Pittman, of the Forum for Youth Investment, addresses outcomes sought in youth programs and the range of other places where young people live, learn, work, play, and make a difference. She noted that "prevention alone is not enough." While avoiding negative behavior is critically important, youth who are "problem free" are not necessarily "fully prepared" or "fully engaged." She urges us to have a higher goal: to go beyond preventing problems and pay attention to promoting competence across domains. Moreover, Pittman and her colleagues outline four other desired outcomes for youth: *confidence, character, connections,* and *contributions.* Having a sense of confidence both influences and directly affects a child's competence. A sense of character often grows out of efforts we make to encourage children to take responsibility for their actions. Connections and contributions develop when we help children and youth go beyond themselves, connecting with others and growing to see that they can make meaningful contributions to their communities and their world.[43]

It is the daily interactions with adults and others that help children develop good character, connections, and contributions—a sense of responsibility for their actions and for the community at large. It often has struck me as a parent that the most important lessons we give to our children occur when we are helping them to reflect on their actions, guiding them in their choices, being honest with them, and modeling what we want to see them become. Good after-school programs help do the same thing. Good after-school programs are not just about filling children up with activities and things to learn; they are about taking the time to listen and talk, to encourage and motivate.

Helping children develop a sense of *character* may seem hard to define. What may look like character-building to some may seem subjective, arbitrary, or even punitive to others. Punishment is not the goal. Instead we want to help children learn from their mistakes, help them understand why they may have taken the wrong turn, and help them celebrate when they take the right one. After-school programs can help develop a sense of autonomy and a set of principles that go beyond oneself. Marian Wright Edelman, president of the Children's Defense Fund, includes in her list of lessons for life: "Don't wait for, expect, or rely on favors. Count on earning them by hard work and perseverance. Keep your word and your commitments."[44] These lessons should be the golden rules of all good after-school programs.

Self-confidence grows in school-age children who have daily support and an increasing sense of responsibility. In the mid-1990s, Save the Children, a national leader in developing innovative grassroots approaches to helping children, developed the "Web of Support," a programmatic approach to assure that children have consistent, caring adults, safe environments, and constructive activities during their out-of school time. Save the Children developed this framework based on the belief that all programs developed *for* young people need to be developed and administered with input *from* young people.[45] In the old neighborhoods, children made decisions all the time: They put on impromptu plays, made up rules for games, and helped plan what they would do during long summer days. Organizing such activities were important first steps in learning principles of democracy and civics. Children should have the same type of input to help decide what goes on in the after-school program.

Moving beyond the walls of the program, building a sense of *connection and contribution* also calls for providing many opportunities to serve the larger community. In April 1997, thousands of Americans felt a sense of excitement as they participated in the call to action made at the President's Summit for America's Future in Philadelphia. Presidents Clinton, Bush, Ford, Carter, and former First Lady Nancy Reagan, representing her husband, endorsed a set of five promises for youth. Led by General Colin L. Powell, America's Promise called on all Americans to make a commitment to provide safe places and structured activities during non-school hours and to ensure opportunities for youth to give back through community service. General Powell's powerful words reflect the goal: "I believe to the depth of my heart that a teenager who has spent a few hours a week helping a younger child learn to read, or spent a few hours at a hospice helping an older person reach the end of their life in dignity, is a changed person."[46]

Today, service learning has become an integral part of many schools and after-school programs. By participating in the community, children test their ideas and explore their interest in real-world activities. Often it is these experiences, more than those that go on inside the school building, that help children develop leadership skills and a sense of confidence and competence.

Together, all of these activities make up the fabric of the after-school program. Unfortunately, such services are still outside the reach of many families, particularly when children have special needs. Too often, after-school staff do not have the training and support to provide optimal services for these children or their families. In his study of inclusive practices of youth with disabilities, Dale Fink found that despite changing laws that no longer permit children with disabilities to be excluded, full participation has not been realized.[47] While promising examples are beginning to emerge across the country, this is an area that will need much more attention as programs continue to expand. It is also an issue that calls for better partnerships among parents, schools, and community based organizations.

Moving Beyond School versus Community

Atelia Melaville writes that "no single institution can create all the conditions that young people need to flourish. . . . The community can expand the opportunities for growth and development that take place not only during school but also before and after school, in the evenings and on the weekends."[48] It is not where the program is or who gets the money to run it that matters. There are good after-school programs in schools and in community centers, but the best programs result from a partnership between the two. In good partnerships, curricula are shared, joint training opportunities are offered, and mutual planning of activities are accomplished.[49] After years of debate, it appears that schools and community-based agencies are finding new and creative ways to work together.

A 1999 survey by the National Governors' Association found that thirty states saw a change in the relationship between school districts and such after-school services. According to one respondent, many principals were initially reluctant to allow after-school providers to use their buildings because of wear and tear and staff costs to keep the buildings open. However, programs have been so successful that principals are now requesting them in their schools. Another respondent pointed to two major reasons for the improved relationships: the knowledge that the needs of children can be better met by schools and community groups working together rather than separately, and the funding incentives to bring the two together.[50]

Joy Dryfoos notes that in the past, less than one-third of all public schools provided space for child care, mostly for kindergarten and primary-age children. More recently, schools have been opening their doors to all age groups. Dryfoos predicts that in the future it is "possible that all schools will be open extended hours, serving as true community hubs."[51] Partnerships between schools and community organizations will make services much stronger.

The idea of creating partnerships between school and community is far from new. More than sixty years ago, Charles Stewart Mott helped pioneer the concept of community education in Flint, Michigan. During the Depression, Mott became deeply concerned with the growing number of "latchkey" children whose parents came to Flint to work in the factories. In 1935 Mott met Frank J. Manley, then a physical-education teacher who spoke about the value of meaningful after-school activities and the potential use of the school building for this purpose. Thus began a lifelong partnership to develop the concept of the community school—"keeping the lights on" after school and using the facility for a range of activities for children and adults. Decades later, the spirit of the community-education movement is reflected in the partnership between the Charles Stewart Mott Foundation and the U.S. Department of Education in their efforts to promote 21st Century Community Learning Centers.[52] This partnership has led to a nationwide effort to improve and expand after-school programs and to promote them for all children.

Similar efforts to forge partnerships have been emerging throughout the past decade. In 1987 Edward Zigler, one of the founding fathers of Head Start, developed the idea of a 21st Century School, a place that would serve as a hub for children and family services. This model includes school-based, year-round child care for preschool children; school-based before-school, after-school, and vacation care for children up to age twelve; comprehensive preventive health; home visiting by trained parent educators; support and training for family child-care providers; nutrition programs and education; and other services. By 1999, this concept had spread to more than six hundred elementary schools across the country.[53]

In New York City, the Beacon schools, started in 1991, are models of school-community-family partnerships. Beacons allow community nonprofits to create community centers in public school buildings, offering a range of activities and services to all ages, including before- and after-school services. Individual Beacons are managed by community-based organizations and work collaboratively with school boards, their host schools, community advisory councils, and a wide range of neighborhood organizations. Many of the Beacon schools are open more than twelve hours a day, seven days a week. Beacons offer sports, recreation, arts and culture, educational opportunities, and a range of other services.[54]

In New York, The After School Corporation (TASC) was established in 1998 by the Open Society Institute to enhance the quality and availability of after-school programming. One of the main goals of TASC is for after-school programs ultimately to become a public responsibility. Toward that ambitious goal, TASC committed up to $125 million for up to seven years, contingent upon a 3:1 match. The initiative is supporting after-school programs operating from three to six P.M. each weekday during the school year for children in kindergarten through twelfth grade. Funds are provided to community-based and other not-for-profit organizations to operate the programs, which are located in public schools.[55] By 2002, the number of TASC-supported programs grew from twenty-five to more than two hundred statewide, and the number of children served increased to more than forty-seven thousand.[56]

On the other side of the country, in 1988, Los Angeles Mayor Tom Bradley launched what has been called one of his most important legacies. He proposed funds to lay the foundation for L.A.'s BEST (Better Educated Students for Tomorrow), which set the stage for a unique public-private partnership between the city, the Los Angeles Unified School District, and the private sector. At the time an estimated one hundred thousand children were believed to be unsupervised after school throughout the city. L.A.'s BEST has developed a combination of activities to keep kids off the streets and interested in doing well at school, including homework assistance and tutoring, science, dance, sports, arts and crafts, computer instruction, reading for recreation, conflict resolution, and community service. By 1998, more than forty thousand children had participated.[57]

Across the country, new partnerships and promising initiatives have emerged. Many community-based organizations, such as YMCAs, YWCAs, and Camp Fire Girls and Boys, have taken the lead, bringing fresh ideas into the schools. For example, by 2000 the YMCA operated eight thousand after-school programs across the country, more than 80 percent of which took place in a school building.[58] Boys and Girls Clubs of America have developed Project Learn, based on the research of Reginald Clark, who argues that low-income youth fail in school because of their activities during non-school hours. He suggests that high-achieving, low-income youth should engage in what he calls "high-yield learning activities" during non-school hours. These activities reinforce skills and information that are critical to academic success in school. "High-yield activities" include homework help and tutoring, leisure reading, writing activities, discussions with knowledgeable adults, helping others, and playing games using cognitive skills.[59]

Given the potential of after-school services for children and families, state policy is beginning to focus on school and community partnerships. For example, one of the earliest statewide efforts was Hawaii's After-School Plus (A+) program, which began in 1990 with fifteen thousand students and had grown by 1998 to more than twenty-two thousand in more than 170 elementary schools. The A+ program attempts to "capitalize on children's natural characteristics and hunger for learning" and requires the cooperation of community agencies and parents. Evaluations indicate a high level of parent satisfaction with the program.[60] In California, through the After-School Learning and Safe Neighborhood Partnership program, schools and communities must develop partnerships to provide academic and literacy support along with safe, constructive alternatives for students in grades kindergarten through nine. Programs must operate on elementary, middle-school, or junior-high campuses, but community organizations must participate in the development, implementation, and evaluation of the program.[61]

Partnerships go beyond the relationship of a school and a single community-based organization. All across the country, communities are beginning to take a look at the overall supply and quality of after-school programs and to launch community-wide efforts to meet the needs. One of the most pioneering efforts to build community-wide systems of after-school services was Making the Most of Out-of-School Time

(MOST), an initiative funded by the DeWitt Wallace Reader's Digest Fund. Began in 1994, MOST was a multimillion-dollar effort in three target cities—Boston, Chicago, and Seattle—to improve the quality and affordability of out-of-school care.

MOST Director Joyce A. Shortt recalled hearing noted futurist Robert Theobald talk about "creating communities anew" in the midst of all the other changes that are occurring. She believes that this notion goes to the heart of what the MOST initiative was all about: "It helps to create a milieu in which local strategies encourage system change so that the needs of children and youth in out-of-school time are supported in ways that work for their community."[62] MOST used a community-based collaborative approach toward improving the quality and quantity of out-of-school services for children and youth, especially those from low-income families. This strategy creates the opportunity to develop local leadership and capacity to plan, create partnerships, and raise and expand resources.

Early findings from an evaluation of the MOST initiative indicate that the three cities have made progress in their efforts to improve quality and expand the availability of school-age programs. For example, approximately six thousand new spaces for school-age care have been created through the initiative, more than $2 million in additional funds have been raised by the cities to support their work, hundreds of staff have been trained, and partnerships have been established with park districts, schools, youth-serving organizations, and cultural institutions.[63]

These collaborative efforts and many others emerging across the country are building community. Some have been initiated in a single area, and others have emerged statewide; some are paid for with public dollars, and others with a combination of public and private resources.

Reaching Out to Parents

One of the strongest reasons to promote partnerships between schools and after-school programs is their potential to support families and to foster deeper involvement by parents in the education of their children. Often it is the after-school staff, more than the teachers in a school, who interact with parents on a daily basis, particularly since children often are picked up from the after-school program rather than directly from their classrooms. After-school staff can help make parents feel welcome and develop a special relationship of trust that is needed to effect change.

Moreover, after-school programs have the untapped potential to be a source of parenting information during middle childhood and early adolescence. Parenting education is more often associated with young children, but the early teen years can be even more challenging.

At The After-School Corporation of New York, parent involvement is crucial to the success of after-school programs. TASC encourages parents to be active in all aspects of the program, from planning to implementation. By the second year of operation, 60 percent of TASC-funded programs employed parents, and more than half had parent volunteers. Many of the programs scheduled regular conferences with parents.[64] A welcoming environment after school often makes the school building more approachable and less intimidating, especially for parents who themselves were not academically successful or who have limited English-language skills.

Heather Weiss and Elena Lopez of the Harvard Family Research Project point to more than thirty years of research that suggests that if you can involve parents in their children's learning, both at home and in school, the children are more likely to succeed at school.[65] Community-based institutions working to involve families can encourage more parents to participate and can help leverage more parent involvement in the education of their children. After-school programs can provide the link between home and school by helping to facilitate communication, sharing information about parenting of older children, and providing support to working families.

Much more attention is needed to understand how best to involve parents of children in after-school and to support their parenting role. While we have new insights into the importance of before- and after-school programs to the parents' ability to work, we still do not have a complete picture of the role that these programs play in the lives of families and in the families' ability to manage their daily lives. We need to continue to reach out to parents, listening to their concerns, training staff in family-centered after-school care, and planning ways to keep parents connected to their children and their schools.

Supporting After-School Staff

We all can remember someone important from our childhood, someone who stood by us, someone who made us feel good about ourselves or taught us something that stayed with us for years. Parents most often fit this description. But like the extended family in days gone by, many other adults also provide role models for children. An after-school program is not just a place to go or a set of fancy equipment: The heart of the program is about someone "being there" for children. All after-school programs should have staff who are specially trained to work with their age groups, and staffing patterns should reflect the range of talents needed to promote a well-rounded education.

As they leave school in the afternoon, children seem to be somewhere on a continuum between "bursting to talk" about their day or "quiet and pensive," not at all ready to share. Naturally, most children have both kinds of days, depending on what is going on in their lives, their personalities, their ages, and their general health. It helps when they enter a space that feels like home and exudes a sense of ease, where the people who greet them really have gotten to know and care about them over a period of time. Those who work with children and their families each day, who mentor and guide, who teach and listen, are the daily heroes in the lives of children.

When an after-school program is effective, its staff works with small groups of children. They know what has been happening in their school, who their friends are, how they like to spend their free time. Moreover, they often know what things are going on at home and how those things may be affecting them. Michelle Seligson and her colleagues believe that the most significant ingredient in a program is the quality of the staff-child relationship. They note that "there is increasing evidence that children's social and emotional needs are as important as their physical needs and that people grow 'in connection' to others." Such relationships with adults can foster social competence, self-esteem, and academic skills.[66]

The National School-Age Care Alliance describes the set of human relationships that are important in a good program. Staff must relate to the children in a positive way, and they must be able to respond to individual needs. This means making children feel welcome and comfortable, accepted, and appreciated. The staff must know the special interests of the children and the range of their abilities and be able to relate to a child's home language and culture. The staff have to encourage children to make choices and to become responsible, and help them learn. They must use positive guidance techniques, which include setting appropriate limits but not using harsh discipline. One eleven-year-old child described a group program this way: "They listen to you, they care what you're saying, they try to understand."[67]

One of the central questions facing after-school programs today is what staffing pattern works best. Although much depends on the setting and type of services that are to be provided, it is clear that new categories of professionals with specialized training are needed to help provide both leadership and direct support to children. Good after-school programs cannot be staffed solely with part-time staff who often cycle in and out of programs. Not only are coordinators or administrators needed to design and implement the overall program, but some number of full-time staff also must work directly with children.

After-school programs often are staffed by a range of adults. Joan Costley, a specialist in professional development, describes three major categories of staff who work in out-of-school programs: the permanent professional, the specialist, and the short-term staff member.[68] The permanent professional usually has made a serious commitment to the field and often takes a leadership role in the after-school program. The specialist comes to the program with expertise in a certain area and usually adds depth to the program. This person may be a coach, an arts teacher, or another adult. Short-term staff often include college students, among others, who may become involved in after-school programs as part of service learning or a short-term job assignment. This list also could include the many mentors who increasingly are working with youth, both in schools and in community-based settings. Such supportive adults often provide important ongoing relationships.

When I was developing small after-school programs in the mid-1970s, we were fortunate enough to be able hire a full-time person in each site. This person held a job that included both working with the children after school and working in the community. Today, such a person would be referred to as having a "blended career."[69] The after-school teacher could work full time and devote the hours when children are in school to liaison work with the school, the community, or families. This "new professional" can play a critical role in education reform: putting people back into the lives of children, bringing the family and the school closer together, and forging linkages between community agencies and the school.

In recent years, statewide professional-preparation initiatives for school-age staff have emerged. For example, the Massachusetts School-Age Coalition, with guidance from the Center for Career Development at Wheelock College, has created a process for developing comprehensive core competencies that reflect the varied perspectives so important in after-school programs. In 2000, the California Commission of Teacher Credentialing established the Child Development Permit with a school-age emphasis. Before this step the permit focused on early-childhood education and did not address the needs of children from age five to fourteen. Other states, such as Florida and New York, also are moving toward credentials that include a school-age focus.[70]

In the upcoming years, the development of a professional-preparation system for after-school staff should emerge from multiple perspectives, including activities focused on traditional youth-serving organizations, traditional school-age child-care professional preparation, and new efforts to prepare teachers and teacher assistants. Since after-school programs themselves are a sort of "blending" of these three approaches, it is just common sense that the new after-school professional would reflect the best of what is known about working with youth, caring for children and families, and education.

When all the expectations for the staff are considered, any program has a tall order to fill. Yet the vast majority of people working in after-school programs are almost invisible to the public. Unlike public-school teachers, the "teachers" who work on "the other side of the day" often go unrecognized. Each September, many articles appear in newspapers about the demand for teachers, yet rarely do they mention those who will need to come to work after school. In his evaluation of the MOST initiative, Robert Halpern found serious concern among program directors who were having difficulty recruiting and retaining good staff.[71] Like preschool teachers, these staff earn low hourly salaries, seldom have benefits, and too often have little training beyond high school. Other studies have found that many after-school teachers have to hold down second jobs just to make ends meet. As discussed in Chapter 6, the time is long overdue for efforts to improve the professional preparation and compensation of after-school staff.

Over the years I have met many after-school providers who tell me that they are not sure how to describe their jobs. When faced with the inevitable question, "What do you do?" they stammer with phrases such as "I work with kids," often reluctant to call themselves teachers. Yet in reality, that is what they are. They may not be standing in front of a chalkboard, eraser in hand, but they are spending important hours with children, guiding them, exposing them to a range of activities, helping them with their schoolwork. Thousands of people will start working in after-school programs this year. Regardless of their titles, it is time they are treated like the important teachers, coaches, and mentors they have become.

Meeting Standards and Achieving Results

Traditionally, accountability in education has been provided by setting standards for both the operation of schools and the content of curriculum. In more recent years, reforms have called for a more outcome-based approach, examining program outcomes as well as outcomes for children. Although the standards-and-outcomes movement has been most clearly focused on the school day, the issue of accountability for these programs is receiving new attention as more and more public dollars are being directed to after-school programs.

Standards for after-school care have come into focus only recently. Historically, state licensing regulations have addressed basic health and safety rather than the range of quality issues. For children in after-school programs, state licensing protections often are as inadequate as they are for younger children. Some states have minimum standards, or few standards appropriate for after-school programs; others have standards focused more on younger children than on older children. Moreover, many programs that are located in schools, or scheduled less regularly, may not even be covered by state licensing.

In the early 1990s, program standards began to emerge. While the National Health and Safety Performance Standards in Child Care included guidance for school-age programs, the school-age community itself also became more active in defining quality. In 1990–91, The National Institute on Out of School Time, or NIOST (then called the School-Age Child Care Project) began developing a self-study guide and observational tool to help programs improve quality ("Assessing School-Age Child Care Quality"). Based on this formative work in developing a self-study process, the National School Age Care Alliance (NSACA), in collaboration with NIOST, began developing a set of standards in 1995. After many focus groups, field testing, and support from the private sector, the air force, and the army, the standards were revised in 1997. In 1998, NSACA launched an accreditation system based on the results of the pilot. These standards provide a framework for program planning at the community level and for public policy at the state and federal levels.[72]

The NSACA standards and its system of accreditation are focused on programs serving children from five- to fourteen years old. The standards are unique in that they reflect both the combination of skills required to do the work well, and the shared nature of many aspects of school-age care, including the sharing of school facilities and staff. The standards cover six key areas: human relationships; indoor environment; outdoor environment; activities; safety, health, and nutrition; and administration. The accreditation process is based on a continuous-improvement model and includes a self-study, the development and implementation of an action plan, a reassessment, and an endorsement by a team of peer reviewers.[73] As was true in early education, accreditation has helped provide a definition of a good program. Although NSACA accreditation is a system less widespread than accreditation for early-childhood programs by the National Association for the Education of Young Children, the fact that there is at last an acceptable set of program standards for school-age services is an important first step. Many states already are beginning to develop public policies that build on the standards. As of the end of 2000, more than a dozen states had recognized NSACA accreditation by offering higher payment rates for accredited programs.[74] By the fall of 2001, more than three hundred programs were accredited by NSACA, and twelve hundred more were engaged in the self-study.[75]

Several challenges are facing accreditation. First, there are not yet enough public or private resources to fully support the infrastructure needed to implement a nationwide accreditation system. While developing core standards is always important for any new field, the actual process of accreditation can be costly and time-consuming. Moreover, after-school accreditation faces special issues because of the difficulty of defining an after-school program. For example, what children do after school, especially when they are older, is often a "virtual" program, consisting of a series of activities, lessons, and a variety of community activities. The real key to quality is not just a set of standards, but the individual requirements and supports provided for the professional development of the staff in the various after-school settings.

While voluntary program standards were emerging, the results-based movement also has caught up with after-school programs. Increasingly, after-school programs are being held accountable for improving educational outcomes, particularly reading and math scores. Much of the new public funding has been premised on achieving exactly these outcomes. Although it is important for there to be continuity and alignment between school and after-school programs, the focus on narrow academic outcomes as the primary goal misses the potential of after-school programs to provide a broader set of competencies. These programs can make important contributions to the overall academic achievement of children, but they must provide a balance of activities and relationships that will complement rather than replicate the school day. The methods and measures used to assess program effectiveness should focus on a broad set of positive youth-development goals, rather than on narrow outcomes. Furthermore, after-school programs should not be held accountable for a poorly functioning school system. Although the time after school is important, it cannot undo or redo what has gone on during the day.

According to a summary by the Afterschool Alliance, many after-school initiatives are showing promising results. For example, higher levels of participation in L.A.'s BEST after-school program led to better school attendance, resulting in higher academic achievement on standardized tests of mathematics, reading, and language arts. Participants in the Boys and Girls Clubs of America's national educational enhancement program, Project Learn, increased their grade averages and showed improved school attendance and study skills. High-school freshman randomly assigned to participate in the Quantum Opportunities after-school and graduation-incentive program were twice as likely to continue their educations beyond high school. Students left out of the program were twice as likely to drop out of school. Every dollar invested in the Quantum Opportunities after-school program produced $3 worth of benefits to youth and the public.[76]

In many programs, children, families, and schools benefit. For example, an independent evaluation supported by The After-School Corporation (TASC) found that students feel that the programs give them a strong sense of belonging and support, that the programs expose them to many new activities, and that they have positive academic benefits. More than half of the parents said they missed less work after their children took part in the program, and that they had more contact with the school as a result of their participation in the program. More than 75 percent of the principals said that the after-school project improved students' attitudes toward the school, their motivation, their attendance, and their overall effectiveness. Moreover, they reported that the programs provided learning opportunities not available during the regular school day.[77]

As more and more evaluations are released, the results must be used to help programs make improvements. The future success of after-school programs will depend not just on the development of standards and outcome measures, but on the use of emerging data and information to help improve the "art and science" of running successful after-school programs that can benefit children, families, schools, and communities.

The New Neighborhood: Still Evolving

As we leave the new neighborhood, the image of what it will become is still evolving. The picture of what the time after school will look like twenty years from now is still being developed. Almost daily, new trends are emerging: State involvement in after-school and youth programs is growing: program models to serve the various developmental levels represented in this age group are emerging; municipal-wide initiatives to assess and plan for out-of-school time are growing. Yet serious challenges remain, particularly the need for increased public support to bring programs to scale, to ensure equity and access to all, and to create a workforce that is specially trained to succeed in these new environments for children.

Finally, an epilogue to any discussion of after-school issues must point out that the ultimate goal should not be just to reform child care so that it is seen as more like education, but rather to help reform the entire education system so that children can indeed attain a well-rounded education. The school day and the after-school program should fit together. Children should be able to take part in a range of activities that contribute to their overall development. Services should be convenient for children and their families. Schools and programs should be connected, not only through co-locations, but through careful planning and communication between the staffs. It is the connections across a child's day that help foster a more holistic approach to their education.

In the decades to come, school and after-school may become integrated into a new kind of day for children, one that is a blend of offerings in the community with more traditional programming in the school. Perhaps if someone reads this years from now, they will wonder what the term "after-school" means, since the entire school day will be changed dramatically. In the meantime, however, the next few years hold much promise for creating new neighborhoods for children that bring together care, education, and youth development while addressing the needs of working families.

5

The Caring Community

Rekindling a Commitment
to Our Children

Just imagine if we all believed in ourselves and worked together—young people, adults, seniors, all cultures, and all religions—all sharing our gifts and talents.... We have everything it takes.

—Craig Kielburger, Founder and Chairman, Kids Can Free the Children

Although my most recent years have been spent working to improve federal and state policy on behalf of early-education and after-school programs, I have always believed that the spirit and strength of this work remains in communities. Child care can provide a reason for caring about other people's children; it can draw people in toward a common purpose. Working to improve care for children has been a struggle, but it is slowly growing into a grassroots movement of people coming together to improve the quality of life for the families in their communities.

Patty Siegel, executive director of the California Child Care Resource and Referral Network, has said, "We need to create a child-care quilt . . . a system that has a deliberate design and is carried out with attention to detail like the quilts we treasure and pass on from generation to generation, warm enough and strong enough and beautiful enough to keep our children safe and healthy."[1]

This chapter is about creating that quilt in three ways: by creating a community-support system for parents and providers; by encouraging citizen participation in the process; and by bringing together the young and the old to create new extended families.

The New Network:
Creating a Community-Support System

Experience with Head Start and the military programs shows that it is not enough to develop a set of programs and allow them to function on their own. There must be a system of support for parents, providers, and the community. This is particularly true in child care, where there are a range of providers, changing parent needs, and a very diversified and decentralized system. Rather than developing a rigid structure to support the child-care system, I suggest a network of extension services, a sort of "virtual agency." I refer to the image of a "network" rather than a single agency, since a number of organizations already may be in place in a community, such as health departments, schools, and other child and family services, that can be coordinated and focused more closely on supporting the community child-care system (see Figure 9).

At the same time, I believe there should be a "door" to child care in every community, a "first stop" for parents, providers, and policy-makers. As I discuss below, this first stop is most often the child-care resource-and-referral agency in a community. Building from this gateway, we can develop "comprehensive child care," linking child care to those critical support services needed by families and providers.

Fragments of a community-support system have been emerging across the country over the past ten years, yet it still is very piecemeal. Since the enactment of the Child Care and Development Block Grant, states and communities have been funding many new initiatives; however, they still are small-scale and fragile. For example, some states have improved consumer education, while others have not; some states have begun to encourage health consultants for child care, yet for others this service is completely unavailable; some states have taken important steps to develop family child-care networks, but such initiatives still are largely beyond the reach of most providers.

By enumerating these functions and documenting some of these initiatives, I hope to begin to form a vision of what is possible and to

> **For Families**
> - Information and referral
> - Family support
> - Outreach to care by family, friends, and neighbors
>
> **For Providers**
> - Health and mental-health outreach
> - Support for children with special needs
> - Training and compensation
> - Family child-care networks
> - Curriculum support and school linkages
>
> **For the Community**
> - Resource development
> - Data collection

FIGURE 9. *Characteristics of a community-support network.*

encourage a more centralized and coordinated approach to the development of this infrastructure. Like the scaffolding of a building under construction, these supports form a platform that hold up child care so it can stand ready to help children and their families.

Parent Services

Child care is not a one-time decision. Rather it is a service that families use over a period of years, changing providers as children grow and schedules change. Families today need advice and support about child care from the time their babies are born through the adolescent years. Once child care has been selected, the process of supporting families has only just begun. Child care can be an important resource to promote positive parenting. Yet, left on their own, few providers have the training or resources to focus on supporting the parent-child relationship or to provide other essential support such as referrals, counseling, or job preparation. Every community should have a system that can help link child-care providers directly to family-support services.

Moreover, similar services are needed for "kith-and-kin" providers. About half of the children in care spend their days or nights with family members, neighbors, or friends. Since these more informal arrangements are used by millions of families, particularly those with very young children, it is important that these caregivers also support healthy child development. I discuss support for kith-and-kin providers as a family service, rather than a provider support, since the role these providers play in the life of a child is more like that of a parent or family member than that of a professional trained to work with a group of children.

Resource and Referral. The first step in supporting families is helping them learn about their options in the community and promoting a better understanding of how to select and monitor the care their children will receive. Every community should have a friendly and inviting place to go to find out about child care. Such a place should be easily accessible in a community, and, like the public library, it should be free and open to all. Although such services still are a long way from being fully funded, the network of child-care resource-and-referral (CCR&R) agencies that has grown up across the country in the last thirty years provides a solid foundation on which to build. Many CCR&Rs grew out of corporate contracts to provide information and referral to the employees of a business; however, over the years, public funds began to support information and referral services. Today, there are more than eight hundred community-based child-care resource-and-referral agencies across the country.

Although many CCR&Rs began as information sources for parents, they have grown to provide several of the functions listed as core elements in any child-care system, including consumer information and support to parents, supply building, data collection, and reporting. Yasmina Vinci, executive director of the National Association of Child Care Resource and Referral Agencies, says, "In the broadest sense, community-based child-care resource and referral defines its mission as doing whatever it takes to make child care work for families and communities."[2]

A nonprofit agency called Bananas, in Alameda County, California, is an example of the important role child-care resource and referral can play in a community. Bananas is a comprehensive family-support and referral agency that serves parents and providers. Founded in 1973 by a small group of mothers with young children, it began as a network of parents interested in cooperative child-care experiences. Today Bananas distributes parenting information, sponsors workshops, provides short-term assistance to families, and has a social worker on staff. Long-term or more intensive service needs are referred to other agencies, and a respite-care program responds to the needs of families in crisis. Along with its family-support activities, Bananas also provides information and technical assistance to child-care providers as well as drop-in workshops in basic baby care for new and expectant parents.[3]

Decades after the first CCR&R was funded, a national initiative was launched to link parents and providers with resource-and-referral agencies across the country. Child Care Aware, administered by the National Association of Child Care Resource and Referral Agencies, is a national initiative to ensure that all parents have access to good information about finding care and resources in their communities. Included is a toll-free hotline funded by the U.S. Department of Health and Human Services that links parents to their local resource-and-referral agency. Local resource and referral agencies have become the heart of a community system of support for child care. It is from this important foundation that other comprehensive services can grow.

Family Support. Beyond basic information and referral, there is a need for additional family-support services linked to child care. Traditionally, child care has not had the staff or training to work effectively with families, nor the resources to provide enhanced family support. Yet such training and support should be available to all child-care programs. This is particularly important as more and more families struggle to balance a range of family issues, from housing needs to health-care coverage and other work support. Their children's child care provides a perfect entry point for the delivery of a range of services.

There are a few glimmers of hope on the horizon. The Parent Services Project (PSP), based in California, is a national nonprofit organization dedicated to integrating family support into early-childhood programs through training, technical assistance, and education. It started as a demonstration project under the creative leadership of Ethel Seiderman in four child-development centers serving low- and moderate-income populations in California's Bay area. By 1999 more than seven hundred organizations nationwide were using PSP principles and techniques. In programs that have embraced PSP's unique approach to strengthening families, parents and staff work side by side to create strong and caring communities where relationships matter and all families are welcomed. PSP offers customized training and technical assistance to child-development centers, child-care resource-and-referral agencies, community schools, family child-care networks, and child-care training centers that work with any child-care program. As they themselves say, PSP "makes places for children, places for families. . . . you can't serve one without the other."[4]

Along with such training, hundreds of CCR&Rs and other agencies are helping to develop systems of care that support the many specialized needs of families, such as care for sick children, backup care during holidays or emergencies, and care for children during nontraditional hours. For example, *Just in Time Care*®, launched in 1995 by the Family and Workplace Connection in Wilmington, Delaware, provides comprehensive emergency backup-care options for families. It links individuals with in-home care, drop-in care at family child-care homes and child-care centers, and work-site programs for snow days, school holidays, and school vacations. Employers subsidize a portion of the cost of the backup care for their employees.[5]

Community-based agencies, or coalitions of businesses or unions, often come together to help develop a special program to recruit providers who can serve families who may work night shifts or weekends. A CCR&R may develop a training program for providers to care for children during natural disasters such as flooding or hurricanes. A hospital or group of community organizations and health providers may develop a system of backup care for children with mild colds or other illnesses that could keep their parents out of work for several days. Without such support, the stress on family members easily can affect their ability to parent young children.

Outreach to Care by Family, Friends, and Neighbors. Since a large segment of the population relies on kith-and-kin care, particularly for very young children, supports for relative caregivers also is needed. Grandparents, aunts, fathers, mothers, or other relatives account for nearly half of child-care arrangements for all children under age five, and for a higher percentage of children in poverty. Since the passage of welfare reform, there has been some evidence that more public funding is going to kith-and-kin providers, particularly because an increasing number of low-income parents work in shifts or during odd hours. Rather than treating relatives and friends like teachers or family child-care providers, we should be taking an approach that better recognizes them as important extended-family members.

While very little research is available on kith-and-kin providers, what is known challenges some common assumptions. For example, there is a misconception that relative caregivers have little interest in improving quality. In fact, surveys conducted across the country have found that many relative providers are very interested in "getting together" and other support that will help them do a better job of caring for children.[6] While regulatory strategies have not traditionally been used with relatives, when public dollars are involved, state and local policy-makers struggle to find the right balance of requirements to ensure safety, supports that encourage better quality, and other policies that allow a wide variety of choices needed by parents.

In 1997, Bank Street College of Education, a longtime leader in early childhood, established the Institute for a Child Care Continuum to conduct research on kith-and-kin child care as well as to provide training and support to organizations that aim to work with them. The Institute identifies and networks programs across the country that are reaching out to support such care. The Institute's work is grounded in the view that child care is a continuum that extends from parents on one end to professional child-care providers on the other, with kith and kin falling between parents and family child care. This view assumes that anyone who provides care to children should have some knowledge of child development and the skills to support healthy child development.[7]

Many community agencies start with focus groups of relative providers as a way of reaching out and learning more about their needs and interests, and then move on to providing various levels of support. In New York, the state contracted with Cornell Cooperative Extension to work with six sites across the state. The Extension helped locate informal providers and conduct focus groups. Based on this information, newsletters were developed to address specific issues of interest to the providers, including health and safety, early literacy, and other topics related to caring for children. A number of similar efforts are underway across the country. For example, in Delaware, Family and Workplace Connection designed a plan to assist caregivers in providing safe and developmentally appropriate environments; relative providers each receive a home health and safety kit and training on a range of issues. In Arizona, the Kith and Kin Project targets friends and family who provide child care, providing training and support and linkages to existing community services. In Pennsylvania, the Relative and Neighbor program recruits and trains neighbors and relative caregivers. Moreover, in addition to the training, every participant is offered three hours of home visits, telephone consultation, or a combination of the two. And in California, the Circles of Caring program is being implemented in some low-income communities to create a multifaceted, community-based support system to stabilize and improve the quality of care, with a special focus on training and support for license-exempt providers.[8]

Provider Services

If a child-care setting is to provide high-quality early-education and after-school services, there must be an infrastructure of support for providers in every community. While some programs are large enough to ensure appropriate curriculum and supervision, health linkages, and other vital supports, many child-care centers and most family day-care providers do not have the resources to provide these essential services. Although there is strength in the fact that the child-care system is very diverse, a missing link in the system has been an organizing mechanism to bring together resources on behalf of child-care providers and to help the providers interact within their communities. Many agencies and organizations will provide a range of services to support child-care providers, but it still is necessary to have a single point of information for the provider community to offer improved training, resources, and support.

Health and Mental-Health Outreach and Support. Child care provides an opportunity to promote better health. An important effort in the movement to link health and child care was kicked off in May 1995 by U.S. Health and Human Services Secretary Donna Shalala. Through a unique partnership between two agencies, the Maternal and Child Health Bureau (MCHB) and the Child Care Bureau, the Healthy Child Care America Campaign was born. The campaign is based on the principle that families, child-care providers, and health-care providers can be partners in promoting the healthy development of young children in child care, with the goal of increasing access to preventive health services and safe environments. In 1996 the American Academy of Pediatrics, with support from HHS, became the coordinator of the campaign. In the same year, health systems development funds from MCHB helped support the campaign through fifty-one projects in the states and territories.[9] Healthy Child Care Campaigns began to grow in almost every state and territory in the country.

At its opening forum in 1995, marking the first official Healthy Child Care event, a ten-step blueprint was developed by a group of health and early-childhood professionals from many organizations and localities across the country. Influenced by the Head Start health-performance standards, this important document frames the agenda for communities interested in promoting health in child care. Its recommendation to use health consultants to help develop and maintain healthy child care is at the heart of all the other steps. Health consultants are health professionals who work in many different ways to improve the health and safety of child care. Angela Crowley, a pediatric nurse-practitioner who has been a pioneer in promoting health consultation in child care, underscored the importance of this approach when she said, "I value my role in clinical settings, but I have very limited time that I can spend with children and families. Child care, on the other hand, affords an extraordinary opportunity to reach children and families. From a health-care perspective, that's been a missed opportunity."[10]

Fortunately, more health professionals are using this opportunity rather than missing it. With funding from the Maternal and Child Health Bureau, a national effort was launched at the University of North Carolina at Chapel Hill to develop and implement a national child-care health-consultant training program. The goal was to train a multidisciplinary team in all the states. Since its inception, the number of child-care health consultants across the country has been growing, and teams from more than three-quarters of the states have participated in the training.

The role of the consultant is to help prevent harm and to promote optimal health in child care. A health consultant may be minimally involved, providing information over the telephone, or more extensively involved by providing advice and educational activities on site. For example, a nurse's on-site consultation may include identification of health and safety risks, comparison of children's records with state immunization requirements, or implementation of infection-control procedures. A one-day on-site assessment might lead to a health-promotion and injury-prevention workshop and a series of telephone consultations.[11] Networks of health consultants have emerged as part of the key infrastructure supporting child care in several states. For example, in Pennsylvania the Early Childhood Education Linkage System of the Pennsylvania chapter of the American Academy of Pediatrics has established a registry that includes more than a thousand health professionals who have volunteered to work with child-care programs on health and safety issues.[12]

Along with general support for health and safety issues, the Healthy Child Care America Campaign and other projects have targeted issues such as immunization, social and emotional health, nutrition in child care, and linkages with children's health insurance. All these efforts demonstrate how child care can serve as a hub of information and support on a range of topics. For example, through its extensive network of health consultants and its work with the state resource-and-referral network, Healthy Child Care Washington was able to ensure outreach, education, and continued training through the distribution of Keep on Track, an immunization-tracking program and resource manual for child-care providers. Several other states have provided information and training through the Back to Sleep Campaign, an effort to ensure that parents and child-care providers put babies to bed on their backs to lower the risk of sudden infant death syndrome. Through partnerships between the USDA's Child and Adult Care Food program and the child-care community, training and support have been provided to improve menu planning and nutrition education for parents and providers. With regard to health coverage for children, the Center on Budget Priorities has coordinated a nationwide effort to link children in child care and other early-childhood programs to the Children's Health Insurance Program in the states.

More recently, new efforts have focused on mental-health issues. A module on mental health has been included in the health consultant training, and specialized mental-health consulting projects and other mental-health initiatives are being implemented in a growing number of communities and states. For example, in 1997, the federal Substance Abuse and Mental Health Services Administration joined with the Casey Family Program to create Starting Early Starting Smart, a public and private initiative aimed at supporting the healthy development of children up to age seven who are affected by alcohol or other substance abuse and serious mental-health issues. Early findings from the demonstration are promising. At the same time, Vermont is developing one of the first statewide early-childhood mental-health initiatives. Already underway in several communities, the Children's Upstream Project has resulted in increased access to mental-health consultants and clinical supervision for child-care providers. Similarly, San Francisco has developed the High Quality Child Care Mental Health Program, which helps provide early-childhood mental-health consultation to local child-care centers and family child-care providers.[13] These and several other communities are using the opportunity provided by child care to bring vital services to children and families.

Supporting the Inclusion of Children with Special Needs. One of the most important goals of the Healthy Child Care America Campaign was to include children with special needs in child care. In 1995, my first year as the director of the Child Care Bureau, wherever I traveled I heard concerns about the care of children with special needs. All families were facing issues accessing good care, but for parents of children with disabilities, finding good child care is particularly challenging. Parents of special-needs children feel overwhelmed, not knowing where to start in their search for child care. Often their search leads to dead ends: few openings, inappropriate placements, programs that do not meet their work schedules, or providers who say they could not handle a particular disability. Feeling rejected and frustrated, many parents are forced to quit work.

Because Head Start has a mandate to include children with special needs, the requirement comes with additional resources and support. However, child-care providers, including those serving very low-income families, often lack the ongoing training and support they need to appropriately address the special needs of young children who are disabled. While states can pay higher rates for special needs child care and can spend their quality funds on supporting inclusive child care, no resources in the Child Care and Development Fund are targeted to support inclusion. Furthermore, up to a few years ago, only limited incentives were available to promote inclusive child care at the federal, state, or local level.

Two federal laws have made a significant difference in the ability of families with children with special needs to obtain services: the Individuals with Disabilities Education Act (IDEA) and Americans with Disabilities Act (ADA). IDEA provides an assurance that all children with disabilities will have access to a free and appropriate public education in the least restrictive environment.[14] The law includes funds for early-intervention services for infants, toddlers, and preschoolers, as well as teacher training and preparation. The ADA is civil-rights legislation designed to protect persons with mental or physical disabilities from discrimination. Title III, which became generally effective in 1992, prohibits discrimination on the basis of disability by public accommodations provided by a variety of businesses and organizations, including child-care centers. Child-care programs must make reasonable modifications in order to accommodate individuals with disabilities, such as revision of policies and procedures, curriculum adaptations, removal of physical barriers, provision of additional staff training, alteration of staffing patterns, and provision of certain adaptive equipment.[15]

While initial early-intervention efforts often focused on inclusion of young children in state-funded pre-kindergarten and Head Start programs, with the establishment of the Child Care Bureau, efforts were stepped up to promote a more targeted focus on inclusion of children in child-care settings—both centers and family child care. Many parents want their children to be in a natural community setting, particularly one that meets their full-day needs, rather than a special program that may meet only a few hours a day. Through IDEA, children with special needs can receive services in child care with funding support from their local public school or education agency. Furthermore, ADA created a new willingness to serve children with special needs. New interest grew in providing a better reimbursement rate through CCDBG for children with special needs.

Although there still is a long way to go in providing the support necessary to adequately address the needs of young children with special needs in child care, over the past few years state and local efforts toward inclusion have multiplied. For example, in 1995 Colorado began a collaborative effort, Colorado Options for Inclusive Child Care, to enhance the quality of services for all children, to increase access to child-care settings by children with special needs, and to provide parents with greater access to a range of child-care settings. Services included linkages with community resources for on-site training and support, problem-solving when care options were limited, tips for parents on interviewing providers, and help in identifying barriers to inclusion.[16] And in Indiana, the Consortium on Professional Development for Educators of Young Children has offered a ladder of training opportunities for all providers and has included special-care workshops as part of its entry-level certificate.[17]

Research shows that developmental gains for children with disabilities may not occur simply by placing them in child care: Success in serving them well depends on continued commitment, planning, and partnerships.[18] The seeds to better child care for children with special needs were planted in the 1990s, but the real challenge still is ahead. Every community should have a focal point to help families find the specialized child care they need, and an ongoing source of support for the providers who care for their children. To provide anything less shortchanges the most vulnerable children and families.

Promoting Training and Compensation Initiatives. Along with linkages to comprehensive services, every community should have a system of ongoing training and support for providers. As recommended in Chapter 6, the higher-education system needs to be redesigned to more adequately address the professional-preparation needs of the child-care community. At the same time, each locality should include a range of training options that can be provided more directly to neighborhood providers. Furthermore, some agency at the state or local level should act as a conduit for scholarships, compensation support, and other benefits (see Chapter 6 for current initiatives and recommendations for professional development).

Networking Family Child Care. One of the key issues facing family child-care providers is a sense of isolation. Working alone in the home with young children is a difficult and demanding job, particularly if you have no backup support or colleagues to share your experiences. Given the number of children being cared for in home-based settings, new strategies are needed to reach out and improve the quality of care given by family child-care providers. However, there are certain challenges to reaching this population. First, it has been estimated that most family child-care homes operate outside any regulatory system,[19] which makes access to such providers more difficult. New strategies are needed to find the places where providers might naturally gather, from the grocery store to the more formal conferences and associations that have emerged over the past decade. Because more and more providers are being paid with public dollars, the state or local agency that manages the funds provides a new point of contact for reaching home-based providers.

Second, new efforts to reach out to home-based providers face the challenge of improving the quality of care in a way that builds upon the strengths of a family setting. The challenge is to ensure that the family child-care provider is using every opportunity available to enrich the experiences of children, just as one would want if the children were home with their own parents. This includes an assurance that children will be safe and healthy, that they will be provided ample opportunities to use language and explore the world around them, and that their parents will be encouraged to stay involved in the things that go on during the time their children are in care.

Finally, home-based settings are not a homogenous group: They include a wide range of providers, from those who see themselves as running a small business in their homes to a friend who may be caring for one or two children. This means that strategies to improve the quality of care must include both career-development training for those who see themselves as part of a profession, and more family-support strategies for those who serve as family members. As has been noted, over the past decade a number of steps have been taken to improve training and accreditation for family child care. In addition, training and support networks are one way of reaching home-based providers.

Family child-care networks should be available in every community. Such networks can emerge from a specific focal point in the community, such as a Head Start program, a school, an employer, a food sponsor, a resource-and-referral agency, or a child-development or family-support program. A network also could be developed through a small provider group that may grow in a neighborhood or through a more formal provider association.

The Child Welfare League of America's standards of excellence for child day-care services define a family child-care system as "a formal network that supports providers by offering training, technical assistance, monitoring, and other support such as equipment-purchasing plans, substitute alternatives for the children when a provider is ill, and access to child-care food programs."[20] A network can provide all or some of these services, depending on available resources. Unfortunately, too many networks are severely underfunded or not funded at all.

Statewide networking efforts have emerged coast to coast. For example, in Georgia, Quality Care for Children has expanded its original Neighborhood Child Care Network to communities across the state. Each network reflects the strengths of its community, includes family child-care specialists who visit the homes, and reaches out to established family child-care providers as well as "exempt" caregivers (relatives, neighbors, and friends).[21] In New York City, Providers United is a network of family child-care providers, working in collaboration with community-based organizations. The network offers workshops and education on child development, training in business development, home visits and technical support, and a resource lending library. It also assists unlicensed providers in the licensing process and connects providers to other resources such as lead-poisoning prevention, voter registration, and Individual Development Accounts.[22]

Many family child-care networks serve to build a communication system across providers. For example, the Oregon Family Child Care Network provides an exchange of information between family child care and other services. The Oregon network began recruiting family child-care providers from across the state in 1994 and then worked with the state university to survey and gather information about the provider community. Since then it has developed a computerized bulletin board, kept providers informed about issues, and represented family child care at statewide meetings.[23]

Supporting Curriculum and School Linkage. Individual child-care programs and providers often work without ongoing program support to help with curriculum or other education issues. In Head Start and the military there is someone on staff, either an education coordinator or a curriculum specialist, to provide this function. Some resource-and-referral agencies and local schools have started to work more directly with the child-care community to provide such program support. Every child-care program should have access to curriculum training and support and linkages to the local school.

Given the number of hours that children are in care, all child-care settings have the potential to promote such key areas as language and math skills among young children. A National Research Council report found that one way to prevent reading difficulties during the preschool years is to ensure that families and group settings for young children offer experiences and support that promote language and literacy.[24] Child-care programs often lack sufficient books and trained staff to adequately address this important issue. Yet there are promising initiatives on the horizon.

The National Head Start Association has launched the Heads-Up Reading program, which uses distance learning to bring training in language and literacy to thousands of Head Start and child-care providers nationwide. Community-based linkages between child care and literacy are now emerging across the country. For example, in Johnson County, Kansas, the public library created the Books to Grow program to reach home providers with books. In Maine, AmeriCorps members are being sent to provide family-literacy training to a number of community agencies, child-care centers, and home providers.[25] Such efforts need to take place in every community.

Along with these initiatives, child-care providers need specialists who can work with them on an ongoing basis. In Kansas, the state child-care agency funded an infant specialist to work in each of the state's sixteen resource-and-referral agencies. The infant specialist provides a minimum of ten hours of training and education specific to infants and toddlers, makes on-site visits and telephone support, works with regulatory agencies, and offers support and training for certification as a child-development associate.[26]

Public schools also can be a key resource in the community for curriculum issues, particularly given the new emphasis on ensuring school readiness and the development of curriculum standards and outcomes. Even when schools do not run preschool programs themselves, they can enhance the school readiness of children by working more directly with child-care providers in the community. This is just beginning to happen across the country. For example, in Maryland, the Model of School Readiness includes eight days of training for public-school prekindergarten and primary-school teachers. The Maryland Committee for Children, in collaboration with the Maryland State Department of Education, the Maryland Department of Human Resources, and several other groups, is sponsoring this training for Head Start and child-care teachers.[27] Similar partnerships with schools are taking place throughout the United States.

Community Services

When new families moves into a neighborhood, they usually can find out what public schools are available, where the libraries are, and a range of other pertinent information on key family services. Every community in the country should have a similar portrait of child care available in its area. Furthermore, at least one agency in each community should have the responsibility to help increase and distribute public and private resources to support parent choices and to help ensure good services. Centralizing these core functions across programs will help bring more cohesiveness to a system that is too often fragmented and uncoordinated.

Resource Development. In recent years, there has been growing recognition of the need for a focal point in the community to help build resources and support for both families and providers. As discussed in Chapter 6, child-care funding comes from a number of sources, both public and private. Increasingly there is a need to better coordinate the existing resources and generate additional funding. Since child care has been funded primarily with federal and state dollars, new efforts are needed to raise local funds and to promote specific projects that will generate additional revenue from the private sector as well. Resource development includes helping to build the supply of care, developing the financing to make renovations or to build facilities, and generating and managing new resources to support parent fees and improve the salaries and benefits of the child-care workforce.

CCR&Rs have been in the vanguard of building community resources. For example, as reported in 1999, the Maryland Committee for Children, which serves as the CCR&R network in Maryland, had assisted thirty-five thousand callers with information on starting and expanding child-care programs, helped create almost three thousand family child-care homes and more than three hundred new or expanded child-care centers, and increased the supply of child care by nearly thirty-two thousand spaces. Thomas Taylor, president of the Maryland State Child Care Association, noted that "this is equal to about $37 million of new business revenue for the state."[28]

Related to resource development, a new concept for child-care financial assistance is emerging. Every community should have an accessible and family-friendly place that provides financial information to parents and describes the range of options available, from tax credits to child-care tuition assistance. Too often the process of applying for child-care assistance includes multiple trips to the welfare office to determine and re-determine eligibility. Moreover, outreach efforts often are limited, and parents rarely find all the information in one place. Putting the management of child-care certificate programs in child-care resource-and-referral agencies and other community agencies is an important first step.

Data Collection and Reporting. Finally, every state and community needs a new system of data collection and reporting for child care. In a nation where instant data has become part of the popular culture, there is a serious information lag in both supply and demand data. Unlike information in other sectors, too often child-care data are fragmented and out of date. No single agency at the community, state, or federal level is responsible for compiling a cohesive picture of child care. Although at least four federal agencies collect data on child care (Commerce, Labor, HHS, and Education), there is no common set of definitions, and little interaction across the data sets. There is no national system for developing data at the community level that would feed into a system of information at the state and then national level.

In recent years, the National Association of Child Care Resource and Referral Agencies has been making significant progress to define common data sets and to develop software that can generate the type of reports and analysis that policy-makers have begun to demand. A growing number of state CCR&R networks, including ones in California, Maryland, and several others, now issue annual reports documenting supply-and-demand data in every county in the state. New mechanisms are needed to combine child-care data with information on the range of preschool, Head Start, and after-school programs.

The New Citizen: Taking Personal Action

The heart of the caring community is found not only in the network of services provided but also in the individual action taken by ordinary citizens. I first realized up close the real power of an individual to effect change when I was working in a Head Start program in Boston in the early 1970s. On a crisp and colorful autumn day, a man named Roland walked into my classroom. He must have been about sixty-five years old. I had heard that a senior volunteer would be joining us two or three days a week, but nothing prepared me for the joy that Roland brought to all of us. When he came into the room, the children would light up, running to greet him, hugs wrapping around his legs. The staff would sigh with relief, knowing that they had those extra hands and eyes that make a room full of children more relaxed. His contribution to the quality of life in our center is a legacy that I hope remains in the memories of the children he cared for. He was the most loyal, consistent, and productive member of our team.

But Roland was only the first. Since that time I have sat and listened to parents, police officers, doctors, and business executives as they worked to improve child care in their communities. There were the parents in California, organizing to have their voices heard at a statewide meeting; the pediatrician in North Carolina who took doctors on rounds to child-care programs; the law-enforcement official who testified with more conviction than any child-development specialist I had ever heard;

and the banker from Colorado who could persuade the most ardent critic about the benefits of investing in quality care.

All of these individuals, and thousands of others, are part of the "caring community." They are the "new citizens" of the twenty-first century. By rekindling a commitment to children, they are addressing the disconnections that most Americans say they experience in our society. The vast majority of Americans agree that connecting with others through volunteer service and other collective actions can bridge the differences that separate people and can help solve community problems. Child care is not just another service in a neighborhood—it can be a community-building institution that helps bring people together. Former Senator Harris Wofford, then CEO of the Corporation for National Service, described the potential of the caring community this way: "We can, in new ways, in a more complicated time, crack the atom of civic power, and take a problem like the crisis of children and youth and ... get things done to solve it."[29]

I can offer only a glimpse into some of the energy being released on behalf of the children and families using child care. These "new citizens" are putting their expertise to work directly through service or by acting as champions of change. Personal involvement with people— whether it is reading to a child or working in a neighborhood to support family child-care providers—brings people together and helps establish community. It is often direct personal action in the lives of those around us that brings about change in others and in ourselves. Yet for some, personal action means advocating for a change by using the power and perspective that comes with their position in the community. Either way, the message is the same: Get connected, make a personal commitment to work on behalf of the children and families, and help build your community.

In Service to the Community

Energy within the caring community is on the rise. According to a study by the League of Women Voters, some 56 percent of Americans describe themselves as involved in community activities and issues, with 15 percent claiming to be very involved. Involvement cuts across racial and ethnic lines.[30] Young Americans often may appear to have given up on the political system, but they are volunteering to work in their communities in record numbers. Service, an American tradition, is having an impact on child care across the country. There are a growing number of examples of adult participation in national-service initiatives related to child care as well as youth participation in service learning that benefits young children.

In 1993 the Corporation for National Service was established to administer AmeriCorps, Learn and Serve, and other national-service initiatives. Shirley Sagawa, an expert on children's policy, became executive vice president of the Corporation for National Service and was determined that AmeriCorps participants would have opportunities to get involved in community efforts to improve conditions for children and expand access to quality child care. One such effort, Action for Children Today (ACT), was launched in 1994.

ACT is an AmeriCorps project run by the National Association of Child Care Resource and Referral Agencies. The program seeks to recruit and train AmeriCorps members to assist local CCR&Rs in expanding the supply and quality of care for children from infancy to school age and to work directly in programs. All ACT members receive initial training on a range of issues related to the delivery of child care. By 2000, AmeriCorps ACT members had provided service to more than twenty-seven thousand children, more than nine thousand families, and more than twelve thousand child-care providers. In 1999–2000, seventy-six ACT members were serving nineteen sites in a dozen states.[31]

ACT members are making a difference for children. In 1999 the Maine Children's Alliance awarded ACT members in that state a Giraffe Award for "sticking their necks out" for kids. In Chapel Hill, North Carolina, ACT members have provided educational-release time for teachers to attend training. Without such support, professional-development opportunities for child-care staff easily can be missed. In Massachusetts, an ACT member developed a homework club at an after-school program for children with learning disabilities and other special needs. Another member developed a multicultural curriculum guide for out-of-school providers. In San Diego, ACT members assisted parents in finding dependable child care by providing information and referral to parents in English and Spanish.[32] The list of successes goes on.

Often a single action by a small group of committed individuals can make all the difference. That is exactly what happened in September 1993, when two college students put their passion to work and ignited a national movement. They believed in a simple idea: that universities and college campuses could provide a natural resource to communities in need of additional support for their young children. Their brainchild,

Jumpstart, began with fifteen Yale students working one-on-one with fifteen struggling preschoolers at the local Head Start Center to teach and reinforce basic academic and social skills. At the end of the year, the teachers reported that all of the Jumpstart children made gains in crucial school readiness areas.[33] By Fall 2000, through Jumpstart, nearly five hundred college students in eight cities nationwide worked with more than fifteen hundred preschool children.[34]

It is not just college students who are getting involved; children from elementary school through high school also are learning through service. As a movement, community-service programs and service learning have become popular with students. The number of high-school students who participate in service-related programs and service learning has increased dramatically.[35]

Community service and service learning are related but not exactly the same. While community service may include one-time activities, service learning usually involves a series of ongoing activities with personal engagement on a regular basis. There is an "intentionality of learning," and some planning and structured reflection to the service activity. Finally, there is a sense of reciprocity between the giver and the receiver, each one learning from association with the other.[36]

Increasingly, service-learning experiences are integrated into the school curriculum or after-school program. Learn and Serve America supports service-learning programs that help students from kindergarten through college meet the needs of their communities, while meeting academic needs and promoting citizenship. Learn and Serve grants are used to create new programs as well as to replicate existing programs and train staff.[37] Planning service-learning projects for the after-school time and integrating the learning that takes place into the school curriculum can help build bridges across the school day and the after-school program.

Hands on Atlanta is an example of community involvement in after-school programs that includes both AmeriCorps volunteers and the promotion of service learning. AmeriCorps members serve in after-school programs in a number of elementary schools, developing and facilitating the activities for the program. AmeriCorps members also are active in after-school service-learning programs in the middle and high schools. The youth serve as "reading coaches" to elementary schools, visit senior homes and child-care centers, work with teachers on school improvement projects, and prepare meals for persons with HIV and AIDS.

These activities are having a real impact on the community and every-one involved. One eighth-grader put it this way: "My attitude towards life, towards people has changed. As I walked into my school Monday morning I felt like a new student. I learned how to work together to get things done. I can do tons of things to improve not only myself, but my community, and anything else that needs improvement."[38]

Champions of Change

Personal service is one way of contributing to the community. But many individuals are helping to improve and expand child care by rais-ing their voices and using the power that comes with their particular roles in the community. Among the new champions for change are parents, business leaders, church officials, doctors and nurses, law-enforcement officials, librarians, media and entertainment personalities, and child-care providers themselves. Each group brings a unique but important perspective to the issue. These multiple perspectives add to the richness and potential of improving early-childhood and after-school services.

Parents have a vested interest in improving services that affect them on a daily basis. Parents' involvement in their children's program often can lead to more active involvement in the community. A Head Start par-ent from Pennsylvania told me that she could hardly raise her eyes up from the floor at her first parent meeting. Slowly she became involved in the center and then in her local and state group. Along the way she gained confidence and a sense of her own abilities to make change.

There is an increasing interest in mobilizing parents to help improve children's services. The Parent Leadership Training Institute (PLTI), which originated in Connecticut almost a decade ago, is helping to turn up the volume and increase the effectiveness of parent voices. PLTI seeks to enable parents to become leading advocates for children. The basic philosophy of the initiative reflects the strong belief that when the tools of democracy are understood and parents are respected, they will actively engage in civic life. Through the Institute, parents are offered leader-ship training that includes a retreat to develop group cohesion, ten weeks of classes on self-concept and perception of leadership, and ten weeks on democracy skill-building with practice of civic skills. Graduation cer-emonies have been held in state capitals. A broad-based community design team implements the PLTI initiative locally, modeling diversity and a commitment to the practice of civil engagement for families.[39]

Now spreading to other states, PLTI has the potential to light a fire of civic action within parents. Elaine Zimmerman, executive director of the Connecticut Commission on Children, believes that parents hold the power to make change both for their own children and for others in the community.[40] After successfully completing the training, one parent from Hartford put it this way:

> I learned to look into my own inner talents and how to use them to my benefit and to my community's also. If it was not for PLTI I would not have discovered these talents—they really pulled it out of us and helped us to recognize them and put them into action. This is the one thing that really changed my life—to discover and put into practice the power within. There are a lot of things we parents can do; we just need a helping hand.[41]

Similarly, in North Carolina, the Parent Leadership Development Project is a model program working to increase family involvement and empowerment in early childhood. The project offers training and support to parents who want to develop their leadership skills. The project has recruited parents and other family members of children with disabilities who are interested in working with professionals to improve services for children and families. The parents, representing a diversity of cultures, language, family constellations, and socioeconomic backgrounds, receive intensive training, including follow-up activities to improve communication, collaboration, and presentation skills, while they learn about the early-intervention system.[42]

Many programs go beyond traditional parent-education messages as they work to empower parents to take charge of their own lives and the lives of their children. The Spirit of Excellence Parent Empowerment Project, developed by the National Black Child Development Institute in 1992, is an example of such an innovation in the field of family support. Started as a demonstration effort in collaboration with African-American parents in Washington, D.C., the project has developed into a complete training curriculum used in several sites across the country. The program focuses on parenting, culture, and life and career planning for parents. Evelyn Moore, president of NBCDI, believes that "when parents are informed and have the skills to be effective, their children will grow and thrive."[43]

When parents gain confidence and begin to organize, they can make important changes in policies related to early-education and after-school services. This has proven to be true for the parents active in Parents

United for Child Care, a parent advocacy group established in Boston more than a decade ago. Elaine Fersh, the founder of Parents United, hoped that the child-care worries of individual parents would become the collective worries of many in the community. Parents United elected its first board of directors in 1988 and launched the Boston School-Age Child Care Campaign with a citywide hearing attended by more than one hundred parents. That same year members of Parents United conducted a petition drive for more extended kindergarten classes in Boston's public schools, and the following year they developed the first directory of after-school programs in Boston to assist parents in finding access to care and transportation.[44] Parents United, along with other advocates in Massachusetts, have been successful in securing more than $100 million in new child-care funding for working families and training parents to work with schools to establish after-school programs that meet their needs.

In the spring of 2000, Parents United released a report produced in conjunction with the Center for Survey Research at the University of Massachusetts. This was the first effort to document the child-care experiences of a sample of families in the state. The survey findings provided a "striking portrait" of the child-care issues faced by parents of all economic backgrounds as they try to juggle work and family. The survey helped policy-makers see the realities of child care through the eyes of parents. One parent said, "I would just like it to be easier for me to afford child care. . . . Sometimes I have to leave them by themselves and I would rather not do it." Another parent summed up the situation this way: "I don't think anyone is helping the average two-parent home with child care. It is almost impossible for families who work: Child care is the biggest obstacle."[45]

Business and Labor. Although parents are central to the effort to move forward the early-childhood and after-school agenda in a community, so are the businesses that employ them and the unions that may represent them. In a survey of more than eleven hundred companies conducted by the Families and Work Institute, two-thirds of the respondents reported that the benefits from child-care programs were greater than the costs or that the programs were cost-neutral.[46] Studies have consistently found that family-friendly policies help reduce absenteeism and staff turnover. Ted Childs, Vice President of Global Workforce Diversity at IBM and a long-standing corporate champion for child care described the importance of business involvement this way: "If you have a workplace that is still reflective of what it looked like in the fifties and sixties, with the same kinds of rules in place, you're not going to be very appealing a place for women to come to work."[47]

More than a decade ago, a senior vice president of GE, and a member of the board of trustees of the Committee for Economic Development, was asked to testify on early education before the Subcommittee on Education and Health of the Joint Economic Committee of Congress. At that time the business community was just beginning to become more interested in issues related to young children. He told the subcommittee that the "quality of childhood education in America is more than an issue of philanthropy and corporate responsibility for us, although it certainly is that: It also is an issue of productivity and profitability in a rapidly changing competitive world." Acknowledging predictions of future labor shortages, he went on to say, "That means that a competitive America—let alone a compassionate America—will need every trained mind and every pair of skilled hands."[48]

Although the private sector still picks up only about 1 percent of the costs of child care, since the early activities of the Committee for Economic Development and other business and labor groups, there have been numerous examples of private-sector involvement in local communities. While pioneering examples tended to be investments in child care by corporations for their own employees, many businesses have since realized that to make a real difference for their employees and others they have to invest in improving and expanding services for the entire community. Perhaps no example stands out more than the group of companies that came together to champion change in the early 1990s, the American Business Collaborative for Quality Dependent Care (ABC).

ABC has been on the forefront of the revolution in family-friendly business practice. This unprecedented collaboration of U.S. companies has worked to increase the supply and enhance the quality of child-care services in communities across the country. Since 1992 ABC has provided more than $100 million to fund child-care, school-age, and elder-care programs. Businesses like those involved in this important coalition now understand that in a tight labor market, becoming part of the "caring community" helps the bottom line. As the title of one report on the ABC coalition put it, "Working together [we can] accomplish what none of us can afford to do alone."[49]

Businesses can be influential change agents not just by dipping into their pockets, but also by wielding their power in the community.

Richard Stolley of Time Inc., former chairman of the Child Care Action Campaign and a tireless advocate of child care, hopes that all business-school students will be taught the benefits, both ethical and financial, of family-friendly policies. Recognizing that businesses have long been interested in public-school reform, he recommends that corporate America include early education in any reform proposals it advocates. In 2000 he wrote:

> As the single most powerful private institution in America, business does not hesitate to use that power to advance its interests within government and society. We want to persuade corporate America that the cause of children is one of its vital interests and to direct its great skills and resources in lobbying, public relations and philanthropy toward that cause.[50]

Toward that end, over the past few years a growing number of business leaders have spoken out for additional public investments in early-childhood and after-school care. Several private-sector advisory groups, established by governors and mayors, have been able to shine the spotlight on issues that had gone unnoticed for years. For example, a group of major American businesses recently have come together to establish "Corporate Voices for Working Families," hoping to bring new attention and increased public investment to early-education, after-school, and other work-family issues. Similarly, business, entertainment, and private philanthropy helped establish the Afterschool Alliance, working to ensure that quality after school programs are available to all children and youth throughout the country.

As Margaret Blood points out, business leaders have a unique ability to get the attention of legislators and the press. When business leaders talk to policymakers about child care and other children's issues, they can serve as "unlikely messengers," lending visibility and important support to these initiatives. Since members of the business community may be seen as fiscally responsible, the messages they carry often get more attention.[51]

Similarly, labor unions can play an influential role in child care, both in contract negotiations and as champions for change in the larger community. Lea Grundy, Lissa Bell, and Netsy Firestein, in a report of the Labor Project for Working Families, point out examples where the championing of an issue by a union made a difference, particularly through a collective bargaining effort or as a lever for organizing. With more than thirteen million members in 1999, unions represented more working families than any other organization in the United States.[52]

Like business leaders, labor leaders can exert real power not only in making change for the members of their own organizations, but also on behalf of the entire community. Labor officials often can use their contacts to gain greater public awareness and increased public investments in child care for all working families.

Health Professionals. But parents, businesses, and employee organizations are not the only champions for change. A growing number of health professionals, law-enforcement officials, and religious leaders are becoming part of the movement to improve and expand services. As shown in Chapter 3, many nurses and other public-health officials are serving as health consultants to child-care programs. The 1999 American Academy of Pediatrics (AAP) survey indicates that 72 percent of pediatricians believe it is their responsibility to be involved in promoting quality child care in their practice communities.

The AAP, which provides technical assistance to Healthy Child Care America, issued a policy statement on the pediatrician's role in promoting the health of patients in early-childhood education and child-care programs: "In order to promote optimal development, pediatricians should work not only with parents, but also with caregivers and representatives from agencies and organizations that are part of the child's and family's support system."[53] Although most child-care programs still do not have access to a regular source of support, some pediatricians are stepping up to the plate and getting involved.

Judy Romano, a pediatric practitioner in West Virginia, realized that many of the children she wanted to reach were in some type of child-care program. She was surprised to find that pediatricians did not take part in many of the activities that were working to improve the health of children. To increase their involvement, she built strong partnerships between the West Virginia chapter of the American Academy of Pediatrics and several children's agencies in the state. She began to develop a network of health professionals in her state who believed, as she does, that "in order to make a difference they needed to step out of their offices and reach out to children in their natural environments."[54]

Law Enforcement. One of the most effective new voices on children's issues is Fight Crime, Invest In Kids, an organization based in Washington, D.C., and started by Sanford Newman, a lawyer and crime victim who became convinced a few years ago that getting children off to a good start was the best way to prevent crime. Since that time, his organization, and the more than fifteen hundred police chiefs, sheriffs, prosecutors, crime victims, and other law-enforcement officials who have joined with him from across the country, have helped build public awareness of the need for early-education and after-school programs.

After culling through the evidence on the benefits of early and sustained investments in children, Fight Crime has released a number of high-profile reports that have helped to spread the word about what it calls "the crime prevention deficit"—the enormous gap between current spending and the public investment it would take to make proven services available.[55] The law-enforcement community makes a strong case for after-school programs by citing FBI data from 1997 showing that the juvenile crime rate increases each day after the school bell rings. In a Northeastern University poll, 92 percent of police chiefs nationwide agreed that America could sharply reduce crime if government invested more in programs to help children and youth get a good start.[56]

Ed Flynn, police chief for Arlington County, Virginia, represents this new voice speaking out on behalf of children and youth. Flynn sums up the growing interest of the law-enforcement community when he says that "the nation's police administrators no longer view their job as just responding to crime, but also as advocating programs to prevent crime."[57]

Faith Communities. Members of many religious denominations have been proactive in helping to expand and improve child-care services. For example, over the past thirty years, the National Council of Jewish Women has helped shine a spotlight on the growing crisis in child care in the United States. Their report, *Windows on Day Care,* appearing in the early 1970s, was one of the first comprehensive pictures of quality and affordability issues faced by working families. Many other faith-based groups, including the National Council of Churches, have played a key role in advocating improved and expanded child care. In addition, for more than a decade the Children's Defense Fund has organized a National Observance of Children's Sabbaths, sponsored by more than two hundred denominations and religious organizations, which unites tens of thousands of religious congregations of many faiths in speaking out for justice for children and families.[58]

A report by the National Council of Churches, *When Churches Mind the Children,* which was released in the early 1980s, documented the significant role that various congregations play in the delivery of child care.[59] In the 1980s, nearly 1.5 million children attended weekday early-childhood programs in religious facilities, and nearly one out of every six child-care centers in the United States was housed in a religious facility.[60] In the mid-1980s, the Ecumenical Child Care Network was established by the National Council of Churches to expand participation of churches in child care, to relieve the isolation felt by many providers working in religious settings, and to stimulate an exchange of ideas and inform child advocates and policy-makers about the needs and contributions of church-based programs. Today, the Ecumenical Child Care Network is an independent organization, sponsoring national and regional conferences and training events, and providing recognition for quality programming.[61]

One of the best examples of faith in action on child care is the North Carolina Rural Economic Development Center's Church Child Care Initiative. Using "church" as a term to refer to all assemblies of faith, the goal of the initiative is to increase the number of church-based child-care centers available to rural children, with a special emphasis on helping children from poor families. In addition to producing a guidebook for congregations on how to begin a child-care program, the initiative's work has included annual forums for the religious community on the needs of children and families, help in determining community needs and program readiness, and workshops for religious leaders in rural areas on regulations and other aspects of planning and administering a faith-based child-care program.[62]

Child-care Providers. Together all of these champions are making a difference for children in child care. But I could not leave the topic of personal action without talking about the quiet heroes who have been working for decades to make child care work for children: the child-care providers themselves. Their own voices for better child care, including better working conditions, also are making a difference in communities across the country. In 1979, the first exposé of the plight of the child-care workforce, "Who's Minding the Child Care Workers?", was written by the founder of what was to become the Center for the Child Care Workforce, Marcy Whitebook, and her colleagues.

Since that time, child-care providers have been struggling to make their voices heard and to gain more recognition for the importance of their work and the need to improve their compensation. Over the past few years, providers have stepped up efforts to build public awareness of these issues. Each year, "Worthy Wage Day" events are held across the country. For example, on May 1, 2000, Worthy Wage Day in Washington, D.C., began with visits to legislators from Maryland, the District of Columbia, and Virginia. In the San Francisco Bay area, a press conference was held in Alameda County to launch a Child Development Corps, and in Madison, Wisconsin, providers attended an all-day in-service training session that included visits to state legislators.[63] But the action for improvements in child care go well beyond a single day. The real struggle occurs day in and day out as child-care providers work on behalf of children and families in a job that remains in the shadows of the economy.

Taken together, through all of these individual and collective actions, we are creating webs of support, civic safety nets for working families. Yet the same families facing child-care issues often are caring for aging parents at the same time. Communities that care in the twenty-first century will have to respond to issues across the generations.

Bringing Together the Generations

The demographics of the population are changing dramatically. The aging of the "baby boomers," born between 1946 and 1964, will accelerate this growth. In 2000, there were an estimated thirty-five million persons age sixty-five or older in the United States, nearly 13 percent of the population. The older population is expected to double to seventy million by 2030. The population age eighty-five and older is expected to grow faster than any other age group. Furthermore, the current generation of older Americans is more highly educated than previous generations, and this trend is expected to continue, while the aging population also becomes more ethnically diverse.[64]

Marc Freedman, author of *Prime Time: How Baby Boomers Will Revolutionize Retirement and Transform America*, believes that the aging population represents one of the country's most valuable natural resources. Rather than seeing these citizens as a drain on the economy, as many social critics have suggested, Freedman argues that such hand-wringing is "blinding us to the benefits of an aging society." He notes that America now posses the "healthiest, most vigorous and best educated" aging population, and, perhaps most important, these older Americans have what everybody else seems to lack—time—particularly "time to care."[65]

This growing resource, coupled with the needs of children today, is giving rise to a renewed interest in the concept of an intergenerational strategy. This strategy—to bring old and young together—grows out of the long-recognized social compact between generations in which there is a reciprocity of need, an interdependence of the generations. A report from a conference on strengthening this social compact put it this way: "Each generation has the responsibility to understand and build on its society's past and to work for a future beyond its lifetime."[66]

Children in child care stand to benefit from this growing movement. In 1998 the Child Care Bureau of the Department of Health and Human Services held a special forum to explore the emerging number of programs focused on bringing together the generations. At that forum, then associate commissioner Carmen Nazario referred to inter-generational child care as "a wonderful blend—the richness of the past and the promise of the future." Many participants in the forum discussed the mutual benefits that occur when young and old come together: Not only does the presence of older people in children's settings teach children about aging and enrich their lives, but active involvement with children also can help sustain older people's physical, mental, and emotional well-being and promote life satisfaction and improved self-esteem.[67]

At least three types of intergenerational activities related to child care are emerging across the country. First, many members of the growing elderly population are serving as caregivers to children, either as caregivers for their own grandchildren or as staff members or volunteers who care for the children of other families. Second, an increasing number of communities are promoting intergenerational connections by co-locating services or sharing sites for children and families with services for the elderly. Moving away from the concept of a gated community where the elderly are clustered together, often isolated from a community, these innovative efforts are beginning to gain public recognition and support. Finally, uniting the generations are the newer efforts to advocate improved services for the elderly and children together, rather than forcing the generations to compete with one another for resources.

Older Adults as Caregivers

Older adults can be caregivers in a wide variety of situations. At the beginning of the twenty-first century, 5.4 million children were living with grandparents or other relatives, 2.1 million of whom were being raised solely by their grandparents or other relatives, with no parent present. Many older individuals today are faced with raising a second family without any extended family or community support.[68] Other grandparents are caring for their grandchildren during the day or at night while the parents of the children work. For example, 30 percent of children under age five are cared for by their grandparents while their parents are at work, in school, or at other times.[69]

In recent years, new efforts also have sprung up to support grandparents who are raising their grandchildren. In Boston, the "Grand-Families House" has been developed, the first effort in the nation to provide apartments that house grandparents raising their grandchildren.[70] And in Chicago, where more than one hundred thousand children are being cared for by their grandparents, the mayor announced that these families will receive priority for city-sponsored child care, providing the children with high-quality programs while giving their elderly caregivers a break from their child-care responsibilities.[71]

Naturally, grandparents have been caring for grandchildren throughout history. On the other hand, over the past thirty years, an increasing number of grandparents have moved to communities that are some distance from their grandchildren, and more children are in formal child-care programs. These two trends call for special efforts to bring the generations back together. At best, child care should be an intimate experience, one that is built on strong relationships. For very young children, it is like an extended family, particularly in modern-day America where families often are geographically separated. Bringing seniors into the child-care setting can help re-create a sense of family. Furthermore, if we value generational diversity and the wisdom that older adults can bring to all of us, we must recognize the value of including older adults in the child-care environment.

In 1963, one of the first reported intergenerational programs was established, the "Adopt a Grandparent" program in Florida. This program involved weekly visits between preschool children from a lab school at the University of Florida and residents of a neighboring convalescence home.[72] A few years later, the Foster Grandparent program emerged as part of the Economic Opportunity Act. The program was designed to provide volunteer opportunities for income-eligible seniors sixty and older to provide services to at-risk children with special needs. Each foster grandparent volunteers twenty hours a week with no more than four children, teaching them how to read, providing support, and functioning as a role model to children who otherwise may not have enough one-on-one adult attention.[73] Foster grandparents, along with other services such as the Retired Senior Volunteer Program, are providing invaluable services to child-care and other community agencies.

Over the years, Sally Newman, founder and executive director of Generations Together, an intergenerational-studies program at the University of Pittsburgh, has been a pioneer in efforts to promote and value the work of older adults in child care. She has initiated intergenerational programs that involve more than one thousand older adults in Allegheny County and have been replicated in communities across the United States.[74]

Newman and her colleagues also initiated the first formal study to examine what can happen when older adults are part of the teaching environment. The older adult participants included in the research worked as volunteers or as classroom aides who were paid a small stipend. The younger adults, including both lead teachers and assistants, were trained in early-childhood practices, educational philosophy, and curriculum. The older adults were not expected to assume professional responsibilities, but were seen as additional support to assist regular staff in the creation of rich and nurturing environments.

The study found that the contributions of older adults were significant, as they appeared to bring a familial dimension to the child-care setting that often complemented the work of the younger adults. Older adults who entered the classrooms without professional training in child development relied on personal experiences with their own families to support children's growth. The older adults did not substitute for the younger adults, but rather brought an added dimension, enriching the child-care setting. Their familial skills included hugging and other kinds of physical affection, teaching skills by modeling, encouraging language development, helping children with personal hygiene and manners, and bonding with individual children.[75]

Although the study included volunteers and foster grandparents, there are seniors who are interested in paid positions with child care. Many seniors, especially women, do not have retirement benefits and live on very modest incomes. Like all child-care workers, these older adults need and deserve to be paid a living wage to support themselves and their families. In addition, as with all caregivers, older adults who assume regular staff positions will need adequate preparation to work with children. With appropriate job selection, job training, and decent compensation, child care can become a productive second career for some seniors from diverse socioeconomic backgrounds.

There is a growing interest in training that is tailored to meet the needs of older adults. For example, as early as 1992, Generations Together gathered a group of experts in child care, child and adult development, gerontology, training, and employment policy to develop guidelines for the productive employment of older adults in child care. The guidelines, which were endorsed by the National Association for the Education of Young Children (NAEYC), outline active recruitment strategies to attract older adults, recommendations for preparing existing staff, procedures for screening, hiring, and placing older adults, and recommendations for the training, education, and appropriate working conditions of older workers.[76]

The voices of those who participate in such programs illustrate the real benefits of intergenerational programs. In describing her experiences in one program, a senior said, "By helping them and playing with them and doing little things with them, [you help them] get used to the idea of the older person." Another said, "I can look out my big windows, and there's a playground for all the children there . . . they have all kinds of toys . . . they sure enjoy using them . . . and I sure enjoy watching them." A young mother put it this way: "My children don't have grandparents close. They have one set in California that they don't have a close relationship with, so this is the only grandparents that they have contact with, and they really think all of [the seniors] are basically grandmas and grandpas. The contact they get is really special."[77]

This growing interest in intergenerational programming in early childhood has only just begun. In recent years, an Intergenerational Caucus of Early Childhood Professionals has been established in cooperation with NAEYC and other professional networks to promote high-quality relationships between young children and older adults. Among its goals, the caucus aims to encourage ongoing professional education, and recognize individuals and institutions that make outstanding contributions to the field of intergenerational programs.[78]

Intergenerational programs are growing, not only between young children and seniors, but also between seniors and youth. For example, the "Grandma Please" program at Hull House in Chicago matches seniors by telephone with children who need after-school assurances and contacts. Unless an emergency occurs, both parties are anonymous to each other. In Washington, D.C., seniors provide tutoring and other support after school to abused and neglected teenagers. In Baltimore, foster grandparents provide a variety of before- and after-school services to nine- to twelve-year-old children of mothers in treatment for substance abuse. And in Lawrence, Massachusetts, Retired Senior Volunteer members are participating in after-school programs, providing one-on-one tutoring.[79]

Shared Sites for Child and Senior Care

Baby boomers have been referred to as the "sandwich generation," caring for their children while also assuming responsibility for their aging parents. Stories about the difficult search for child care have given way to similar difficulties finding suitable elder-care services. Once found, the concern, as in child care, becomes how to ensure programs that promote the continued development and learning of the participants. Age segregation is not a natural state in most cultures. While many seniors are able to become actively engaged in volunteer activities, those confined to nursing homes too often are not able to reach out or actively engage in community activities. Yet this may be exactly what they need and want.

In 2000, about seventeen thousand nursing homes in the United States were caring for 1.5 million elders.[80] These older adults do not want to be isolated and alone; they need avenues to stay productive and connected. Co-locating services for children with seniors is one way to make this happen.

In 1995 the American Association of Retired Persons formed an advisory committee to study what they referred to as Intergenerational Shared Site Programs. They found approximately 280 such programs across the country and more than one hundred organizations planning to open similar programs. The study also found that the most common programs are nursing homes co-located with child-care centers and adult day services co-located with child-care centers. It also found that one of the most beneficial aspects of the programs was the frequency of positive, informal intergenerational interactions at the sites. The challenges to these programs include funding and a high need for opportunities to network and share information, ideas, and strategies for success.[81]

Seeing and hearing about co-located services can reinforce belief in the possible. An article on such programs in the *Chicago Tribune* highlighted "a growing care trend to forge bonds across the generations." One such program, situated in a five-story, turn-of-the-century building in Seattle, teams a nursing home, an assisted-living facility, and adult day care with a day-care center for seventy-five children. One mother with a five-year-old and an eight-year-old in the program remarked that her children grew up "without fear of wheelchairs, walkers, or frail seniors," and each child established a friendship with an older resident. Many of these programs bring children and elder residents together at specified times, while others may use a more spontaneous approach. Either way, the programs require planning and attention but can reap benefits for all. The director of the Seattle center remarked that she sees bonds form as babies are placed in the arms of seniors; she noted, "You get a lot of laughter—some of the residents get tears in their eyes as they remember their own children or think of grandchildren who may live far away."[82]

Similar efforts continue to spring up. In Norwalk, Connecticut, the Marvin Center Children's Center is managed by Bright Horizons Family Solutions, a top provider of employer-sponsored child care. Supported by state school-readiness funds, the program draws children from a diverse group of families. Operating from seven-thirty.A.M. to six P.M., the center shares a building with "the Marvin," which includes forty-nine apartments for senior citizens. The children and the seniors interact both formally and informally. Although the seniors are free to visit the center to watch, read, or talk to the children, once a week the center holds a special activity with the seniors.[83] Putting the wisdom of age together with the spirit and energy of the computer generation can lead to wonderful and productive experiences for all.

Working Together for Change

The presidential campaign of 2000 reverberated with concerns about senior issues, from Social Security to prescription drugs. Lost in the din of debates was the hope of uniting the generations to work together to improve services for children and seniors. In 1986, the American Association of Retired Persons, the National Council of the Aging, the Child Welfare League of America, and the Children's Defense Fund came together to launch Generations United, a national organization advancing ideas of generational interdependence. Today, Generations United includes about one hundred national, state, and local organizations representing more than seventy million Americans, and is the only national organization advocating for the mutual well-being of children, youth, and older adults.

Donna Butts, executive director of Generations United, puts it this way: "Our philosophy is quite simple; we believe in intergenerational approaches that use the strength of one generation to meet the needs of the another. At Generations United, we focus on the bookend generations—our children, youth, and elderly. We believe that through this effort we support the middle generations."[84]

Today, a growing number of state and local intergenerational coalitions and networks are working to provide coordinated programs, training, and networking opportunities. From coast to coast, these groups are promoting the spirit and renewal that comes with bringing together the generations. In partnership with Generations United, many of these organizations are focusing on public-policy issues and legislation that may affect children and the elderly.[85]

Perhaps the real hope of changing public opinion about the need to improve child care and other services may in the end lie with what some have referred to as the "longevity revolution," the voices of those who have lived the longest but who are the most concerned about the future. In the winter of 2000, Marc Freedman wrote: "Transforming the aging of America will require new ideas and new policies—and new constituency for change—but it will especially require new institutions. If we can devise creative new roles and opportunities at the community level, there is much reason to believe that people will respond."[86]

The Caring Community: Still Converging

After discovering hundreds of examples of community initiatives, citizen action, and intergenerational programs, I remain convinced that "community" is not just a geographic location: It is a spirit, an attitude of caring. It is something that happens when you take a step forward on behalf of others, when you make even the smallest attempt to care. Yet when it comes to child care, many communities are just getting started.

The United States needs to "wire" its child-care system and create the connections that will make it work for families, providers, and the community. Every community should have a well-developed set of resources to help families to make better choices, whether parents are young and just starting out or whether they have teenagers and continue to need support. The health department and the mental-health community should see child care as their portal to reaching children and families. The schools should reach out and help child-care providers promote the skills children will need to be ready to enter school. Special attention should be paid to building resources and information systems. We should expect nothing less.

Furthermore, every community should provide many opportunities for everyone to become involved, to share their expertise, to work on behalf of children. It is through these civic investments, both individual and collective, that the caring community emerges. The need for child care provides an important opportunity for building this new sense of community, particularly across the generations. Child care provides an enormous opportunity for positive change. We should not let it slip away.

6

Toward Redesigned Child Care
A Call for Investment and Reform

Child-care policies in the United States are long overdue for reform. We live in a world where most developed nations recognize that parents need time and support to care for their newborn infants, as well as better options when they return to work, and where preschool is recognized as a fundamental part of education. Yet the United States ranks among industrialized countries that spend the fewest public dollars per child on early education.[1] In order to continue building a strong and competitive nation, we simply must catch up and begin to make the type of investments that recognizes new realities.

Over the course of the twentieth century, the economics of child care in the United States have changed dramatically. What began mostly as an uncompensated support, provided by relatives and close friends or through charitable institutions, increasingly has evolved into a paid service purchased in the marketplace. In 1997 the Council of Economic Advisers called child care a rapidly growing industry that involves substantial costs to large numbers of parents.[2] In the twenty-first century, we need to usher in a third phase, one that recognizes that child care is a public good with long-term implications for children. Our current system of financing is outdated and underfunded, shortchanging both children and families. Any serious education debate, or concern with the stability and well-being of families, has to squarely face and embrace this issue.

The call for child-care reform is growing. Two recent publications, *The Child Care Problem: An Economic Analysis* by David Blau, and *America's Child Care Problem: The Way Out* by Suzanne W. Helburn and Barbara R. Bergmann, provide exhaustive reviews of the economics of child care.[3] While the policy recommendations offered by these two perspectives may differ, what is significant about these two books, appearing within months of each other, is that both are written by economists, both outline the inadequacy of current child-care policies, both recognize that child-care policy must address the quality of care and the well-being of children, and both call for significant new investments. While offering different financing strategies, my own book joins this chorus in an appeal to the nation to modernize our child-care policies.

Based on my experience administering federal child-care assistance, and working in the child-care field for more than three decades, I believe there are three goals that should guide new child-care policy in the United States:

Care and Education Should Be Integrated

The fact that child care has twin goals—to serve as a work support for families and to promote the education of children—contributes to the challenge of creating a new financing strategy. The schedules of working families come in all shapes and sizes. Children and their child-care needs come in all ages and stages. Working families need extended and flexible hours. Parents must have choices that fit these realities, but they should be good choices, not just the "default mode" that too many parents now face.

Currently, most support for child care responds to the work goal, providing portable assistance to families so they can purchase the type of care that best meets their needs. However, funds are so limited, and policies so out of touch with the actual costs of care, that most eligible families do not benefit in any substantial way relative to their need. Moreover, since child-care funding builds largely on a free-market approach, very little attention is being given to building the supply or safeguarding quality to ensure good education or family-support services.

On the other hand, traditional preschool funding and some of the new after-school programs do address the education goal. However, too often they do not meet the needs of working families. Child care should not be designed to fit a banker's schedule or an outdated nine-month calendar year. Half-day programs do not satisfy the needs of a full-day world. Despite increased interest in preschool, often it does not cover the hours needed by working families. Similarly, there is a growing interest in developing tutoring and mentoring programs after school to improve academic achievement. These services may be designed (and funded) to meet twice or three times a week for an hour or two after school. However, for working parents such activities must be integrated into a program that also meets the needs of their children for adult supervision every afternoon.

Parents Should Have Access to Quality Options

The integration of care and education has been the hallmark of child-care policy in many other countries. As noted in Chapter 3, while some countries have developed high-quality, full-day child-care programs for children from birth to six, others provide free universal preschool on a school-day schedule, with wraparound after-school services on a fee basis. Although we can learn much from other countries, our system will reflect our own values and history. This means that the American child-care system will have to build the quality of services into its current diverse delivery system.

I propose a mixed approach to financing that includes supply-side and demand-side strategies. This proposal draws upon innovations taking place across the country and recent thinking in child-care financing that has emerged over the past few years.[4] First, we should build quality (education, health, and family support) into the supply of care through direct investments in programs and the development of an infrastructure of supports. This approach is less like the financing strategies historically used in the public education system, with a single delivery system, and more akin to publicly supported higher-education institutions or publicly supported "charter schools." In both cases public funds are provided directly to a range of providers, with built-in quality protections. This should allow families more access to a range of quality options. At the same time, we need to expand and reform the current system of child-care assistance and tax policies.

I argue for this mixed approach—investing in supply-building and expanding and reforming portable assistance—because I do not believe that either one of these financing mechanisms alone will be able to respond to the dual goals of supporting working parents and promoting education. Tax or subsidy policies *alone* will not be able to provide the safeguards that we need to protect the quality of care for children. While we have seen some important progress in recent years in raising reimbursement rates within our subsidy policies, such progress has been slow and sporadic, with minimum quality oversight and limited reach. Moreover, while I advocate a significant amount of new funding, sooner rather than later, I recognize that these investments will not be realized overnight. Although phasing in supports for the supply of care will provide immediate progress, subsidy improvements are not direct enough to make the kind of improvement we need in the near future.

At the same time, reliance on supply-building *alone* will not allow working parents enough choice. Even when additional dollars are invested in child-care programs, as when pre-kindergarten funding is channeled into child care, it is not likely that such funding will cover free full-day, full-year programs. Pre-k policies are emerging in a more employment-neutral way and therefore are being funded to cover only part of the day, or the school day at best. Moreover, it is easier to make a direct investment in center-based and family child care. However, families will continue to need portable assistance in order to access the full range of services, including other family members and neighbors, particularly when children are very young or when parents work evenings or at night.

All Adults Caring for Children Should Have the Support Needed to Be Successful

As a country, we need to begin to value caregiving. Child care in the United States represents a continuum from parents, to family, to friends and neighbors, to family child care, to center-based teachers. The research is clear; all of these adults have an important influence on our children. Our policies therefore have to recognize that all caregivers should have the supports needed to be successful. For parents, this means time to be with their babies during the first year of life, flexible work schedules, good benefits, economic security, decent health and housing benefits, and educational opportunities to support their parental role when their children are young and when they are adolescents. Family, friends, and neighbor caregivers also should have economic security and other benefits as well as a community infrastructure that

20th Century Child Care →	Turning Point: Promising Initiatives Emerging →	Recommendations for 21st Century Child Care
Unpaid leave, with limited coverage	Growing interest and demand for paid parental leave	Paid parental leave as an available choice for first year of a baby's life
Strained and under-funded programs for children from birth to age 5	Expansion of Pre-school, Head Start, and community part-nerships, growing interest in universal pre-K and birth-to-3 services	Early Learning Pro-grams accessible to all, and a more cohesive system (diverse providers: Head Start, schools, child care)
Strained and under-funded programs for school-age children (6–17)	Growth of 21st Century Community Learning Centers and state after-school initiatives; growing interest in youth develop-ment	Neighborhood After School Programs accessible to all (community/school partnerships)

FIGURE 10a. *Recommendations for redesigning child care: Infants, preschool and school-age children.*

supports their caregiving. Family child-care providers and teachers in all types of centers should have professional training, adequate compensation and working conditions, and supports that allow them to respond to the special health and family needs of the children in their care.

Based on these goals, I offer six recommendations to redesign child-care policies in the United States (see Figure 10a and b). Figure 10a provides recommendations for specific age groups (babies, preschool children, and school-age children). The next three recommendations, in Figure 10b, are meant to build a system of support for care across the age spectrum.

20th Century Child Care	Turning Point: Promising Initiatives Emerging	Recommendations for 21st Century Child Care
Limited child-care assistance with minimum coverage for children and families	Growth in child-care assistance, improved reimbursement rates, and interest in child-care financing	Expanded and Reformed Child-Care Assistance
Limited information and supports for parents, providers, and community	Expansion of child-care resource and referral, family child-care networks, health and disability linkages, new champions, and cross-generation activities	Community Support Network (comprehensive resource and referral; family child-care networks; outreach to family, friend, and neighbor caregivers; health consultation; school linkages; and other community involvement)
Undeveloped professional preparation system; underpaid staff	State professional development planning and compensation initiatives	Professional Development System

FIGURE 10*b*. *Recommendations for redesigning child care: All age groups.*

Although no attempt has been made to estimate the cost of the entire set of recommendations, cost estimates are available from other sources.[5]

1. Provide Paid Parental Leave as a Choice During the First Year of a Baby's Life

Most industrialized countries provide some form of paid family leave upon the birth or adoption of a child, although the number of weeks and the percentage of wages covered by the benefit may vary. The

United States provides only limited coverage of family leave and no financial support to parents who choose to remain at home to care for their babies. New thinking on child-care financing recognizes that the child-care continuum should include support so that one parent can choose to stay home to care for an infant for up to one year. Poll after poll indicates widespread support for parental leave.[6]

In a review of cross-national leave policies, Sheila Kamerman notes that in nearly all developed countries, job-protected leaves for childbirth have become the norm, paid for through sickness (temporary disability) benefits, unemployment or family-allowance systems, or as a separate social insurance benefit. These policies vary in eligibility criteria, leave duration, benefit level, and take-up, or usage. One of the major trends in the 1980s and the 1990s was to extend leave policies to create a real alternative to out-of-home infant care.[7]

Extend Family and Medical Leave

While the United States has made some limited progress in the past few years, we still have a long way to go to join our peers in other countries. In 1993, Congress passed the Family and Medical Leave Act (FMLA), providing many working families the right to take up to twelve weeks of unpaid, job-protected leave to care for their new babies or sick family members and to recover from their own serious illnesses. FMLA has allowed an estimated four million working family members each year to care for their loved ones without putting their jobs or their health insurance at risk.[8]

Despite these successes, too many people in the country are not covered because they work for businesses with fewer than fifty employees. Furthermore, providing time off is not enough in itself. Many families, particularly low-income families, cannot take advantage of FMLA without additional support. Because FMLA only guarantees unpaid leave for childbirth or family illness, millions of families who qualify do not take time off, and more than seven out of ten of those say it is because they cannot go without pay.[9]

The United States should move forward on parental leave by extending FMLA to all families, regardless of the size of the companies they work for, and by providing incentives for states to use creative new financing strategies to provide paid leave for families during the first year of a child's life. In response to the need for financial assistance during the leave period, the Clinton administration requested that the Department of Labor evaluate the effectiveness of using state unemployment compensation systems as a means to provide partially paid parental leave for the birth or adoption of a new child. Final regulations became effective in 2000.

In 2001, several states were considering legislation to allow the use of unemployment compensation for parental leave. A few states use temporary disability insurance as a partial wage replacement for circumstances that include pregnancy and childbirth. A few states are considering broadening coverage, while other states are establishing tax credits for employers who provide family-leave benefits. More and more states are conducting studies of the costs and benefits of providing leave benefits, and others are holding hearings on family-leave proposals.[10]

Promote At-Home Infant-Care Programs

While we are moving forward with expanding FMLA, through federal or state action, we should step up efforts to ensure that low-income families with babies have access to the kind of support that would allow them to take time off from work. Low-wage jobs typically do not provide paid parental leave, so parents of infants often cannot reduce hours or take time away from work. Many families cannot afford to go without a paycheck, even for a few weeks. While Aid to Families with Dependent Children (the former welfare program) used to provide an exemption for families with young children, current policies under the Temporary Assistance to Needy Families program (TANF) allow states to exempt women who have children under age one from work-participation requirements. Yet more than one-third of the states still do not take advantage of this exemption, therefore requiring women with children under age one to participate in a work activity.[11] I propose that all women who have children under age one should be exempt from work requirements. At the same time, however, women should not have to go on welfare to receive the support they need to remain home with their babies. Other alternatives should be explored.

A few states have begun to experiment with using state dollars to provide resources to low-income families who choose to stay home after the birth of a baby. These initiatives, known as At Home Infant Care (AHIC) programs, show promise. At least two states have launched AHIC programs. In 1997 the Minnesota legislature added a new component to the state's child-care assistance program by establishing the At Home Infant Child Care program. This program allows families to receive a subsidy in lieu of child-care assistance if they have a child under age one, if they are eligible for or currently receiving child-care assistance, and if they provide full-time care for their infant child.[12] One hundred and one families participated in the program in its first eighteen months. Parents who participated reported both bonding and developmental benefits as well as financial benefits.[13]

In 2001, Montana started a similar pilot program for families with infants under age two. Eligibility is set at 150 percent of poverty. Families interested in the Montana At Home Infant Care program are not allowed to obtain child-care assistance for other children in the family and cannot access TANF cash assistance even if income-eligible. The rate of the AHIC payment is established according to the market rate for infant child care. Parents are required to complete a child-development education plan that is parent-directed. The plan may include activities in health, child development, nutrition, and other related areas.[14]

States should be given incentives both to create At Home Infant Care programs and to improve the out-of-home care provided to the youngest children. Funds to run AHIC programs could be made available to those states that agree to increase child-care expenditures, develop plans for improving the quality of out-of-home infant care, and ensure that families have resource-and-referral support to make informed choices. Parents choosing AHIC should not get preference over parents who choose to return to work. At the same time, both types of parents should have access to parent education, well-baby visits and a host of other services linked to child care or to programs that support mothers or fathers who choose to remain home with their babies.

2. Develop Early-Learning Programs that Are Accessible to All

The drumbeat to expand early education is growing. Over the past century, the United States created a system of public education and higher education. Given the growing number of working mothers, and the importance of the early years, the next logical step is to develop a more coherent system of early education. In recent years we have seen historic growth in state pre-kindergarten programs as well as increased investments in Head Start and Early Head Start. Most recently, the Committee for Economic Development, an independent, nonprofit, and nonpartisan organization of more than two hundred of the nation's top business and education leaders, issued a call for the United States to invest in universal access to preschool for all three- and four-year-olds.[15]

As discussed in Chapter 3, the expansion of state preschool and other early-childhood programs into child care represents an important step forward. The federal government has two important roles in early education. First, it must ensure equal access to high-quality programs for the most vulnerable children. At the same time, however, it has a responsibility to stimulate state investments in innovation and expansion of services, and to promote a more cohesive system of services for children from birth to age five.

Expand Head Start and Early Head Start for Children from Birth to Age Five

At a minimum, in a nation as wealthy as the United States, high-quality comprehensive services should be provided for all eligible young children, particularly the most vulnerable infants and toddlers. Head Start today is a discretionary program that receives an annual appropriation from Congress and represents the nation's largest financial commitment to early-childhood services. In fiscal year 2002 the federal appropriation for Head Start was $6.5 billion. In addition, in 1999, eighteen states invested state funds in Head Start.[16] In 2001, Head Start served 905,000 children.[17] However, the program still does not serve all of the eligible preschool children, and serves only a fraction of eligible children under age three.

Head Start, administered at the federal level by the Head Start Bureau of the U.S. Department of Health and Human Services, is a federal-to-local program that distributes funds to a network of grantees that have been selected to serve designated areas in local communities. The proportion of funds distributed in each state is established by formula in statute. The federal grant can fund 80 percent of the costs, with a required 20 percent local match. Grantees can choose to delegate certain programmatic and administrative responsibilities to sub-grantees, referred to as delegate agencies. Funds are distributed directly to communities and are administered by some fifteen hundred grantees locally based in every state, the District of Columbia, Puerto Rico, the Virgin Islands, the Outer Pacific Islands, and 150 tribal nations.

Head Start serves children of families whose income is below the federal poverty line at the point of entry in the program. Services are free to families; unlike services provided through the Child Care and Development Fund, no co-payment is expected. The majority of Head Start children are four years old, and about one-third are three years old. Less than 10 percent of the children are under age three and are served by both Migrant Head Start and Early Head Start, which began in 1995. Although Head Start has begun to branch out and serve children in family child-care homes, it remains primarily a center-based program. Furthermore, many programs remain part day, although this is changing rapidly.

Head Start should be expanded in three important ways. First, given the inadequacy of the poverty line to truly reflect the needs of low-income families, eligibility for Head Start should be expanded to at least 150 percent of poverty. This will help poor families in higher-income areas remain eligible for this critical service.

Second, Head Start grantees should be allowed the flexibility to assess community needs and serve children from birth through age five, depending on the availability of other services. Along with this increased flexibility, Early Head Start programs should continue to be added. This will allow new providers to participate in the Head Start model. Given the increase in state preschool programs and the demand for infant and toddler services, particularly due to welfare reform, the need to serve children under age three is more important than ever. One word of caution: Such expansion must be accompanied by a strong training and technical-assistance component. Traditional preschool programs need teacher-preparation and additional resources to provide quality comprehensive services to very young children.

Third, Head Start programs should be allowed to serve families full day, all year, by using Head Start funds or through creative partnerships with the child-care community. Providing funding directly to Head Start for full day programs will provide an easier mechanism to plan and manage services. Providing incentives for Head Start to partner with child care will help improve services for children served by other programs. While Head Start-child care partnerships can help improve the overall quality of care, additional training and technical assistance will be needed to support Head Start as it moves forward with collaborative arrangements.

Provide Incentives for States to Expand and Improve Early Education and Develop a More Cohesive Early-Education System

Over the years, states have become laboratories for creative early-childhood initiatives. Prompted by findings in the mid-1980s that touted the benefits of early education, and spurred on by more recent research on the importance of the early years, the number of preschool initiatives has grown steadily over the past decade. Four out of five states now fund a state pre-kindergarten initiative. State funding for prekindergarten rose from $190 million in 1988 to more than $1.9 billion in 2001.[18]

These pre-kindergarten programs take various forms and can be classified by several characteristics. Some states focus on one age range, such as three- and four-year-olds, while others target children from birth to five years old. As discussed earlier, at least one state (Georgia) provides universal coverage for four-year-olds, while most states attempt to target funds to low-income families to ensure access to services. Funding may flow from a state in a variety of ways. Some states fund pre-kindergarten programs that are delivered through the schools or contracted out to a wide variety of child-care providers. Other states fund Head Start or similar programs that are delivered through Head Start or a wider network of providers. Finally, some states fund community-wide initiatives that provide funding to a range of providers based on a menu of early-childhood services. Almost all of these state initiatives provide funds directly to programs, rather than to parents.

In addition to state efforts, some Title I funds are being used for preschool services. Title I of the Elementary and Secondary Education Act is the single largest source of federal funding for elementary and secondary education. Administered by the U.S. Department of Education, its primary purpose is to help local education agencies and schools improve the teaching and learning of children who are failing or who are at the greatest risk of failing. In fiscal year 1999, Title I provided about $7.9 billion, primarily to high-poverty schools, to serve about twelve million children.

Historically, most children served by Title I have been in kindergarten through grade twelve; however, a growing number of schools also are now serving younger children. A stratified, nationally representative survey, drawn from sixteen thousand school districts found that during the 1990–2000 school year, an estimated $407 million was spent on preschool, serving an estimated 313,000 children. Only about 17 percent of all school districts that received Title I funds used a portion of these funds to serve preschool children during that year. Almost all preschool children served were between the ages of three and five.[19] Although Title I funding recently increased, it is still too early to tell if this expanded funding will be used to serve additional preschool children.

New incentives are needed for states to expand early-education services while also creating a more cohesive system. A state incentive-grant program could be developed to stimulate state investments in universal pre-K for three- and four-year-olds, or to improve and expand services for children from birth to five. In order to qualify for additional funding, a state would have to agree to establish a state council on early childhood, representing a broad group of experts, various state agencies, and the private sector. This group would be charged with conducting a review of the state's early-childhood programs and developing a plan for systematic improvements in five key areas: standards; training and compensation; curriculum; data collection; and comprehensive service linkages (health, mental-health and disability services). These five areas can serve as "unifiers," supporting providers in all types of programs, to create a more holistic early-childhood system.

At the same time, better planning and coordination are needed at the federal level between the Department of Education and the Department of Health and Human Services. Although an interagency work group has been established, the two departments should step up efforts to develop more articulated data sets, a joint public-awareness campaign about the importance of the early years, and better mechanisms for sharing promising practices across programs.

3. Create Neighborhood After-School Programs Accessible to All

Like early education, after-school programs have experienced enormous growth. While we need to continue to expand programs, this growth must be accompanied by more systematic efforts to ensure quality. Furthermore, new programs should reflect the differing needs of young children in early elementary school, middle-schoolers, and teens. In order to do this, federal, state, and community-planning efforts should help coordinate the various services that will be needed to meet the developmental needs of this age range.

Expand and Improve 21st Century Community Learning Centers

The largest source of support for after-school programs ($1 billion in 2002) is the 21st Century Community Learning Centers program, or 21st CCLC. As discussed in Chapter 4, funds for the program are authorized under the Elementary and Secondary Education Act. In March 2002, 1.2 million children were being served in about sixty-eight hundred centers across the country.[20] Yet thousands of other schools have applied over the past few years and have been unable to obtain services due to limited funds. For example, in 2001, more than twenty-seven hundred applicants requested $1.9 billion in new after-school programs dollars, but only 11 percent of those requests could be filled.[21]

The 21st CCLC program should more than double over the next few years. Moreover, as the administration of the 21st CCLC moves to the states in 2002, and the program is opened up to community-based organizations, an important opportunity arises to expand services and promote a more coordinated approach to planning. In addition, partnerships between school and community-based organizations should be encouraged. The federal role should focus more directly on increasing funds to states, promoting innovation, setting standards, and ensuring training and technical assistance. Evaluation results should be used to help strengthen and inform a continuous improvement plan for after-school programs.

Promote State Investments in After-School and Youth Services and Develop More Cohesive Planning

According to the National Conference of State Legislatures, in 2000–2001 at least twenty states passed legislation pertaining to after-school policies. These policies range from the creation of new programs to financing and regulating existing ones.[22] California, Maryland, and several other states have moved to increase resources for after-school programs. At the same time, community-wide projects are emerging through state and local efforts to plan systems of service delivery, rather than just creating separate and isolated programs. New incentives are needed to promote such efforts.

The Younger Americans Act (YAA), which has been introduced in Congress, would provide important new funds for youth services, including after-school programs, while also creating an infrastructure of support for youth-serving programs at the state and local levels. YAA would establish, for the first time in our nation's history, a comprehensive, coordinated national youth policy. It would authorize $2 billion by 2006. Ninety-five percent of the funds would be allocated by the states to eligible community-based and youth-development organizations.[23] Passage of this important legislation is long overdue.

Given the fact that after-school services can grow from education, youth and child-care funding, it is critically important that coordination take place at every level. At the federal level, an interagency coordinating mechanism should be established to bring together the Department of Health and Human Services (which currently administers both youth programs and child care) with the Department of Education, the Department of Justice, and the Department of Agriculture. While some efforts have been made in the past to promote such coordination, such efforts should be increased. Moreover, now that the administration of the 21st Century Community Learning Centers is at the state level, new incentives need to be put in place to promote better collaboration between state education departments and state child-care administrators in charge of CCDBG funding.

4. Expand and Reform Child-Care Assistance to Parents

Even with increased program supports, parents need additional resources to help pay for care. The two main sources of support to parents, the Child Care and Development Fund and the Dependent Care Tax Credit, should be expanded and modified to better meet the needs of low- and middle-income families. Furthermore, new efforts are needed to reform the child-care financial-aid system in every state.

Increase the Child Care and Development Fund

The lack of child-care subsidies often puts families in serious financial jeopardy. For example, a survey of families waiting for child-care assistance in Minneapolis in 1995 found that 71 percent of the parents who had to pay for child care fell into significant debt; 47 percent depleted their accumulated savings; about one-quarter of the families turned to public assistance; one out of seven were forced to quit their jobs; and several parents experienced bankruptcy or eviction.[24] Similarly, in 1999 the Children's Aid Society of New York surveyed a sample of families waiting for child-care assistance in New York City. They found that 77 percent of the families believed that their current child-care situations were harming their children; 41 percent reported having to cut back on other household expenses such as food and children's clothing; nearly half the very poor families paid between 20 and 50 percent of their incomes on child care; and 36 percent of the parents said they were either unable to work or had lost their jobs. At the time, it was estimated that forty thousand working families were on waiting lists in the city, with an estimated two hundred thousand eligible children whose parents would utilize child-care assistance if it were available.[25]

Since 1996, combined federal and state funding for child care under the Child Care and Development Block Grant (CCDBG) and the Temporary Assistance to Needy Families block grant (TANF) has more than doubled. Most of this growth in spending has been attributable to federal funds, and a high percentage of those funds became available through TANF as welfare caseloads dropped. In fiscal year 2000, states spent $9 billion on child care ($6.5 in federal funds, including CCDF, TANF transfer, and TANF direct, and $2.5 in state dollars).[26]

Despite this increased funding, there continued to be a significant unmet demand for child-care assistance. In 1999, HHS estimated that 14.7 children from birth to age thirteen were eligible for child care according to federal guidelines. Yet in 2002, child-care funding serves an estimated average 2.2 million children per month.[27] Only one out of seven eligible children is served.

This demand for child-care assistance has been fueled by the dramatic growth in the number of low-income working families. For example, Mark Greenberg has pointed out that welfare caseloads dropped by 1.8 million families from 1996 to 1999, and studies consistently found that the majority of those who left the welfare rolls were employed, typically in low-wage jobs. At the same time, the percentage of families working or participating in work activities while still receiving TANF also grew significantly. By fiscal year 1999, nearly nine hundred thousand adults receiving assistance were employed or engaged in work activities. Moreover, during this time period there was a large increase in labor-force participation by low-income single parents. Between 1996 and 1999, the number of employed single mothers grew from 1.8 million to 2.7 million.[28]

While the number of children served in the child-care subsidy system grew, it could not keep up with growing demand. In November 2000, HHS released the first results of *The National Study of Child Care for Low Income Families*, a five-year research effort to examine child care in seventeen states and twenty-five communities. The study was designed to examine how states and communities formulate and implement policies and programs to meet the child-care needs of families moving from welfare to work, as well as those of other low-income parents; how these policies change over time; and how these policies, as well as other factors, affect the type, amount, and cost of care in communities.[29]

The study showed that states appeared to be able to meet the demand for child care for TANF families, since caseloads have declined dramatically. Yet CCDF funding was not intended to serve only welfare families. Instead, in 1996, Congress recognized that low-income working families would have a continual need for child-care assistance, and expanded the income eligibility from 75 percent of median income to 85 percent. Yet according to the national study, on average states served only about 15 or 20 percent of eligible children in April 1999, and no state served more than one-quarter of the eligible families. In fact, twelve of the seventeen study states had waiting lists for families needing child-care assistance.[30] According to a survey by the Children's Defense Fund, as of March 2000, in two out of five states, a family earning as little as $25,000 could not qualify for child-care assistance.[31] In 2002, a report on five states, released by the Center for Law and Social Policy, found a similar pattern of unmet need, with states reporting only from 8-to 28 percent of eligible children served.[32]

Moreover, the Children's Defense Fund survey found that states have been forced to make various trade-offs with regard to parent co-payments and payment rates. While regulations for CCDF suggested that states pay reimbursement rates at the 75th percentile of the market rate, nearly half the states set their provider-reimbursement rates at levels below the 75th percentile or based them on outdated rates. Moreover, the regulations also suggested that states set co-payments at no more than 10 percent of family income in order to provide equal access to families. Yet in 2000, two-thirds of the states required families with incomes at 150 percent of poverty level to pay more than 7 percent of their income in fees or did not even allow a family at this income level to qualify for assistance.[33] A 1998 HHS inspector general's report on payment rates and co-payments concluded that state child-care certificate policies may be restricting parental choice.[34]

Already facing growing demand for child care and limited resources, by the end of 2001 states also experienced an economic downturn and tight budgets. In January 2002, according to the National Conference of State Legislatures survey, forty-five states reported that their revenues were below forecasted levels at the beginning of the fiscal year, while many states reported that their spending in key budget areas was above forecasted levels.[35] Moreover, rising TANF caseloads threatened child-care gains: Between March and September 2001, TANF caseloads increased in thirty-two states.[36] Finally, proposed increases in the work requirements, without significant new investments in child care, can only worsen the situation for low-income working families.

To meet this increasing need, the Child Care and Development Fund must continue to be expanded. In 2002, a coalition led by the Children's

Defense fund recommended a CCDBG expansion of $20 billion over the next five years. States should be encouraged to raise eligibility to the levels allowed by federal law, to set co-payments at no more than 10 percent of family income, to allow reimbursement rates to better reflect the full cost of care, and to invest additional dollars in other quality improvements.

Reform Child-Care Assistance

Despite increasing resources, many families are not taking advantage of available subsidies. For example, a review of "leaver" studies, examining the situations of families whose welfare cases have been closed, indicated that most respondents who had left welfare and were working were not receiving a child-care subsidy. Lack of awareness of the child-care subsidy system appeared to be a contributing factor to limited use of available funds by welfare families.[37] Similarly, a survey of one hundred women applying for welfare in New York City found that nearly half the women were threatened with sanctions if they could not find child care and were not told they could not be sanctioned if they could not find appropriate care. Yet the majority received no assistance from their caseworker in finding child care.[38]

Research on how low-income mothers navigate and experience the child-care subsidy system continues to document the complex issues facing families. A study by The Urban Institute found that a number of factors affected whether families could obtain and retain child-care assistance, including state and local management styles, the process of application and reapplication, and the availability of outreach and information.[39] Many families are unaware that child-care assistance is available, or they assume that subsidies are not available if they are working.

Child-care assistance (which I think we should rename "child-care tuition assistance") needs to be totally reinvented so that it is more user-friendly. Special outreach efforts should be made to inform families about the availability of child care through many media sources and in the languages spoken in the community. Families should be able to apply for such assistance in multiple locations throughout a community, receiving the same application and information on all subsidy and tax provisions available. Families should be able to have their eligibility determined once a year, so that there is continuity of care for their children. Furthermore, providers should be paid regardless of whether children are out sick.

Innovations in financial assistance, rate policy, and a host of other administrative issues should be included in any expanding child-care resources.

Expand the Dependent-Care Tax Credit

One of the oldest forms of support for child care is the dependent-care tax credit, which is estimated to be worth $2.7 billion.[40] Tax allowances for child and dependent care were first authorized in 1954, when Congress enacted comprehensive tax reform. The credit was adopted in 1976, but few changes have been made over the past two decades. Starting in 1982, expense limits were raised, the maximum credit was increased, and a sliding scale based on family income was established to determine the amount of the credit. In 1983 the credit became available to taxpayers filing the short form. Beginning in 1989, the federal government required that all taxpayers claiming the credit provide the care provider's name, address, and taxpayer identification number on their tax returns; the maximum age for a qualifying child was lowered from under fifteen to under thirteen; and taxpayers receiving tax-free assistance from their employers under a dependent-care assistance program were required to reduce by the amount of that assistance the amount they claimed under the dependent-care tax credit. The 1989 changes resulted in fewer families claiming the dependent-care tax credit for tax year 1989 than for tax year 1988.[41]

The tax credit is available to individual taxpayers for employment-related expenses incurred for the care of a dependent child under age thirteen or a spouse or dependent who is physically or mentally incapacitated. Families may claim work-related expenses of up to $2,400 for one child or dependent and up to $4,800 for two or more children or dependents. Beginning in 2003, these expense limits increase to $3,000 and $6,000 respectively. Any expenses above these amounts are not eligible for the credit. Although no income cap prevents higher-income families from claiming the credit, the credit targets the greatest amount of assistance to lower-income families. Only a portion of eligible expenses may be taken as a credit, decreasing on a sliding scale from 30 percent to 20 percent as the taxpayer's income rises. In 2003, the upper limit of 30 percent will increase to 35 percent.[42] There are serious limitations to this tax credit. First, the credit is not refundable, so families who qualify for a credit that is larger than their tax liability receive only a portion of the credit, up to the amount of tax owed. Families whose income is so low that they owe no tax receive no federal credit at all. Furthermore, the provisions are not adjusted for inflation, unlike other tax provisions that determine tax liability, such as the personal exemption, the standard deduction, and the earned income-tax credit. Because of this, the targeting to low-income families benefits fewer families over the years. Moreover, the dollar limits on what can be claimed as child-care expenses do not reflect the true cost of care.

All three of these issues should be addressed. First, the dependent-care tax credit should be refundable for families who do not have a tax liability. Second, it should be adjusted for inflation. Third, the percentage of expenses that families can claim should be raised to at least 50 to 75 percent of the costs, and a higher percentage of families should be able to claim the full amount allowable.

Finally, special incentives should be given to states to enact state tax-credit provisions. Currently, more than half the states (and the District of Columbia) have made provisions for child and dependent care in their income-tax laws. The provisions may be credits, which offset against state tax liability, or deductions, which reduce the amount of income subject to the state tax. Most state provisions are dependent upon or tied to the federal credit, with the state credit or deduction determined by some or all of the provisions of the federal credit. Less than a dozen states have established tax provisions that are refundable.[43]

5. Develop a Community Support System

Child care in the United States is missing an infrastructure of support for parents, programs, and policy-makers at the community and state levels. Currently, the main source of infrastructure support is the quality set-aside in the Child Care and Development Fund (CCDF). All states are using their quality funds for a range of activities, including consumer education and resource-and-referral services, health outreach, training and compensation initiatives, and a wide array of efforts to build the supply of care. However, spending on quality is limited. Unfortunately, key infrastructure supports, such as consumer education and licensing, have been forced to compete for limited funds with important quality enhancements such as training and compensation. The *National Study of Child Care for Low Income Families* reported that in fiscal year 1999, median spending on child-care quality per child of employed parents was only $11.42 per year.[44] Moreover, since quality funds can be spent on care for all children, there is no special focus on improving the quality of services for very low-income children, who could benefit the most from enriched environments. In addition, although efforts have been made to increase supply, such as recruiting family child-care providers, this expansion often is offset by attrition.[45]

The quality funds in CCDF should be expanded, from a minimum of 4 percent to from 15 to 20 percent of overall funding. These resources, in combination with other federal, state, local, and private dollars, should be used to develop a more coherent infrastructure of support.

Fully Fund Child-Care Resource and Referral in Every Community

The Child Care and Development Fund should include enough resources to fully fund a network of child-care resource-and-referral agencies in every state. At a minimum, CCDF funds should help support the three core functions that every community should have in place: free information and referral for parents, resource development, and data collection and reporting. From this core, other enhanced services and provider supports can grow, using child-care quality funds and resources from other sectors.

Provide Incentives to Improve Health and Safety

Providing parents with information and referral is not enough to ensure the health and safety of children in child care. Incentives are needed to help states improve their licensing requirements and to ensure that every child-care provider has access to a health consultant. Such improvements should be funded both from child-care and health resources. For example, in 2000 important provisions that had bipartisan support were introduced in Congress to improve the health and safety of children in child care settings. Such incentives are long overdue. Congress should act to fund these provisions and ensure that all states review their licensing standards based on recommended guidelines, expand their enforcement policies, and provide health-outreach services. At the same time, maternal and child-health dollars and other state public-health resources should be used to establish a network of health consultants in every state.

Expand Provider Supports to Improve Quality

Every community should have a system of provider supports in place, including resources to expand accreditation, family child-care networks, infant and toddler specialists, and access to comprehensive services. Yet child-care funding alone will not be enough to improve quality. Other federal and state resources should be used to provide the range of other important support services needed. For example, mental-health consultation should be included in any new legislation regarding mental-health services; disability outreach in child care should be covered under the Individuals with Disabilities Education Act; curriculum support and school linkages should be included in an education bill; training initiatives should be included in higher-education legislation; and incentives to bring together the elderly and children's programs should be included in the Older Americans Act.

6. Strengthen the Professional Development Systems for Early-Childhood and After-School Staff

Because early-childhood and after-school services have grown so rapidly in the past two decades, the support to help develop the workforce has not yet been put in place. We need a comprehensive study of higher education in each state and a plan for retooling the system to help prepare the early-education and after-school workforce of the twenty-first century. While some efforts have been made to move forward, they have been very limited. More than any other issue, the professional preparation and compensation of the child-care workforce is the key to unlocking the door to quality improvements.

Designing a system of professional preparation for early-childhood staff requires pulling together many bits and pieces of a disconnected and fragmented system. This includes developing ways to track individual training experiences, link informal training to the traditional systems of higher education, and ensure some level of articulation along the way. Federal incentives are needed to build the capacity of and access to higher education, to increase compensation, and to launch new research efforts to better understand the best way to staff early-childhood and after-school programs.

Improve the Capacity and Access to Higher Education and Credentials

Training of early-childhood and after-school staff takes place at various levels, from certificate programs to graduate education. Higher-education institutions should recognize this progression by ensuring articulation across certificate, associate, bachelor's, and graduate programs. Furthermore, funds should be made available to develop professional-preparation programs that reflect the emerging roles in the field, including family child-care providers, classroom staff for various age groups, infant and toddler specialists, family child-care network coordinators, early-childhood literacy specialists, resource-and-referral counselors, and other new roles.

New resources should build on the initiatives that have taken place over the past few decades. In the mid-1970s the Office of Child Development launched an effort to develop a set of competencies and a training-and-assessment system to help prepare people to work in early-childhood programs. Anticipating the growth in Head Start and child care, the Child Development Associate (CDA) credentialing system was designed to provide a cadre of early-childhood professionals who could be in charge of a group of young children. One of the most important steps in this process was the development of the CDA competencies for early-childhood providers. Today, more than one hundred thousand caregivers have earned their CDA credential—including thousands of family child-care providers and infant-toddler providers. A CDA credential is available for school-age staff working in the army child-care system, and discussions are underway to develop a credential for the civilian community.[46]

In 1999, the federal government took another step forward when the Department of Labor moved to expand the development of child-care apprenticeship programs in the states. Apprenticeships are used by many industries to train and credential their workforce by combining on-the-job training with related academic instruction leading to a recognized credential. Based on the success of an apprenticeship program in West Virginia and a handful of other states, the department awarded grants to ten states and the District of Columbia to develop apprenticeship programs to train child-care workers. Since then several other states have been added. Funds should be made available to all states interested in developing apprenticeship programs.

States should be encouraged to recognize the CDA credential or to develop apprenticeship or state credentials based on the CDA competency standards for staff working with children. Efforts should be made to require all child-care providers to pursue higher-education degrees and to obtain appropriate AA and BA degrees.

States have taken a number of important steps to improve the professional preparation of the child care workforce. In 1989 the state of Delaware convened the first planning process to create a statewide comprehensive career-development system. The report from this initiative was widely disseminated and served as an impetus to many other states to take a similar comprehensive approach, involving many stakeholders in the process. By 1998, forty-eight states and the District of Columbia had an active early-childhood career-development planning and implementation initiative underway.[47]

In 2002, the Bush administration proposed that all states create professional-development plans. However, new funding will be needed to help the states implement this proposal. Currently, dedicated funds for professional preparation in early education or after-school are extremely limited. For example, although Congress did include an Early Childhood Educator Professional Development Program as part of the reauthorization of the Elementary and Secondary Education Act, in 2002 only $15 million was appropriated.[48] While this was an important first step, a new national initiative is needed to provide funds for statewide planning for professional development, and to build the capacity of the higher-education institutions to train the child-care workforce of the twenty-first century.

Provide Scholarships and Link Training to Compensation

While we build the capacity of the higher-education system to prepare the workforce of the future, we also need incentives for states to invest in scholarships and specific compensation initiatives. North Carolina has served as a model for the entire country. The state has at least three important initiatives that directly affect the professional development and compensation of child-care providers: the T.E.A.C.H. Early Childhood® Project, the T.E.A.C.H. Early Childhood® Health Insurance Program, and the Child Care WAGE$® Project.

Begun as a pilot in 1990 to provide a single scholarship model to twenty-one child-care teachers in North Carolina, T.E.A.C.H. (Teacher Education and Compensation Helps Early Childhood) is now an umbrella for a variety of scholarship programs in the state. In 2000, its tenth year, more than five thousand child-care providers across the state utilized scholarships to take college courses leading to credentials or two- or four-year degrees in child development or early-childhood education. Scholarships for teachers working toward an associate's degree cover a substantial portion of tuition and book costs, include a travel stipend, and provide for release time. Employers must agree to provide a raise or bonus upon completion of the required credit hours. In turn, participants must pay part of the costs of their education and must commit to remain an additional year in their sponsoring center after they complete their required courses. The results have been promising. Teachers receiving a scholarship to work on an associate's degree in early-childhood education complete an average of thirteen to fifteen credits a year while continuing to work full time in their sponsoring programs. Their earnings increase by an average of 10 percent a year, exceeding earlier expectations.[49] By 2002, twenty-one states were implementing the T.E.A.C.H. program, providing more than eighteen thousand scholarships to be used at any one of nearly 450 universities and community colleges.[50]

To extend these efforts, the T.E.A.C.H. Early Childhood® Health Insurance program was created to help fund the cost of health insurance for workers in child-care programs that have made a commitment to supporting the education and compensation of their staff. Child-care providers are eligible to have up to one-third of the cost of individual (not family) health-insurance coverage reimbursed through a special fund if they meet the conditions of the program. The health-insurance program is available statewide. Similar efforts are being considered by other states.[51]

The Child Care WAGE$® project provides a salary supplement linked to the education of participating child-care providers. Participants include child-care teachers, directors, and family child-care providers who work in licensed programs, have credentials or degrees, and whose earnings fall below a maximum limit. Applicants are assigned a WAGE$ education level, based on a screening of their transcripts, and each level carries with it an annual supplement paid directly to participants in six-month installments as long as the provider remains in the program.[52] In FY 2000–01, data from sixty-one participating counties indicate lower turnover rates for WAGE$ participants and an increasing level of education. There are three salary-supplement scales that counties may choose. The range for the lowest scales is from $200 to $3,000 per year; the highest scale ranges from $300 to $6,250 per year.[53]

While North Carolina has the most comprehensive set of policies, other states and communities have promising initiatives. For example, Rhode Island became the first state to offer paid health insurance to family child-care providers who care for children through the state's subsidy program. The benefits were later extended to cover half the health premiums for centers devoting at least 50 percent of their licensed capacity to serving children receiving a subsidy.[54] By the end of 2001, eight states had compensation initiatives. These compensation initiatives follow two basic models—providing rewards directly to individuals in the form of stipends (not part of their regular compensation) or providing grants to programs to improve overall compensation through improved salaries and benefits.[55] Many counties in California are implementing a version of the Child Development Corps, a component of the California CARES program (Compensation and Retention Encourage Stability). The program provides a professional-development stipend, typically ranging from $500 to $6,000 a year, to child-care teachers, directors, and home-based providers who meet certain education and training qualifications and who commit to continuing their professional development.[56]

The United States should provide scholarship programs designed to support professional preparation at several levels. Both federal and state higher-education legislation should make the development of these sectors a priority. Yet resources for scholarships are not enough; they also must be coupled with compensation initiatives. In 2001 and 2002, several bills were introduced in Congress to provide state incentives for training and compensation and to expand the quality set-aside in the Child Care and Development Fund. These quality improvements must be made a national and state priority if we are to build a stable child-care workforce.

Launch New Research on Staffing Issues

Given the size and importance of the early-childhood and after-school workforce, we have relatively little data that provides even basic information on this sector of the labor force. While related data is collected by the Department of Labor, the Census Bureau, Health and Human Services, and Education, we still do not have an ongoing and coherent data-collection system that describes and tracks trends in the workforce. Nomenclature is outdated, and information over time is not available. Although we need to create new mechanisms to collect data on the supply of providers, we also need to launch new research that will provide us with information on the most effective staffing patterns and professional-preparation strategies.

A Final Reflection

As I close this book, I wonder what child care will be like when my own grandchildren arrive. I hope that all new parents have more time, less stress, and a system of services to help them build stronger families and caring communities. I hope that when my grandchildren enter child care, they will spend their days in beautiful spaces with caring, smart, well-supported, and creative providers. I hope that their teachers will be valued and respected by their community and that they will have warm, friendly, and productive relationships with the children and families they serve. More than anything, I hope that some day we will be able to claim that the United States is doing the very best for all of our children, particularly the most vulnerable. The door is open for us to redesign child care. Like the children in child care themselves, we do not have a moment to waste.

Notes

Chapter One

1. U.S. House of Representatives, Committee on Ways and Means, *2000 Green Book, Background Material and Data on Programs within the Jurisdiction of the Committee on Ways and Means,* 106th Cong., 2nd sess., WMCP 106–14 (Washington, D.C.: Government Printing Office, October 6, 2000), pp. 572, 573.

2. Ibid., p. 573.

3. Robert B. Reich, "Working Principles: From Ending Welfare to Rewarding Work," *American Prospect,* June 19–July 3, 2000, p. 23.

4. Ellen Goodman, "The End of Motherhood as We Knew It," *Boston Globe* (September 17, 1995), p. 39.

5. "What the Polling Tells Us," Communications Consortium Media Center, Washington, D.C. Web site, <www.earlycare.org/pollingtellsus.htm>, February 16, 2002.

6. Ellen Galinsky, *Ask The Children* (New York: William Morrow, 1999), pp. xiv–xv.

7. Unpublished tabulations prepared by Donald Yarosz, "Percentage distribution of children 0–5 according to hours per week in center-based child care, by child and family characteristics: 1999" calculated from the National Household Education Survey (New Brunswick, N.J.: National Institute for Early Education Research, Rutgers University, February 15, 2002).

8. National Research Council and Institute of Medicine, *From Neurons to Neighborhoods: The Science of Early Childhood Development,* Jack P. Shonkoff and Deborah A. Phillips, eds. (Washington, D.C.: National Academy Press, 2000), p. 297.

9. Linda Giannarelli and James Barsimantov, "Child Care Expenses of America's Families," Occasional Paper No. 40 (Washington, D.C.: The Urban Institute, January 2000), pp. 3–4.

10. Deborah Vandell and Barbara Wolfe, *Child Care Quality: Does it Matter and Does It Need to be Improved?* (Washington, D.C.: U.S. Department of Health and Human Services, Executive Summary), pp. 5–6, <http://aspe.hhs.gov/hsp/ccquality00/execsum.htm>, October 20, 2000.

11. Ibid.

12. *The 2002 Child Care Center Licensing Study* (Washington, D.C.: The Children's Foundation, 2002), p. iv; and *The 2001 Family Child Care Licensing Study Summary Data* fact sheet (The Children's Foundation, 2001).

13. Kay Hollestelle, Executive Director, The Children's Foundation, personal communication, March, 2002.

14. Deborah A. Phillips, *Child Care for Low-Income Families: Summary of Two Workshops* (Washington, D.C.: National Academy of Sciences, 1995), p. 13. For further information, see G. L. Siegel and L. A. Loman, "Child care and AFDC Recipients in Illinois: Patterns, Problems, and Needs," prepared for the Division of Family Support Services (Illinois Department of Public Aid, St. Louis, Mo.: Institute of Applied Research, 1991).

15. *Welfare Reform: Implications of Increased Work Participation for Child Care*, GAO/HEHS 97-75 (Washington, D.C.: General Accounting Office, 1997), p. 8.

16. U.S. Department of Health and Human Services, "Child Care Bureau Focuses on School Age Care," *Child Care Bulletin*, March/April 1995, Issue 2, p. 1.

17. Harriet B. Presser, "Toward a 24-Hour Economy," *Science*, Vol. 224, June 11, 1999, p. 1778.

18. "Cost of Child Rearing Rises by 2 percent," Reuters, April 27, 2000. This article reports that child-care costs rose by 5 percent between 1998 and 1999, contributing to the overall rise in the costs of child-rearing.

19. Kristin Smith, *Who's Minding the Kids? Child Care Arrangements, Fall 1995 Current Population Reports*, P-70-70 (Washington, D.C.: U.S. Bureau of the Census, October 2000), p. 27.

20. Anne Mitchell, Louise Stoney, and Harriet Dichter, *Financing Child Care in the United States: An Expanded Catalogue of Current Strategies* (Kansas City, Kans.: The Ewing Marion Kauffman Foundation, 2001), pp. 3–4.

21. Karen Schulman, *The High Cost of Child Care Puts Quality Out of the Reach of Many Families* (Washington, D.C.: Children's Defense Fund, 2000), p. 1.

22. Robert Halpern, Sharon Deich, and Carol Cohen, *Financing After-School Programs* (Washington, D.C.: The Finance Project, May 2000), p. 9.

23. Smith, *Who's Minding the Kids?*, p. 27

24. Giannarelli and Barsimantov, "Child Care Expenses of America's Families," pp. 8, 10.

25. Testimony of Vicky Flamand before the U.S. Senate Finance Committee, "Child Care Supporting Working Families, March 19, 2002, p. 2.

26. Remarks of U.S. Treasury Secretary Robert Rubin, *Proceedings of the White House Conference on Child Care*, Washington, D.C., October 23, 1997, p. 36.

27. Isabel Sawhill and Adam Thomas, *A Hand Up for the Bottom Third: Towards a New Agenda for Low-Income Working Families* (Washington, D.C.: The Children's Roundtable, The Brookings Institution, May 2001), p. 36.

28. Statement by Olivia Golden, Assistant Secretary for Children and Families, Administration for Children and Families, U.S. Department of Health and Human Services, to the U.S. House of Representatives Committee on Ways and Means, Subcommittee on Human Resources, March 16, 1999, p. 5.

29. Personal communication with Marcy Whitebook, former director of the Child Care Employee Project, December 1999.

30. "Current Data on Child Care Salaries and Benefits in the United States" (Washington, D.C.: Center for the Child Care Workforce, March 2001), p. 4.

31. Marcy Whitebook, Carollee Howes, and Deborah Phillips, *Who Cares? Child Care and Teachers and the Quality of Care in America—The National Child Care Staffing Study, Executive Summary* (Oakland, Calif.: Child Care Employee Project, 1989), p. 4.

32. *Cost, Quality, and Child Outcomes in Child Care Centers, Public Report, 2nd Ed.* (Denver: University of Colorado Economics Department, 1995), pp. 44–45, 75.

33. Marcy Whitebook, Carollee Howes, and Deborah Phillips, *Worthy Work: Unlivable Wages—The National Child Care Staffing Study, 1988–1997* (Washington, D.C.: Center for the Child Care Workforce, 1998), p. 7.

34. Ibid., pp. 7–8.

35. Marcy Whitebook, Laura Sakai, Emily Gerber, and Carollee Howes, *Then and Now: Changes in Child Care Staffing 1994–2000* (Washington, D.C.: Center for the Child Care Workforce, 2001), pp. v–vii.

36. Pauline D. Koch, "The Role of Licensing in Child Care: Licensing as an Element of Quality," statement to the Child Care Bureau Conference on Licensing, Department of Health and Human Services, Washington, D.C., November 2, 1998, p. 2.

37. "Child Care Licensing Qualifications and Training Requirements for Roles in Child Care Centers and Family Child Care Homes," Summary Sheet, Institute for Leadership and Career Initiatives (Boston: Wheelock College), January 2002.

38. *Child Care: State Efforts to Enforce Safety and Health Requirements*, GAO/HEHS-00-28 (Washington, D.C.: GAO, January 2000), Table 4, p. 20.

39. William Gormley Jr., "Regulating Child Care Quality," *Annals*, AAPSS 563, May 1999, p. 118. See also B. Willer et al., *The Demand and Supply of Child Care in 1990* (Washington, D.C.: National Association for the Education of Young Children), 1991.

40. Office of the Inspector General, *States' Child Care Certificate Systems: An Early Assessment of Vulnerabilities and Barriers* (Washington, D.C.: U.S. Department of Health and Human Services, February 1998), OEI-05-97-00320, p. 14.

41. Koch, "Role of Licensing in Child Care."

42. GAO, *Child Care*, Table 3, p. 14.

43. Gormley, "Regulating Child Care Quality," p. 123.

44. GAO, *Child Care*, pp. 17–19.

45. National Association of Child Care Resource and Referral Agencies, "NACCRA at a Glance" (Washington, D.C.: NACCRA, n.d.), updated through personal communication with Yasmina Vinci, March 2002.

46. Office of the Inspector General, *States' Child Care Certificate Systems*, p. 12.

47. Ibid., p. 13.

48. Carol Copple, *Quality Matters: Improving the Professional Development of the Early Childhood Workforce* (Washington, D.C.: National Association for the Education of Young Children, 1990), p. 7.

49. Center for Early Childhood Leadership, "Research Notes: A Profile of Early Childhood Center Directors" (Wheeling, Ill.: Center for Early Childhood Leadership, National–Louis University, 1998), p. 1.

50. Gwen Morgan, Sheri Azer, Joan Costley, Andrea Genser, Irene F. Goodman, Joan Lombardi, and Bettina McGimsey, *Making a Career of It: The State of the States Report on Career Development in Early Care and Education* (Boston: Center for Career Development in Early Care and Education, 1993), pp. 96–98.

51. Center for Early Childhood Leadership, "Research Notes: Investing in Teachers' Professional Development: A Comparison of Elementary Schools and Child Care Centers" (Wheeling, Ill.: Center for Early Childhood Leadership, National–Louis University, 1999), p. 2.

52. Arlene Skolnick, "Changes of Heart: Family Dynamics in Historical Perspective," in *Family, Self and Society: Towards a New Agenda for Family Research*, Philip A. Cowan, Dorothy Field, Donald A. Hansen, Guy Swanson, and Arlene Skolnick, eds. (Norwood, N.J.: Lawrence Erlbaum Associates, Inc., 1998), pp. 56–57.

53. Kathleen Sylvester, *Listening to Families: The Role of Values in Shaping Effective Social Policy* (New York: Carnegie Corporation of New York, 2000), p. 3.

54. For a full discussion of the history of child-care advocacy, see Sally S. Cohen, *Championing Child Care* (New York: Columbia University Press, 2001).

55. Amy Dombro and Patty Bryan, *Sharing the Caring: How to Find the Right Child Care and Make It Work for You and Your Child* (New York: Simon and Schuster, 1991), pp. 13–14.

56. Mona Harrington, *Care and Equality: Inventing a New Family Politics* (New York: Knopf, 1999), p. 114.

57. "The Parent Vote: Moms and Dads Up for Grabs," Web site of the National Parenting Association, <www.parentsunite.org>, November 2000.

58. *Women's Voices 2000* (Washington, D.C.: Center for Policy Alternatives and Lifetime Television, 2000), p. 3.

59. Barbara Bowman, M. Suzanne Donovan, and M. Susan Burns, eds., *Eager to Learn: Educating Our Preschoolers* (Washington, D.C.: National Academy Press, 2000), Executive Summary, p. 2.

60. National Institute of Child Health and Human Development, "The Study of Early Child Care" (Washington, D.C., April, 1998), Pub. 98-4318, April 1998, pp. 1–24.

61. S. Peisner-Feinberg et al., "The Children of The Cost, Quality, and Child Outcomes Study Go to School," Executive Summary (Washington, D.C.: National Institute of Early Child Development and Education, June 1999), p. 1.

62. The Carolina Abecedarian Project, Executive Summary, University of North Carolina Web site, <www.fpg.unc.edu/~abc/>, October 31, 1999.

63. Mary B. Larner, Lorraine Zippiroli, and Richard E. Behrman, "When School is Out: Analysis and Recommendations," in *The Future of Children: When School is Out*, Richard E. Behrman, ed., Vol. 9, No. 2 (Los Altos, Calif.: The David and Lucile Packard Foundation, Fall 1999), p. 16.

64. Lorie Dorfman and Katie Woodruff, *Child Care Coverage in U.S. Newspapers*, Issue 7 (Berkeley, Calif.: Berkeley Media Studies Group, May 1999), p. 9.

65. *A Nation of Spectators: How Civic Disengagement Weakens America and What We Can Do About It—The Final Report of the National Commission on Civic Renewal* (College Park, Md.: University of Maryland, 2000), p. 6.

66. "What Is the Purpose of Connect America?" overview document, The Points of Light Foundation Web site, <www.pointsoflight.org>, February 3, 2000.

67. Ibid.

68. "Public Attitudes Toward Community, Citizenship and National Service," conducted for *Blueprint* by Mark Penn, May 11, 1999, Web site, <www.servenet.org/resources/research/blueprint.php3>, March 30, 2000.

69. "Giving and Volunteering in the United States: Findings from a National Survey," Independent Sector Web site, <www.independentsector.org>, June 3, 2000.

70. "Working Together: Community Involvement in America, A Summary of Recent Research," League of Women Voters Web site, <www.lwv.org>, March 20, 2000, p. 5.

71. Michael Sherraden, *Assets and the Poor: A New American Welfare Policy* (Armonk, N.Y.: M.E. Sharpe, 1991), pp. 3–7.

72. Larry W. Beeferman, "Asset Development Policy: The New Opportunity," Asset Development Institute, Center on Hunger and Policy, Heller School of Social Policy and Management, Brandeis University, Waltham, Mass., Web site, <www.centeronhunger.org/adipubs.html>, 2001.

Chapter Two

1. *Proceedings of the White House Conference on Child Care*, Washington, D.C., October 23, 1997, p. 9.

2. Sonya Michel, *Children's Interests/Mothers' Rights: The Shaping of America's Child Care Policy* (New Haven: Yale University Press, 1999), p. 20.

3. Ibid., p. 40.

4. Barbara Beatty, "The Politics of Preschool Advocacy: Lessons from Three Pioneering Organizations" in Carol J. DeVita and Rachel Mosher-Williams, *Who Speaks for America's Children?* (Washington, D.C.: The Urban Institute, September 2001), p. 167; Barbara Beatty, *Preschool Education in America: The Culture of Young Children from the Colonial Era to the Present* (New Haven: Yale University Press, 1995).

5. Gilbert Y. Steiner, *The Children's Cause* (Washington, D.C.: The Brookings Institution, 1976), pp. 120–21, citing *Proceedings of the Conference on the Care of Dependent Children*, January 25–26, 1909 (Washington, D.C.: Government Printing Office) p. 192.

6. Elizabeth Rose, *A Mother's Job: The History of Day Care, 1890–1960* (New York: Oxford University Press, 1999), pp. 74–75.

7. Steiner, *The Children's Cause*, p. 122.

8. Beatty, *The Politics of Preschool Advocacy*, p. 169.

9. Personal correspondence with Sonya Michel, June 14, 2002.

10. Steiner, *The Children's Cause*, pp. 16–17.

11. Edward F. Zigler and Mary E. Lang, *Child Care Choices: Balancing the Needs of Children, Families, and Society* (New York: Free Press, 1991), pp. 34–35.

12. Steiner, *The Children's Cause*, pp. 16–17.

13. Ibid., pp. 17–18.

14. Ibid., p. 20.

15. Zigler and Lang, *Child Care Choices*, p. 35.

16. Emily D. Cahan, *Past Caring: A History of U.S. Preschool Care and Education for the Poor, 1820–1965* (New York: National Center for Children in Poverty, Columbia University, 1989), p. 46.

17. Michel, *Children's Interest/Mothers' Rights*, pp. 174, 177.

18. Ibid., p. 209.

19. Ibid., pp. 210, 226.

20. Ibid., pp. 219–20.

21. Mary Jo Bane and David Ellwood, *Welfare Realities: From Rhetoric to Reform* (Cambridge: Harvard University Press, 1994), pp. 12, 20.

22. Edward Zigler and Susan Muenchow, *Head Start: The Inside Story of America's Most Successful Educational Experiment* (New York: Basic Books, 1992), p. 123.

23. Steiner, *The Children's Cause*, p. 112.

24. Ibid., p. 115. Kilpatrick's column is reprinted in the *Congressional Record*, daily ed., December 2, 1971, p. E12897.

25. Ibid., p. 113. The text of the president's veto message (H.Doc. 92-48) is contained in *Congressional Record*, daily ed., December 10, 1971, pp. S21129–30.

26. Alfred J. Kahn and Sheila Kamerman, *Child Care: Facing the Hard Choices* (Dover, Mass.: Auburn House, 1987), p. 3.

27. "What Price Day Care?" *Newsweek*, September 10, 1984, p. 14.

28. *Child Care and Development Block Grant: First Annual Report to the Congress on State Program Services and Expenditures* (Washington, D.C., U.S. Department of Health and Human Services, Administration for Children and Families, Child Care Bureau, 1995), p. 5.

29. Ibid., p. x.

30. For further details on child-care provisions in the Personal Responsibility and Work Opportunity Reconciliation Act of 1996, see "A Summary of Key Child Care Provisions of H.R. 3734: The Personal Responsibility and Work Opportunity Reconciliation Act of 1996" (Washington, D.C.: Center for Law and Social Policy, August 1996).

31. "Child Care Bureau Mission" fact sheet, Child Care Bureau (Washington, D.C.: U.S. Department of Health and Human Services, 1995).

32. For a full discussion, see John T. Bruer, *The Myth of the First Three Years: The New Understanding of Early Brain Development and Lifelong Learning* (New York: Free Press, 1999).

33. "Proceedings of the White House Conference on Child Care," pp. 76–77.

34. Governor Bill Clinton and Senator Al Gore, *Putting People First* (New York: Times Books, 1992), p. 101.

35. *Proceedings of the White House Conference on Child Care*, p. 12.

36. Ibid, p. 42.

37. "President Clinton Announces Child Care Initiative," fact sheet, January 7, 1998.

38. "Mrs. Bush's Remarks Before The Senate Committee on Health, Education, Labor and Pensions, January 24, 2002," Web site, <www.whitehouse.gov/firstlady/news-speeches/fl20020124.html>.

39. *The President's State of the Union Address*, January 29, 2002, Web site, <www.whitehouse.gov/news/releases/2002/01/20020129-11.html>.

40. "Working Towards Independence," Executive Summary of the administration's welfare policy, February 27, 2002, White House Web site, <www.whitehouse. gov/news/releases/2002/02/welfare-reform-announcement-book.html>.

41. Testimony of Jack P. Shonkoff, M.D., before the U.S. Senate Committee on Health, Education, Labor, and Pensions, Washington, D.C., February 12, 2002, p. 3.

42. "Early Childhood Education Initiative," White House Web site, <www. whitehouse.gov/infocus/earlychildhood/> April 2, 2002.

43. Anne E. Kornblat, Globe Staff, "Bush, Kennedy Work on Preschool Plan, Quiet Cooperation Despite Tax Dispute," *The Boston Globe*, January 22, 2002, p. A2.

44. "Kennedy–Voinovich Early Care and Education Act" press statement, office of Senator Edward M. Kennedy, Washington, D.C., April 2, 2002.

45. Statement of Senator Kennedy at the introduction of Senate Bill 2566, The Early Care and Education Act, 107th Cong., 2nd sess., May 23, 2002, referred to the Senate Committee on Health, Education, Labor, and Pensions. Office of Senator Kennedy Web site, <http://Kennedy.senate.gov/kennedy/statements/02/05/2002524312.html>, May 24, 2002.

Chapter Three

Epigraph: National Research Council and Institute of Medicine, *From Neurons to Neighborhoods: The Science of Early Childhood Development*, Jack P. Shonkoff and Deborah A. Phillips, eds. (Washington, D.C.: National Academy Press, 2000), p. 297.

1. National Research Council and Institute of Medicine, *From Neurons to Neighborhoods: The Science of Early Childhood Development*, Jack P. Shonkoff and Deborah A. Phillips, eds. (Washington, D.C.: National Academy Press, 2000), p. 297.

2. Based on data from 1999 National Household Survey. Unpublished tabulations prepared by Donald J. Yarosz, National Institute for Early Education Research (New Brunswick, N.J.: Rutgers University, 2002).

3. The Urban Institute, National Survey of American Families, 1999, unpublished tables (Washington, D.C.: February 2002). Figure from Sonenstein et al., "Primary Child Care Arrangements of Employed Parents: Findings from the 1999 National Survey of America's Families," Occasional Paper No. 59 (Washington, D.C.: The Urban Institute, June, 2002), p. 4.

4. Barbara Beatty, "The Politics of Preschool Advocacy: Lessons from Three Pioneering Organizations" in Carol J. DeVita and Rachel Mosher-Williams, *Who Speaks for America's Children?* (Washington, D.C.: The Urban Institute, September, 2001), pp. 165–190.

5. Emily D. Cahan, *Past Caring: A History of U.S. Preschool Care and Education for the Poor, 1820–1965* (New York: National Center for Children in Poverty, 1989), p. 48.

6. Irving Lazar and Richard B. Darlington, *Lasting Effects after Preschool*, DHEW (OHDS) 79-30178 (Washington, D.C.: U.S. Department of Health, Education and Welfare), 1978), p. 3.

7. W. Steven Barnett, "Benefit-Cost Analysis of Preschool Education: Findings from a 25-Year Follow-up," *American Journal of Orthopsychiatry*, Vol. 63, No. 4 (1993), pp. 500–508; and Lynn A. Karoly et al., *Investing in Our Children: What We Know and Don't Know About the Cost and Benefits of Early Childhood Interventions* (Santa Monica, Calif.: Rand Corporation, 1998).

8. Donald J. Hernandez, "Changing Demographics: Past and Future Demands for Early Childhood Programs," in *The Future of Children: Long-Term Outcomes of Early Childhood Programs*, Richard E. Behrman, ed., Vol. 5, No. 3 (Los Altos, Calif.: The David and Lucile Packard Foundation, Winter 1995), p. 147, Fig. 1.

9. Deanna S. Gomby, Mary B. Larner, Carol Stevenson, Eugene Lewit, and Richard E. Behrman, "Long-Term Outcomes: Analysis and Recommendations," in *The Future of Children: Long-Term Outcomes of Early Childhood Programs*, Richard E. Behrman, ed., Vol. 5, No. 3 (Los Altos, Calif.: The David and Lucile Packard Foundation, Winter 1995), p. 19.

10. Carnegie Corporation of New York, *Starting Points: Meeting the Needs of Our Youngest Children* (New York, 1994), pp. xiv–xvii, 7–9.

11. National Institute of Child Health and Human Development, *The NICHD Study of Early Child Care*, NIH Pub. 98-4318 (April 1998), p. 5.

12. Ibid., p. 15.

13. Suzanne Helburn and the Cost, Quality and Child Outcomes Study Team, *Cost, Quality and Child Outcomes in Child Care Centers, Public Report*, 2d ed. (Denver: University of Colorado, Economics Department, 1995), p. 1.

14. Ellen Galinsky, Carollee Howes, Susan Kantos, and Marybeth Shinn, *The Study of Children in Family Child Care and Relative Care* (New York: Families and Work Institute, 1994), p. 4.

15. NICHD Early Child Care Research Network (2000), abstract, "The Relation of Child Care to Cognitive and Language Development," <http://public.rti.org/secc/abstracts.cfm?>, June 14, 2002.

16. S. Peisner-Feinberg et al., *The Children of the Cost, Quality and Outcomes Study Go to School*, Executive Summary, 1999, <www.fpg.unc.edu/~NCEDLPAGEScqes.htm>.

17. The Carolina Abecedarian Project Web site, <www.fpg.unc.edu/~abc>, 7/01/02.

18. National Commission on Children, *Beyond Rhetoric: A New American Agenda for Children and Families* (Washington, D.C.: National Commission on Children, 1991), pp. 48–49.

19. Sue Bredekamp and Carol Copple, eds., *Developmentally Appropriate Practice in Early Childhood Programs, rev. ed.* (Washington, D.C.: National Association for the Education of Young Children, 1997), pp. 10–15.

20. National Research Council and Institute of Medicine, *From Neurons to Neighborhoods*, Shonkoff and Phillips, eds., pp. 1–15.

21. The National Head Start Association, *Fulfilling the Promise: Report of the Head Start 2010 National Advisory Panel* (Alexandria, Va., 2000), p. 1.

22. Nancy Duff Campbell, Judith C. Appelbaum, Karin Martinson, and Emily Martin, *Be All That We Can Be: Lessons from the Military for Improving Our Nation's Child Care System* (Washington, D.C.: National Women's Law Center, April 2000), pp. 2–10.

23. Ibid., p. 1.

24. "DOD—Making a Difference in Child Care: Lessons Learned While Building the Military Child Development System" (Washington, D.C.: U.S. Department of Defense, n.d.), p. 2.

25. Gail L. Zellman and Ann S. Johnson, *Examining the Implementation and Outcomes of the Military Child Care Act of 1989* (Arlington, Va.: Rand National Defense Research Institute, 1998).

26. Campbell, Appelbaum, Martinson, and Martin, *Be All That We Can Be*, pp. 11–19.

27. Ibid.

28. Ibid.

29. Ibid.

30. Personal communication with Linda Smith, former director of family policy, Department of Defense, Washington, D.C., December 2000.

31. "Early Childhood Education and Care: International Perspectives," testimony of Sheila B. Kamerman, Compton Foundation Centennial Professor, Columbia University School of Social Work, and Director, Columbia University Institute for Child and Family Policy, to the U.S. Senate Committee on Health, Education, Labor, and Pensions, Washington, D.C., March 27, 2001, p. 2.

32. Ibid., p. 4.

33. Ibid., p. 2.

34. Sarane S. Boocock, W. Steven Barnett, and Ellen Frede, "The Long-Term Outcomes of Early Childhood Programs in Other Nations: Lessons for Americans," *Young Children*, Vol. 56, No. 5 (Washington, D.C.: National Association for the Education of Young Children, September, 2001), p. 44.

35. Personal correspondence with Gwen Morgan, June 26, 2002.

36. American Public Health Association and American Academy of Pediatrics, *National Health and Safety Performance Standards: Guidelines for Out-of-Home Child Care Programs* (Arlington, Va.: National Center for Education in Maternal and Child Health, supported by the Maternal and Child Health Bureau, U.S. Department of Health and Human Services, 1992).

37. U.S. Department of Health and Human Services, Maternal and Child Health Bureau, *Stepping Stones to Using Caring for Our Children: Protecting Children from Harm* (Denver: National Resource Center for Health and Safety in Child Care, 1997).

38. K. Alison Clarke-Stewart, "In Search of Consistencies in Child Care Research," in Deborah Phillips, ed., *Quality in Child Care: What Does Research Tell Us?* (Washington, D.C.: National Association for the Education of Young Children, 1987), p. 118.

39. Barbara Bowman, M. Suzanne Donovan, M. Susan Burns, eds., *Eager to Learn: Educating Our Preschoolers* (Washington, D.C.: National Academy Press, 2000), Executive Summary, pp. 6–7.

40. Scott Groginsky, Susan Robison, and Shelley Smith, *Making Child Care Better: State Initiatives* (Denver: National Conference of State Legislatures, 1999), p. 26.

41. National Association for the Education of Young Children, *Accreditation Criteria and Procedures* (Washington, D.C., 1998), p. 13.

42. National Association for the Education of Young Children Web site, <www.NAEYC.org>, April 18, 2000.

43. Marcy Whitebook, "NAEYC Accreditation as an Indicator of Program Quality: What Research Tells Us," in S. Bredekamp and B. Willer, eds., *NAEYC Accreditation: A Decade of Learning and the Years Ahead* (Washington, D.C.: National Association for the Education of Young Children, 1996), pp. 31–46.

44. Kathy Modigliani, "Promoting High-Quality Family Child Care," working paper, Quality 2000 Initiative (New Haven: Yale University), p. 1.

45. National Association for Family Child Care, "Fact Sheet on NAFCC and Accreditation," NAFCC Web site, <www.nafcc.org>, April 1999.

46. National Research Council and Institute of Medicine, *From Neurons to Neighborhoods*, Shonkoff and Phillips, eds., p. 7.

47. Emily Fenichel, Abbey Griffin, and Erica Lurie-Hurvitz, *Quality Care for Infants and Toddlers* (Vienna, Va.: National Child Care Information Center, U.S. Department of Health and Human Services, 1999), p. 11.

48. American Public Health Association and American Academy of Pediatrics, *National Health and Safety Performance Standards*, p. 8.

49. Sharon L. Kagan and Nancy E. Cohen, *Not by Chance: Creating an Early Care and Education System for America's Children* (New Haven: Bush Center in Child Development and Social Policy, Yale University, 1997), p. 26.

50. Bowman, Donovan, and Burns, eds., *Eager to Learn*, p. 10.

51. Lilian G. Katz, "Another Look at What Young Children Should Be Learning" fact sheet, ERIC DIGEST, EDP-PS-99-5 (Champaign, Ill.: Clearinghouse on Elementary and Early Childhood Education, June 1999).

52. Sue Bredekamp, "Developmentally Appropriate Practice: The Early Childhood Teacher as Decisionmaker," in Bredekamp and Copple, eds., *Developmentally Appropriate Practice in Early Childhood Programs*, pp. 33–52.

53. Personal communication with Diane Dodge, President, Teaching Strategies, Inc., Washington, D.C., August 2000.

54. *Accreditation Criteria and Procedures of the National Association for the Education of Young Children* (Washington, D.C., 1998), pp. 22–23.

55. Bowman, Donovan, and Burns, eds., *Eager to Learn*, p. 6.

56. Karen Schulman, Helen Blank, and Danielle Ewen, *Seeds of Success: State Prekindergarten Initiatives 1998–1999* (Washington, D.C.: Children's Defense Fund, 1999), pp. 91–92.

57. Bowman, Donovan, and Burns, eds., *Eager to Learn*, p. 7.

58. Campbell, Appelbaum, Martinson, and Martin, *Be All That We Can Be*, pp. 18–19.

59. Douglas R. Powell, "Preparing Early Childhood Professionals to Work with Families," in *New Teachers for a New Century: The Future of Early Childhood Professional Preparation* (Washington, D.C.: U.S. Department of Education, March 2000), p. 62.

60. "What Does the Latest Research About Fathers Tell Us?" Child Trends Web site, <http://www.childtrends.org/n-aboutfathers.asp>, June 15, 2002.

61. For further examples of involvement by fathers in early childhood, see James Levine, Dennis Murphy, and Sherrill Wilson, *Getting Men Involved: Strategies for Early Childhood Programs* (New York: Scholastic, 1993).

62. Judy Pfannenstiel, *School Entry Assessment Project: Report of Findings for Missouri Department of Elementary and Secondary Education* (Overland Park, Kans.:

Research and Training Associates, Inc., for Missouri Department of Elementary and Secondary Education, 1999), p. iii.

63. "Abstract of Early SESS Findings" (Seattle, Washington: The Casey Family Programs, March 2002).

64. "Frequently Asked Questions About Military Child Care," <http://military~childrenandyouth.calib.com/mm-fag.htm>.

65. Personal communication with Helen Taylor, Associate Commissioner, Head Start Bureau, U.S. Department of Health and Human Services, April 2000.

66. Barbara Warman, "Trends in State Accreditation Policies," *Young Children* (Washington, D.C.: National Association for the Education of Young Children, September 1998), pp. 52–55.

67. Schulman, Blank, and Ewen, *Seeds of Success*, p. 186.

68. Anne W. Mitchell, "Historical Perspectives on Early Childhood Care and Education in New York," a paper prepared for the Early Care and Education for All working conference, Rensselaerville, N.Y., November, 2001. Available at <http://www.ceceny.org/publications.php>. Updated by Anne Mitchell, February 2002.

69. Testimony of Olivia Golden, Assistant Secretary, Administration for Children and Families, to the U.S. House of Representatives Government Reform and Oversight Committee, Human Resources Subcommittee, Washington, D.C., February 19, 1998, p. 2.

70. *The Statement of the Advisory Committee on Services for Families with Infants and Toddlers* (Washington, D.C.: U.S. Department of Health and Human Services, September 1994), p. 13.

71. J. T. Bond and the Research and Evaluation Department of the Ewing Marion Kauffman Foundation, *Full Start: An Evaluation of a Head Start/Community Child Care Collaboration* (Kansas City, Mo.: Ewing Marion Kauffman Foundation, July 1998), pp. 1–3, 25.

72. "Why Smart Start: Needs and Challenges of Smart Start Communities" fact sheet (Raleigh: North Carolina Partnership for Children, 1999).

73. Schulman, Blank, and Ewen, *Seeds of Success*, p. 163.

74. Kelly Maxwell, Donna Bryant, and Shari Miller-Johnson, *A Six County Study of the Effects of Smart Start Child Care on Kindergarten Entry Skills* (Chapel Hill: Frank Porter Graham Child Development Center, University of North Carolina, September 1999), Executive Summary, p. 14.

75. Rachel Schumacher, Mark H. Greenberg, and Joan Lombardi, *State Initiatives to Promote Early Learning: Next Steps in Coordinating Subsidized Child Care, Head Start and State Prekindergarten* (Washington, D.C.: Center for Law and Social Policy, 2001), pp. 77–95.

76. For more information on community-wide planning efforts, see Laurie Miller, Atelia Melaville, and Helen Blank, *Bringing it Together: State Driven Community Early Childhood Initiatives* (Washington, D.C.: The Children's Defense Fund), 2002.

77. "What Is Success By 6®?" fact sheet (Alexandria, Va.: United Way of America, n.d.).

78. "Keep on Moving: 1999 Annual Report" (Boston: Associated Day Care Services, 1999), p. 1.

Chapter Four

Epigraph: Lisbeth B. Schorr with Daniel Schorr, *Within Our Reach: Breaking the Cycle of Disadvantage* (New York: Anchor Press, 1988), p. xx.

1. Laura Sessions Stepp, "Keeping Kids Occupied After School," *Washington Post,* October 21, 1999, p. C4.

2. Michelle Seligson, "Foreword," in Marlene A. Bumgarner, *Working with School Age Children* (Mountain View, Calif.: Mayfield Publishing Company, 1999), p. xi.

3. Stepp, "Keeping Kids Occupied After School."

4. The Afterschool Alliance, "Afterschool Alert: Poll Report No. 4 (Washington, D.C.: July/August 2001), pp. 1–2.

5. "Fact Sheet on School Age Children's Out of School Time" (Wellesley, Mass.: National Institute on Out of School Time, Center for Research on Women), January 2000.

6. "After School Fact Sheet" developed by Jane Quinn for The Children's Aid Society in *School Age Review, The Journal of the National School Age Care Alliance,* No. 4 (Fall 2001), pp. 20–21.

7. James Traub, "What No School Can Do," *New York Times Magazine,* January 16, 2000, p. 52.

8. U.S. Department of Education and U.S. Department of Justice, "Working for Children and Families: Safe and Smart Programs" (Washington, D.C., April 2000), p. 5 (citing Bureau of Labor Statistics, 1997 Annual Average Figures from the Current Population Survey, U.S. Department of Labor, Washington, D.C.).

9. U.S. Department of Education and U.S. Department of Justice, *Working for Children and Families: Safe and Smart After School Programs* (Washington, D.C.: Government Printing Office, April 2000), p. 6.

10. Jeffrey Capizzano, Kathryn Tout, and Gina Adams, *The Patterns of Child Care for School Age Children with Employed Mothers* (Washington, D.C.: The Urban Institute, September 2000), pp. viii, 6, 8. Because the National Survey of America's Families measures "regular" child-care arrangements—those arrangements used at least once a week for the most recent month—a certain percentage of parents reporting "no care" for their children also may be using a week-to-week patchwork of child-care arrangements that would not fall under the definition of regular care.

11. Personal communication with Beth M. Miller, National Institute on Out of School Time, September 2000.

12. Judith Bender, Charles H. Flatter, and Jeanette Sorrentino, *Half A Childhood: Quality Programs for Out-of-School Hours,* 2d ed. (Nashville: School Age Notes, 2000), p. 1.

13. Michelle Seligson, Andrea Genser, Ellen Gannett, and Wendy Gray, *School-Age Child Care: A Policy Report* (Wellesley, Mass.: School-Age Child Care Project, 1983), p. 21.

14. Ibid., pp. 21–22.

15. Ibid., pp. 15–19.

16. Alice H. Hall, "Interview with Michelle Seligson," *School Age Review: The Journal of the National School-Age Care Alliance,* No. 1 (Spring 2000), p. 35.

17. "A Letter from the President of NSACA, Eddie Locklear," *School-Age Review: The Journal of the National School-Age Care Alliance,* No. 3 (Spring 2001), p. 2.

18. *Standards for Quality School-Age Care* (Alexandria, Va.: National Association of Elementary School Principals in collaboration with Wellesley College School-Age Child Care Project, 1993), p. 1.

19. Carnegie Council on Adolescent Development, *A Matter of Time* (Carnegie Corporation of New York, 1992), p. 79.

20. Patricia Seppanen et al., *National Study of Before and After School Programs*, prepared for the U.S. Department of Education (developed by RMC Research Corporation, Portsmouth, N.H.; the Wellesley College School Age Child Care Project; and Mathematica Policy Research, 1993), pp. 15, 157.

21. U.S. Department of Education and U.S. Department of Justice, *Safe and Smart: Making the After-School Hours Work for Kids* (Washington, D.C.: GPO, 1998), p. 6.

22. "Expand Learning: Making Every Minute Meaningful: Results of a 1999 Survey by The National Governors' Association, Center for Best Practice" (Washington, D.C.: National Governors' Association, n.d.).

23. 21st Century Community Learning Centers Program Grant Application Package, CDFA #84.287, Office of Educational Research and Improvement (Washington, D.C.: U.S. Department of Education), p. 7.

24. Afterschool Alliance, "America's Afterschool Funding Gap Grows," <www.afterschoolalliance.org>, July 2001.

25. Barbara Hanson Langford, *State Legislative Investments in School Age Children and Youth* (Washington, D.C.: The Finance Project, June 2001). A state-by-state catalogue can be found on pp. 31–67.

26. Mary B. Larner, Lorraine Zippiroli, and Richard E. Behrman, "When School Is Out: Analysis and Recommendations," in *The Future of Children: When School Is Out*, Richard E. Behrman, ed., Vol. 9, No. 2 (Los Altos, Calif.: The David and Lucile Packard Foundation, Fall 1999), p. 16.

27. Jodie Morse, "Mo' Time, Mo' Better Schools," <www.time.com/time/education/>, January 20, 2001.

28. Deborah Lowe Vandell and Hsiu-chih Su, "Research in Review: Child Care and School-Age Children," *Young Children*, Vol. 54, No. 6 (November 1999), p. 62.

29. Slide presentation by Terry K. Peterson, Counselor to the Secretary, U.S. Department of Education, to the National Academy of Sciences, Washington, D.C., October 21, 1999.

30. Beth M. Miller, Susan O'Connor, Sylvia W. Sirignano, and Pamela Joshi, *"I Wish the Kids Didn't Watch So Much TV": Out-of-School Time in Three Low-Income Communities* (Wellesley, Mass.: Center for Research on Women, 1996), p. 7.

31. National Child Care Information Center, "Child Care Bureau Focuses on School Age Care," *Child Care Bulletin*, Issue 2 (March/April 1995), p. 1. Tracey Ballas referred to school-age child care as the "new neighborhood" in her presentation to a leadership institute sponsored by the Child Care Bureau, U.S. Department of Health and Human Services, January 1995.

32. Jacquelynne S. Eccles, "The Development of Children 6–14," in *The Future of Children: When School Is Out*, Richard E. Behrman, ed., Vol. 9, No. 2 (Los Altos, Calif.: The David and Lucile Packard Foundation, Fall 1999), pp. 30–44. Sources regarding Erickson's stages of development are taken from K. S. Berger, *The Developing Person through the Life Span* (New York: Worth Publishers, 1988), p. 37.

33. National Research Council and Institute of Medicine, *Community Programs to Promote Youth Development*, Jacquelynne Eccles and Jennifer Appleton Gootman, eds. (Washington, D.C.: National Academy Press, 2002), p. 4. In this report, The National Research Council examined youth programs that target young people ages ten to eighteen.

34. Ibid.

35. "Positions for Youth: Public Policy Statements of the National Collaboration for Youth" (Washington, D.C., 1999), p. 3.

36. National Research Council and Institute of Medicine, Eccles and Appleton Gootman, eds., pp. 6–7.

37. Beth M. Miller, "Power of the Hours: The Changing Context of After School," *School Age Review: The Journal of the National School-Age Care Alliance*, No. 2 (Fall 2000), pp. 18–23.

38. Carnegie Council on Adolescent Development, *Turning Points: Preparing American Youth for the 21st Century, A Report of the Carnegie Task Force on the Education of Young Adolescents* (Carnegie Corporation of New York, June 1989), p. 15.

39. Howard Gardner, *Frame of Mind: The Theory of Multiple Intelligences* (New York: Basic Books, 1983).

40. "Evaluating After-School Care; Labor and Population Program," Rand Research Brief, Rand Web site, <www.rand.org/publications/rb/rb2505/>, March 9, 2002.

41. Healthy Weight 2010: Objectives for Achieving and Maintaining a Healthy Population" Washington, D.C.: American Obesity Association, January 2000), p. 9.

42. "Afterschool and Technology Training: Afterschool Alert Issue Brief" of the Afterschool Alliance, Issue Brief No. 5—21st Century Community Learning Centers Version (Washington, D.C.: August 2001), p. 1.

43. These concepts were presented by Karen Pittman at the Summer Seminar for After-School Program Professionals, Wellesley College, National Institute on Out-of-School Time, July 9–12, 2000. They are based on numerous publications, including Karen Pittman, Merita Irby, Joel Tolman, Nicole Yohalem, and Thaddeus Ferber, "Preventing Problems, Promoting Development, Encouraging Engagement: Competing Priorities or Inseparable Goals?" (Takoma Park, Md.: The Forum for Youth Investment, International Youth Foundation, September 2001); a working paper based on the 1996 working paper by Karen Johnson Pittman and Merita Irby, "Preventing Problems or Promoting Development: Competing Priorities or Inseparable Goals (Takoma Park, Md.: International Youth Foundation, 1996); and Karen Pittman, Merita Irby, and Thaddeus Ferber, "Unfinished Business: Further Reflections on a Decade of Promoting Youth Development" (Takoma Park, Md.: The Forum for Youth Investment, International Youth Foundation, 2000).

44. Marian Wright Edelman, *Lanterns: A Memoir of Mentors* (Boston: Beacon Press, 1999), p. x.

45. Wendy Nadel, *The Web of Support: Providing Safe, Nurturing, Learning Environments during Out-of-School Time* (Westport, Conn.: Save the Children, n.d.), pp. 135–37.

46. General Colin L. Powell, America's Promise Web site, <www.americaspromise. org>, September 19, 2000.

47. Dale Borman Fink, *Making a Place for Kids with Disabilities*" (Westport, Conn.: Bergin and Garvey, 2001), p. 9.

48. Atelia Melaville, *Learning Together: The Developing Field of School-Community Initiatives* (Washington, D.C.: Institute for Educational Leadership and National Center for Community Education, September 1998), p. 6.

49. Personal communication with Linda Zang, President of the National School Age Child Care Alliance, March 2, 2002.

50. National Governors' Association, "Making Every Moment Meaningful: Results of a 1999 Survey by NGA" (Washington, D.C., n.d.), pp. 4–5.

51. Joy Dryfoos, "The Role of the School in Children's Out of School Time," in *The Future of Children: When School Is Out*, Richard E. Behrman, ed., Vol. 9, No. 2 (Los Altos, Calif.: The David and Lucile Packard Foundation, Fall 1999), p. 131.

52. Andrea Warren, "21st Century Community Learning Centers: Expanding Educational Opportunities," *Afterschool Makes the Grade: In Focus* Vol. 2, No. 3 (Flint, Mich.: The Charles Stewart Mott Foundation), September, 1999, pp. 4–5.

53. Matia Finn-Stevenson and Edward Zigler, *Schools of the 21st Century: Linking Child Care and Education* (Boulder, Colo.: Westview Press, 1999), pp. ix, 78.

54. Constancia Warren, Prudence Brown, and Nicholas Freudenberg, "Evaluation of the New York City Beacons: Summary of Phase I Finding," Academy for Educational Development Web site, <www.aed.org>, November 22, 1999; U.S. Department of Education and U.S. Department of Justice, *Safe and Smart*, p. 41.

55. "The After-School Corporation: Application for Round IV Funding" (New York: The After-School Corporation, 1999), p. 1. Updated by Mary Bleiberg, Director of Policy and Planning, The After-School Corporation, April 2002.

56. Personal communication with Mary Bleiberg, The After-School Corporation, April 2002.

57. "L.A.'s BEST After School Enrichment Program 1997–98 Annual Report" (Los Angeles: Office of the Mayor and Los Angeles Unified School District), pp. 4, 6.

58. Personal communication with Tom Campbell, YMCA of the USA, September 2000.

59. "Project Learn: A Generation-Changing Program," presentation by Julian Savage, Senior Director of Education Programs, Boys and Girls Clubs of America, December 14, 1999.

60. Mark Ouellette, "Extra Learning Opportunities That Encourage Healthy Lifestyles," National Governors' Association, Center for Best Practices, Washington, D.C., January 25, 2000, p. 6, NGA Web site, <wwwnga.org/Pubs/Issuebriefs/2000/0001/25ELO.asp>, March 10, 2000.

61. Council of Chief State School Officers, *Extended Learning Initiative: Opportunities and Implementation Challenges* (Washington, D.C.: Council of Chief State School Officers, May 2000), pp. 8–15.

62. Joyce A. Shortt, "Building Communities in These Times," *Spotlight on Most*, Vol. 2, No. 2 (April 1997), pp. 1, 6.

63. "The MOST Initiative: Making the Most of-Out-of-School Time," Web site of the National Institute on Out-of-School Time, <www.NIOST.org>, November 21, 2000.

64. *Time After School, The After-School Corporation Report on Activities* (New York: The After-School Corporation, April 2001), p. 22.

65. Heather B. Weiss and M. Elena Lopez, "An Elementary Lesson: It's Community that Keeps Students in School," *Boston Globe*, September 10, 2000, p. 4F.

66. Michelle Seligson, Kathryn A. Wheeler, and Patricia Stahl, with Mary E. Casey and Jennifer Ekert, "Redefining Caregiver-Child Relationships in After-School Programs: Final Report on Phase One, Bringing Yourself to Work," *Executive Summary* (Wellesley, Mass.: National Institute on Out-of-School Time, February 1999), p. 1.

67. Janette Roman, ed., NSACA *Standards for Quality School-Age Care* (Boston: National School-Age Child Care Alliance, 1998), back cover.

68. Joan Costley, "Building a Professional Development System That Works for the Field of Out-of-School Time" (Wellesley, Mass.: National Institute on Out-of-School Time, November 1998), p. 8.

69. Gwen Morgan, "Credentialing in Out-of-School Time Programs," (Wellesley, Mass.: National Institute on Out-of-School Time, November 1998), p. 14

70. Ellen Gannett, Judy Nee, and Darci Smith, "Professional Development Systems: The State of the States," *School Age Review: The Journal of the National School Age Care Alliance*, No. 3 (Spring 2001), pp. 26–31.

71. Robert Halpern, "After-School Programs for Low-Income Children: Promise and Challenges," in Behrman, ed., The *Future of Children: When School Is Out*, p. 88.

72. Linda Sisson, "Advancing and Recognizing Quality," *School Age Review: The Journal of the National School-Age Care Alliance*, No. 1 (Spring 2000), pp. 6–7; and personal communication with Ellen Gannett, Joyce Shortt, Linda Zang, and Susan O'Connor, March 2002.

73. Roman, ed., NSACA *Standards for Quality School-Age Care*, pp. 1–8.

74. Personal communication with Louise Stoney, Principal, Stoney Associates, September 2000.

75. "Advancing and Recognizing Quality in After School," *School Age Review: The Journal of the National School Age Care Alliance*, No. 4 (Fall 2001), p. 32.

76. "Afterschool Outcomes" summary, Afterschool Alliance Web site, <www.afterschoolalliance.org/after_out.cfm>, March 16, 2002.

77. *Time After School*, pp. 36–40.

Chapter Five

Epigraph: "Interview with Craig Kielburger, Founder of Free the Children," by John Terry and Donna Woonteiler, CYD *Journal*, Vol. 1, No. 1 (Winter 2000), pp. 15–19. ("Free the Children" later was changed to "Kids Can Free the Children.")

1. Remarks by Patty Siegel, Executive Director, California Child Care Resource and Referral Network, White House Conference on Child Care, Washington, D.C., October 1997.

2. Personal communication with Yasmina Vinci, Executive Director, National Association of Child Care Resource and Referral Agencies, April 2000.

3. Bananas Web site, <www.bananasinc.org>, April 2000.

4. "Parent Services Project," Parent Services Project brochure (Fairfax, Calif., 1999).

5. "Just in Time Care," Family and Workplace Connection, Wilmington, Del., Web site, <www.familyandworkplace.org/intime.htm>, June 17, 2002.

6. Ann Collins and Barbara Carlson, *Child Care by Kith and Kin—Supporting Family, Friends and Neighbors Caring for Children* (New York: National Center for Children in Poverty, 1998), pp. 5–6.

7. Personal correspondence with Toni Porter, Director, Institute for a Child Care Continuum, Bank Street College of Education, New York, April 2000.

8. For further information, see Tony Porter and Sena Rice, *Lessons Learned: Strategies for Working with Kith and Kin Caregivers* (New York: Bank Street College of Education, 2000).

9. Phyllis Stubbs-Wynn, ed., *Building Healthy Child Care Partnerships: Success Stories from Health Systems Development in Child Care Projects* (Denver: National Resource Center for Health and Safety in Child Care, 1998), p. 2.

10. "Missed Opportunities," *Yale Nursing Matters*, Vol. 1, Issue 2 (Spring 2000), p. 11.

11. Margaret S. Ulione and Angela A. Crowly, "Nurses as Child Care Health Consultants," *Healthy Child Care America Newsletter*, Vol. 1, No. 2 (September 1997), pp. 1, 4.

12. Stubbs-Wynn, ed., *Building Healthy Child Care Partnerships*, p. 16.

13. National Center for Children in Poverty, *Promoting the Emotional Well-Being of Children and Families: Using Mental Health Strategies to Move the Early Childhood Agenda and Promote School Readiness, a Policy Reprint* (New York: NCCP, n.d.), pp. 7, 9, 14.

14. Bernadette Knoblauch and Kathleen McLane, "An Overview of the Individuals with Disabilities Education Act Amendments of 1997, Update 1999," ERIC *Digest* E576 (Reston, Va.: ERIC Clearinghouse on Disabilities and Gifted Education, June 1999), p. 1.

15. "Child Care Settings and the Americans with Disabilities Act," *The Arc's Q & As*, #101–33 (Silver Spring, Md.: rev. April 1994), pp. 1–2, The Arc Web site, <http://thearc.org/faqs/ccql.html>.

16. "Collaborative Efforts Promote Inclusive Child Care in Colorado," *Child Care Bulletin*, Issue 5 (September/October 1995), <www.nccic.org>.

17. "Inclusive Child Care—Quality Child Care for ALL Children," *Child Care Bulletin*, Issue 21 (January/February 1999), p. 2.

18. Ibid., p. 1.

19. David A. Corsini, Steven Wisensale, and Grace-Ann Caruso, "Family Day Care: System Issues and Regulatory Models," *Young Children*, Vol. 43, No. 6 (September 1988), p. 17.

20. Child Welfare League of America, "Family Child Care System, A Model for Expanding Community Services," n.d., p. 1, CWLA Web site, <www.cwla.org>.

21. "National Family Child Care Network: Promising Practices Project" (Atlanta: Quality Care for Children, n.d.), pp. 1–2.

22. Jane Knitzer and Fida Adely, *The Role of Community Development Corporations in Promoting the Well-Being of Young Children* (New York: National Center for Children in Poverty, 2002), pp. 11–12.

23. "Oregon Family Child Care Network" brochure (Salem, Ore.: Oregon Family Child Care Network, n.d.).

24. Catherine Snow, Susan Burns, and Peg Griffin, *Preventing Reading Difficulties in Young Children* (Washington, D.C.: National Academy Press, 1998), pp. 8–9.

25. Joan Lombardi, "Promoting Language, Literacy, and a Love of Learning Makes a Difference," *Child Care Information Exchange*, No. 129 (September/October 1999), pp. 44–47.

26. "Infant/Toddler Project" brochure, Kansas Association of Child Care Resource and Referrals, August 2000.

27. Donna Hinkle, *School Involvement in Early Childhood* (Washington, D.C.: U.S. Department of Education, National Institute on Early Childhood Development and Education, July 2000), p. 28, and personal communication with the Maryland Committee for Children, April 2002.

28. Remarks of Thomas Taylor in *Child Care Bulletin*, Issue 22, National Child Care Information Center, n.d., p. 5.

29. *Who Gives and Who Gets: A Dialogue on Community and National Service: A Summary of Regional Dialogue, Seattle, January 1998* (Berkeley, Calif.: Grantmaker Forum on Community and National Service, September 1998), p. 6.

30. League of Women Voters, "Working Together: Community Involvement in America," League of Women Voters E-Library, <www.lwv.org>, March 30, 2000.

31. "AmeriCorps: Action for Children Today National Service Program" brochure (Washington, D.C.: National Association of Child Care Resource and Referral Agencies, Summer 2000), and personal communication with Jane Adams, NACCRRA, April 2002.

32. "Summary of AmeriCorps ACT Program Impacts" (Washington, D.C.: National Association of Child Care Resource and Referral Agencies, Summer 2000.

33. "Jumpstart Is," Jumpstart Web site, <www.jstart.org>, March 13, 2000.

34. "Jumpstart Today", <www.jstart.org>, October 30, 2000.

35. Robert Shumer and Charles Cook, "The Status of Service-Learning in the United States: Some Facts and Figures" (National Service Learning Clearinghouse, June 1999), p. 3.

36. *Making an Impact on Out-of-School Time: A Guide for the Corporation for National Service Programs Engaged in Afterschool, Summer and Weekend Activities for Young People* (Wellesley, Mass: National Institute on Out-of-School Time, and Washington, D.C.: Corporation for National Service, June 2000), Sec. 4, p. 3.

37. Corporation for National Service Web site, <www.cns.gov/learn>, November 2, 2000.

38. *Making an Impact on Out-of-School Time*, pp. 13–14, 17.

39. "The Parent Leadership Training Institute" brochure (Hartford: Connecticut Commission on Children, n.d.); and personal communication with Elaine Zimmerman, April 2002.

40. Personal communication with Elaine Zimmerman, October 2000.

41. "Parent Leadership Training Institute Graduates Leaders," *Hartford News*, July 7–14, 1999, p. 10.

42. "Parents Take the Lead: Seeking Input from Constituents," *ED: Early Developments—Outreach Bridges to Excellence*," Vol. 4, No. 3 (Winter 2000), pp. 10–12.

43. "The Spirit of Excellence Parent Empowerment Project" brochure (Washington, D.C.: National Black Child Development Institute, n.d.); and personal communications with Evelyn Moore and Andrea Young, July 1, 2002.

44. Personal communication with Elaine Fersh, Executive Director, Parents United for Child Care, November 13, 2000; and "Building Parent Power" (Boston: Parents United for Child Care, October 2000).

45. "Choices and Tradeoffs: PUCC's Statewide Parent Survey," in *Parent Power: The Newsletter of Parents United for Child Care*, Vol. 11, No. 11 (Spring 2000), p. 3. For the full report, see "Choices and Tradeoffs—The Parent Survey of Child Care in Massachusetts, a report for Parents United for Child Care by Randy Albelda and Carol Cosenza (Boston: University of Massachusetts, March 2000).

46. *Investing in Child Care: Challenges Facing Working Parents and the Private Sector Response* (Washington, D.C.: U.S. Department of the Treasury, 1998), p. vii.

47. "*Working Mother* Releases 'Best 100 Companies' List," *USA Today* Web site, <www.usatoday.com/careers/special/womstor16.htm>, November 12, 1999.

48. Testimony of Frank Doyle, Senior Vice President, General Electric, and member, Board of Trustees, The Committee for Economic Development, to the Joint Economic Committee of Congress, Subcommittee on Education and Health, Washington, D.C., February 26, 1990, pp. 1–2.

49. "Working Together to Accomplish What None of Us Can Afford to Do Alone" (Boston: WorkFamily Directions, n.d.), cover and p. 1.

50. Richard B. Stolley, "Chairman's Corner," *Child Care Action News*, Vol. 17, No. 6 (November/December 2000), p. 2.

51. Margaret Blood, "Reflections on Successful Legislative Advocacy for Children" in Margaret Blood and Melissa Ludtke, *Business Leaders as Legislative Advocates for Children*, Working Paper Series (New York: Foundation for Child Development, September 1999), p. 1.

52. Lea Grundy, Lissa Bell, and Netsy Firestein, "Labor's Role in Addressing the Child Care Crisis," Working Paper Series (New York: Foundation for Child Development, December 1999), p. 6.

53. "Pediatricians Make Significant Gains in Child Care Outreach," *Healthy Child Care America* (Fall 1999), p. 1.

54. Ibid., pp. 1 and 4.

55. Personal correspondence with Sanford Newman, February 3, 1999.

56. "From America's Front Line against Crime: A School and Youth Violence Prevention Plan" (Washington, D.C.: Fight Crime, Invest in Kids, n.d.), p. 4.

57. "Afterschool Programs Backed by Police Chiefs," *Denver Post*, November 1, 1999, p. A6.

58. "Every Child Deserves a Moral Start," Children's Defense Fund Web site, <www.childrensdefense.org/moral-children-sabbath.htm>, March 26, 2002.

59. For a detailed discussion of faith-based groups and child care, see "A Survey of Congregation Based Child Care in the United States" by Mary Bogle in *Sacred Places, Civic Purposes: Should Government Help Faith Based Charity?*, E. J. Dionne, Jr., and Ming Hsu Chen, eds. (Washington, D.C.: Brookings Institution Press, 2001), pp. 216–251.

60. Roger Neugebauer, "Religious Organizations Taking Proactive Role in Child Care," *Child Care Information Exchange*, No. 133 (May/June 2000), pp. 18–20.

61. Ibid.

62. *A Child at The Door: A Guidebook for Starting a Child Care Program in Your Church* (Raleigh: North Carolina Rural Economic Development Center Church Child Care Initiative, 2000).

63. "Worthy Wage Network," Center for the Child Care Workforce Web site, <www.ccw.org>, November 1, 2000.

64. *Older Americans 2000: Key Indicators of Well Being* (Washington, D.C.: Federal Interagency Forum on Aging Related Statistics, n.d.), p. xii.

65. Marc Freedman, *Prime Time: How Baby Boomers Will Revolutionize Retirement and Transform America* (New York: Public Affairs, 1999), pp. 16–17.

66. Eric Kingson, Jack Cornman, and Judith Kline Leavitt, *Strengthening the Social Compact: An Intergenerational Strategy* (Washington, D.C.: Generations United, n.d.), p. 5.

67. "Intergenerational Child Care" brochure, National Child Care Information Exchange for the U.S. Department of Health and Human Services, Child Care Bureau (Washington, D.C.: 1998).

68. "Fact Sheet: Grandparents and Other Relatives Raising Children: Challenges of Caring for the Second Family" (Washington, D.C.: Generations United, August 2000).

69. Kristin Smith, "Who's Minding the Kids? Child Care Arrangements," *Fall 1995 Current Population Reports*, P-70-70 (Washington, D.C.: U.S. Bureau of the Census, October 2000), p. 6. This includes primary, secondary, and tertiary child care arrangements for preschoolers.

70. "First-in-the-Nation GrandFamilies House—Open Summer 1998," *Together, The Generations United Newsletter*, Vol. 3, No. 3 (Summer 1998), p. 14.

71. "Chicago's Ambitious Child Care Plan Targets Kids in Grandparent Care," *Child Care Action News*, Vol. 17, No. 6 (November/December 2000), p. 5.

72. Sally Newman, Elizabeth Larkin, and Thomas Smith, *To Help Somebody's Child: Complementary Behaviors of Older and Younger Child Care Providers* (Pittsburgh: Generations Together, n.d.), p. 43.

73. "The Foster Grandparent Program," Generations United Web site, <www. generationsunited.org>, November 24, 2000.

74. Biographical sketch of Sally Newman distributed at the Ninth Family Reunion: Families and Seniors Across the Generations conference, Vanderbilt University, Nashville, Tenn., November 20, 2000.

75. Newman, Larkin, and Smith, *To Help Somebody's Child*.

76. Sally M. Newman, Karen Vander Ven, and Christopher R. Ward, *Guidelines for the Productive Employment of Older Adults in Child Care* (Washington, D.C.: National Association for the Education of Young Children, 1992), pp. 7–19.

77. Quoted in Newman, Larkin, and Smith, *To Help Somebody's Child*, p. 25, and videotape, *Old Friends Are the Best Friends: Intergenerational Child Care*" (Stanwood, Wash: Josephine Sunset Home, 1992).

78. "National Intergenerational Caucus of Early Childhood Professionals" brochure (Des Plains, Ill.: Oakton Community College, n.d.).

79. National Senior Service Corps, "Afterschool Activities," (Washington, D.C.: January 19, 2000), pp. 1–2.

80. Remarks by Robert Mayer at the Ninth Family Reunion.

81. "The Draft Final Report of the Intergenerational Shared Site Project, A Study of Co-Located Programs and Services for Children, Youth and Older Adults," *AARP* (Washington, D.C.: American Association of Retired Persons, n.d.), pp. v–vi.

82. Chad Graham, "Growing Care Trend Tries to Forge Bonds Across the Generations," *Chicago Tribune*, October 20, 1999, Tribune Web site, <www.chicagotribune.com/news/nationworld/article/02669.SAV,-9910200221,FF.html>.

83. "Intergenerational Center: New Model in the Making," *Work-Life Today News*, trial issue (McLean, Va.: National Institute of Business Management, n.d.), p. 4.

84. Generations United Web site, <www.generationsunited.org>, November 24, 2000.

85. Marti Long, "Intergenerational Policy Update," *Together: The Newsletter of Generations United*, Vol. 5, No. 2 (Summer 2000), pp. 6–7, 13.

86. Marc Freedman, "New Possibilities for the Longevity Revolution," *Exchange: A Newsletter of Intergenerational Issues, Programs and Research*, Issue 15 (Winter 2000), p. 2.

Chapter Six

1. Marcia K. Myers and Janet C. Gornick, "Cross-National Variation in ECEC Service Organization and Financing," in *Early Childhood Education and Care: International Perspectives*, Sheila B. Kamerman, ed. (New York: Columbia University Institute for Child and Family Policy, 2001), pp. 141–176.

2. Council of Economic Advisers, "The Economics of Child Care: A Report by the Council of Economic Advisers" (Washington, D.C.: unpublished report, December 1997), p. 5.

3. See David Blau, *The Child Care Problem: An Economic Analysis* (New York: Russell Sage Foundation, 2001); and Suzanne W. Helburn and Barbara R. Bergmann, *America's Child Care Problem: The Way Out* (New York: Palgrave for St. Martin's Press, 2002).

4. By the mid-1990s, child-care experts began looking for lessons from other fields and other countries to bring fresh thinking and new perspectives to the child-care dilemma. Gradually new players were brought into the discussions, including economists, business and union leaders, and others from the private sector. New financing ideas began to emerge. For a more detailed discussion of emerging ideas on child-care financing, see: "Financing the Early Childhood "Education System, NAEYC Policy Brief," *Young Children*, Vol. 56, No. 4 (July, 2001), pp. 54–57; Anne Mitchell, Louise Stoney, and Harriet Dichter, *Financing Child Care in the United States: An Illustrative Catalog of Current Strategies* (Kansas City, Mo.: Ewing Marion Kauffman Foundation, and Philadelphia, Pa.: Pew Charitable Trusts, 1997); Teresa Vast, *Learning Between Two Systems: Higher Education as a Model for Financing Early Care and Education, The Financial Aid Think Tank Report, 1998*; Louise Stoney, *Looking into New Mirrors: Lessons for Early Childhood Finance and System Building* (Boston: The Horizon Initiative, 1998); Richard Brandon, Sharon Lynn Kagan, and Jutta M. Joesch, "Design Choices: Universal Financing for Early Care and Education," Human Services Policy Brief (Seattle: Human Services Policy

Center, June 2000); and *Stepping Up Together: Financing Early Care and Education in the 21st Century* (Kansas City, Mo.: Ewing Marion Kauffman Foundation; and Los Altos, Calif.: The David and Lucile Packard Foundation).

5. Although no attempt was made to cost out the recommendations proposed in this book, several cost estimates made in other books or reports are relevant, although the proposals use different financing mechanisms. For example, Suzanne Helburn and Barbara Bergmann, in *America's Childcare Problem*, estimate that affordable child care at improved quality would cost $30 billion in new funds per year, and free universal care would cost $102 billion new money per year. David Blau, in *The Child Care Problem*, calls for means-tested child allowance, a means-tested child-care voucher with a value that depends on the quality of the child-care provider at which it is redeemed, and subsidizing the cost of accreditation and information to parents. He estimates his plan would cost $207 billion a year. After accounting for the elimination of programs that would be redundant with his new system, and other savings, he estimates that the net annual cost of the new system would be $95.6 billion. James Walker calls for a child-allowance plan that would cover the first three children in families up to 175 percent of poverty (more than 22 million children) at an annual cost of $45 billion. He proposes the redirection of some income-support programs, tax credits and tax deductions to cover these costs. He also proposes the development of Parental Leave Accounts in "Funding Child Rearing: Child Allowance and Parental Leave," in *The Future of Children: Financing Child Care*, Richard Berhman, ed. (Los Altos, Calif.: The Lucile and David Packard Foundation, 1996).

6. National Partnership for Women and Families, "State Family Leave Benefit Initiatives in 2001: Making Family Leave More Affordable, "National Partnership for Women and Families Web site, <www.nationalpartnership.org/content>, March 5, 2002.

7. Sheila Kamerman, "Parental Leave Policies: An Essential Ingredient in Early Education and Care Policies", *Social Policy Report, A Publication of the Society for Research in Child Development*, Vol. 14, Number 2, 2000, p. 1.

8. National Partnership for Women and Families, "State Family Leave Benefit Initiatives," March 6, 2002.

9. "New Labor Department Study Finds Family and Medical Leave Act a Resounding Success," National Partnership for Women and Families Web site, <www.nationalpartnership.org/content>, January 9, 2001, p. 2.

10. National Partnership for Women and Families, "State Family Leave Benefit Initiatives," March 5, 2002.

11. Gretchen Kirby, Christine Ross, and Loren Puffer, *Welfare-to-Work Transitions for Parents of Infants: In-Depth Study of Eight Communities* (Washington, D.C.: U.S. Department of Health and Human Services, July 27, 2001), p. iv.

12. *At Home Infant Child Care Program: Report to the Legislature*, Minnesota Department of Children, Families and Learning (Roseville, Minn: February 2000, Executive Summary), p. 1.

13. Donna R. Lenhoff et al., citing "At Home Infant Child Care Program Report to the Legislature," Minnesota Department of Children, Families and Learning, St. Paul, Minnesota, p. 3, in *Family Leave Benefits: A Menu of Policy Mod-*

els for State and Local Policy Leaders (Washington, D.C.: National Partnership for Women and Families, September 2001), p. 16.

14. "Do You Think Parenting Your Children Is an Important Job? So do we. The At-Home Infant Care Program" fact sheet, developed by Working for Equality and Economic Liberation and the Montana Early Childhood Services, Missoula, Mont., n.d.

15. *Preschool for All: Investing in a Productive and Just Society* A statement by the Research and Policy Committee of the Committee for Economic Development (Washington, D.C.: 2002), p. 36. The Committee estimated that at a minimum, $25 to $35 billion annually in additional funding would be needed to provide universal preschool to all eligible three- and four-year-olds.

16. Karen Schulman, Helen Blank, and Danielle Ewen, *Seeds of Success: State Prekindergarten Initiatives 1998–99* (Washington, D.C.: Children's Defense Fund, 1999), p. xx.

17. Statement by Wade Horn, Assistant Secretary for Children and Families, Department of Health and Human Services, to the U.S. Senate Committee on Finance, Subcommittee on Social Security and Family Policy, and the Senate Committee on Health, Education, Labor, and Pensions, Subcommittee on Children and Families,, Washington, D.C., March 19, 2002, p. 9.

18. "Quality Counts 2002, Building Blocks for Success," *Education Week*, No. 17 (January 10, 2002), p. 43

19. *Title I Preschool Education: More Children Served, but Gauging Effect on School Readiness Difficult*, GAO/HEHS-00-171 (Washington, D.C.: General Accounting Office, September 2000), pp. 3–4.

20. Statement by Wade Horn, p. 12.

21. "America's Afterschool Funding Gap Grows," The Afterschool Alliance, July 2001, The Afterschool Alliance Web site, <www.afterschoolalliance.org>.

22. National Conference of State Legislatures, "Before and After School Legislative Enactments 2000–2001," <www.ncsl.org/programs/cyf/>.

23. "The Younger Americans Act" summary fact sheet, developed by Fight Crime, Invest in Kids (Washington, D.C.: n.d.).

24. *Valuing Families: The High Cost of Waiting for Child Care Sliding Fee Assistance* (Greater Minneapolis Day Care Association, 1995), p. 4.

25. Natasha Lifton and Myrna Torres, *The Human Cost of Waiting for Child Care: A Study* (New York: Children's Aid Society, 1999), pp. 1–3.

26. Jennifer Mezey, Rachel Schumacher, Mark H. Greenberg, Joan Lombardi, and John Hutchins, *Unfinished Agenda: State Child Care Policies For Low-Income Families since 1996* (Washington, D.C.: Center for Law and Social Policy, 2002), p. 21.

27. Statement by Wade Horn, p. 4.

28. Testimony of Mark H. Greenberg, Senior Staff Attorney, Center for Law and Social Policy, to the U.S. Senate Committee on Finance, Subcommittee on Social Security and Family Policy, and the Senate Committee on Health, Education, Labor, and Pensions, Subcommittee on Children and Families, March 19, 2002, Washington, D.C., p. 6.

29. Ann M. Collins, Jean I. Layzer, J. Lee Kraeder, Alan Werner, and Fred B. Glantz, *National Study of Child Care for Low-Income Families: State and Community*

Substudy Interium Report (Cambridge, Mass.: Abt Associates for the U.S. Department of Health and Human Services, November 2000), p. 4.

30. Ibid, p. 36.

31. Karen Schulman, Helen Blank, and Danielle Ewen, "A Fragile Foundation: State Child Care Assistance Policies" (Washington, D.C.: Children's Defense Fund, November 2001), p. x.

32. Mezey, Schumacher, Greenberg, Lombardi, and Hutchins, *Unfinished Agenda*, p. 30.

33. Karen Schulman, Helen Blank, and Danielle Ewen, *A Fragile Foundation: State Child Care Assistance Policies* (Washington, D.C.: The Children's Defense Fund, November, 2001), p. xi.

34. Office of the Inspector General, *States' Child Care Certificate Systems: An Early Assessment of Vulnerabilities and Barriers*, OEI-05-97-00320 (Washington, D.C.: U.S. Department of Health and Human Services, February 1998), p. ii.

35. National Conference of State Legislatures, "State Fiscal Outlook for FY 2002," January Update <http.www.ncsl.org/programs/fiscal/sfo2002htm>, Feb. 6, 2002.

36. Testimony of Mark H. Greenberg, p. 9. While the overall national caseload remained flat over that period, under the block grant structure the fact that caseloads were continuing to fall in one state did not result in fiscal relief to other states with rising caseloads.

37. Rachel Schumacher and Mark H. Greenberg, *Child Care after Leaving Welfare: Early Evidence from State Studies* (Washington, D.C.: Center for Law and Social Policy, 1999), p. ii.

38. "Child Care: Reports Demonstrate Poor Children Do Not Have Access to Good Child Care," *Women and Welfare Watch* (New York: NOW Legal Defense and Education Fund, Winter 2000), p. 5.

39. Gina Adams, Kathleen Snyder, and Jodi R. Sandfort, "Navigating the Child Care Subsidy System: Policies and Practices that Affect Access and Retention," Series A, No. A–50 (Washington, D.C.: The Urban Institute, March 2002), pp. 1–3.

40. Internal Revenue Service, *Statistics of Income* Bulletin (Washington, D.C., Spring 2001), Table 1, p. 221.

41. National Women's Law Center, "Tax Relief for Employed Families Improving the Dependent Care Tax Credit," July 2000, National Women's Law Center Web site, <www.nwlc.org>, and personal communication with Christina Martin Firvida, NWLC, June 2002.

42. National Women's Law Center, "New Tax Law Increases Assistance to Families with Child and Adult Dependent Care Expenses," <www.nwlc.org>, June 2001.

43. National Women's Law Center, "State Child and Dependent Care Tax Provisions, Tax Year 2001," <www.nwlc.org>, January 2001.

44. Collins, Layzer, Kraeder, Werner, and Glantz, *National Study of Child Care for Low-Income Families*, p. 32.

45. Ibid., p. 88.

46. Personal communication with Carol Phillips, Executive Director, Council for Professional Recognition, April 2000.

47. Sheri Azer and Cristina Hanrahan, *Early Care and Education Career Development Initiatives in 1998* (Boston: Wheelock College Center for Career Development in Early Care and Education, 1998).

48. National Association for the Education of Young Children, "Early Childhood Educator Professional Development Program", a fact sheet on the new federal grant program (Washington, D.C.: January, 2, 2002), p. 1.

49. "TEACH Early Childhood: Celebrating Ten Years July 1, 1990–June 30, 2000" (Chapel Hill, North Carolina: Child Care Services Association), p. 3; and personal correspondence with Susan Russell, Executive Director, Child Care Services Association, March 2000.

50. Testimony of Susan Russell, Executive Director, Child Care Services Association, to the U.S. Senate Committee on Health, Education, Labor, and Pensions, Washington, D.C., February 12, 2002, p. 3; updated by Susan Russell April 2002.

51. "TEACH Early Childhood Health Insurance Program" fact sheet, n.d.; and personal correspondence with Susan Russell, April 2002.

52. "Child Care WAGES Project: Statewide Implementation" fact sheet, n.d.; and personal correspondence with Susan Russell.

53. Testimony of Susan Russell, updated by Susan Russell April 2002.

54. "Rhode Island Expands Health Benefits for the Child Care Workforce," *Rights, Raises, Respect: News and Issues for the Child Care Workforce*, Vol. 3, No. 1 (Winter 1999), p. 5.

55. Anne Mitchell, "Compensation/Retention Initiatives—An Update, December 2001," unpublished notes.

56. Marcy Whitebook, "Finding a Better Way: Defining and Assessing Public Policies to Improve Child Care Workforce Compensation," unpublished manuscript (Oakland, Calif.).

Index

Page references followed by *t* and *f* refer to tables and figures respectively.

219